Matthew D. Jensen is a visiting lecturer
at Moore Theological College,
Sydney Australia.

AFFIRMING THE RESURRECTION OF THE INCARNATE CHRIST

The first letter of John is commonly understood to contain no reference to Jesus' resurrection. Matthew D. Jensen argues that, far from this being absent from the theology of 1 John, the opening verses contain a key reference to the resurrection which undergirds the rest of the text, and is bolstered by other explicit references to the resurrection. The book goes on to suggest that the author and the readers of this epistle understand themselves to be the authentic Israel from which faithless Jews had apostatised when they denied that Jesus was 'the Christ' and left the community. Jensen's interpretation calls for a new understanding of the historical context in which 1 John was written, particularly the question of Jesus' identity from the perspective of his fellow Jews. An innovative and provocative study, of interest to scholars and advanced students of New Testament studies, Johannine theology, and Jewish history.

MATTHEW D. JENSEN is a visiting lecturer at Moore Theological College, Sydney Australia.

SOCIETY FOR NEW TESTAMENT STUDIES

MONOGRAPH SERIES

General Editor: John M. Court

153

AFFIRMING THE RESURRECTION
OF THE INCARNATE CHRIST:
A READING OF 1 JOHN

SOCIETY FOR NEW TESTAMENT STUDIES

MONOGRAPH SERIES

Recent titles in the series:

Affirming the Resurrection of the Incarnate Christ: A Reading of 1 John

MATTHEW D. JENSEN

CAMBRIDGE
UNIVERSITY PRESS

CAMBRIDGE UNIVERSITY PRESS
Cambridge, New York, Melbourne, Madrid, Cape Town,
Singapore, São Paulo, Delhi, Mexico City

Cambridge University Press
The Edinburgh Building, Cambridge CB2 8RU, UK

Published in the United States of America by Cambridge University Press, New York

www.cambridge.org
Information on this title: www.cambridge.org/9781107027299

© Matthew D. Jensen 2012

First published 2012

Printed and bound in the United Kingdom by the MPG Books Group

A catalogue record for this publication is available from the British Library

Library of Congress Cataloguing in Publication data
Jensen, Matthew D.
  Affirming the resurrection of the incarnate Christ : a reading of 1 John /
  Matthew D. Jensen.
     p. cm. – (Society for New Testament Studies monograph series ; 153)
  Revision of the author's Ph.D. thesis, submitted to the University of Sydney in 2010.
  Includes bibliographical references and index.
  ISBN 978-1-107-02729-9
  1. Bible. N.T. Epistle of John, 1st–Commentaries.   I. Title.
  BS2805.53.J46   2012
  227'.9406–dc23   2012018829

ISBN 978-1-107-02729-9 Hardback

CONTENTS

ACKNOWLEDGEMENTS

This monograph is a revised version of my PhD thesis submitted to the University of Sydney in 2010. I would like to acknowledge and thank some of the many people who helped throughout the period of its research.

My two supervisors, Professor Iain Gardner and Revd Dr Bill Salier, gave clear guidance and support. Alison Woof, David Scarratt and my mum proofread the original thesis minimising the typing errors. In partnership with the University of Sydney, the faculty, staff and other postgraduate students at Moore College provided a rich place to undertake the study. In particular, Revd Dr Peter Bolt encouraged me to pursue the research from start to end, Revd Dr Michael Jensen read the first draft, the library staff obligingly procured the desired books and articles, and Revd Dr Michael Clark discussed the state of the thesis acting as a sounding board at some crucial times.

Since the submission of the thesis and this revised version, two further works on 1 John have been released that unfortunately I have not interacted with – U. C. von Wahlde, *The Gospel and Letters of John* (2010) and U. Schnelle, *Die Johannesbriefe* (2010).

Finally, I would like to thank the three groups of people from whom I have learned, and continue to learn, so much – my family, the members of my local church, and my year at college. These people generously spent time talking with me about the research, enquiring about its progress and praying for its results.

INTRODUCTION

It is often claimed that 1 John contains no references to Jesus' resurrection. For example:

> Except for the singular fact of its silence as to the Resurrection, the Epistle, in its eschatology, covers exactly the same canvas as the Gospel.[1]

> In connection with the doctrinal standpoint of the Johannine Epistles, one further factor merits discussion. While the death of Jesus is important (cf. e.g. i.7; ii.2), there are no references whatsoever to the resurrection (except indirectly perhaps in ii.1, and there it is to the results not the fact itself). The living Christ, in whom his people now dwell, is in the forefront of the writer's mind, but of the resurrection itself he is silent.[2]

> [T]here are no references to his [Jesus'] birth, resurrection or exaltation, and even his death is more implied in the concern for what it achieves than proclaimed as a fact to confront, stumble over or struggle to interpret.[3]

Some scholars have found the absence of references to the resurrection puzzling given its emphasis in John's Gospel and the other New Testament documents.

> It is interesting to notice that neither 1 John nor Hebrews emphasizes the resurrection of Jesus … This is a strange contrast with the literature of the New Testament in general. The complete absence of reference to the resurrection of Jesus in 1 John has

---

[1] Law 1979: 353.   [2] Houlden 1973: 21.
[3] Lieu 1991: 75. See also O'Neill (1966: 66): 'There is no specific reference to Jesus' resurrection'; and von Wahlde (1990: 197): 'It is curious … that the final eschatology of 1 John does not discuss physical resurrection from the dead, as does the gospel.'

> to be seen over against the strong emphasis on this event in the Gospel of John.[4]
>
> It is not clear whether they [the false teachers] disbelieved in the resurrection of Jesus; one of the curious facts about this Epistle is that the resurrection is not mentioned, although John clearly presupposes it.[5]
>
> The absence of any real interest in the life of Jesus, including his resurrection, sits oddly with the emphasis on belief that he is the Christ or Son of God.[6]

However, there are some who see an allusion to the resurrection in the opening verse of 1 John.[7] This allusion moved Jones to ask: 'While the resurrection is apparently not an issue in 1 John, it appears more than likely that v.1 includes in its scope appearances of the risen Christ as recounted in John ... Could it be that 1 John 1:1–4 is more related to the resurrection than normally thought?'[8]

This monograph presents a reading of 1 John that flows from understanding the opening verses of the book to be affirming the resurrection of the incarnate Christ. Since the opening of a document is integral to establishing its framework for interpretation, this research explicates the text of 1 John in light of the opening resurrection allusion. It argues that the resurrection is explicitly mentioned on three other occasions (4:2; 5:6–7, 20). Further, it also proposes that these resurrection affirmations are made in the historical context of an intra-Jewish disagreement over the identity of Jesus as the Christ, a disagreement in which the vital proof is Jesus' resurrection.

This 'resurrection' reading of 1 John has not been presented before because the allusion to the resurrection in the opening verses has generally been discarded for three reasons. First, under the influence of the historical reconstructions that dominate the interpretation of 1 John, the opening verses of 1 John are often understood to affirm the incarnation and not the resurrection. Brown exemplifies this when he disregards the possible allusion with the reasoning: '[T]here is no evidence that the epistolary author and his adversaries were quarrelling over the

[4] Painter 1975: 113.   [5] Marshall 1978: 15.   [6] Lieu 1991: 101.
[7] Haupt 1879: 7, 11; Plummer 1911: 73; Gore 1920: 59; Ross 1954: 135; Richter 1977: 141; Bruce 1979: 36; Barker 1981: 307; Stott 1988: 65; Klauck 1991: 61–4; Beutler 2000: 37; Thomas 2003: 65; Heckel 2004: 436–8; Kinlaw 2005: 99, 106; Morgen 2005a: 50–3; Yarbrough 2008: 38.
[8] Jones 2009: 21.

reality of the risen Jesus.'[9] Second, the allusion to the resurrection is ignored because of the similarity between the prologues of the Gospel of John and 1 John. Since John 1:1–14 affirms the incarnation, so too must 1 John 1:1–4. Thus Johnson comments: 'Just as the Gospel of John begins with a prologue (John 1:1–18), so do the letters. In both, the Word (logos) is the central theme. Here too the Elder introduces some of his principal concerns: the reality of the incarnation, eternal life, and fellowship with the community of believers.'[10] Third, the allusion to the resurrection is discarded due to the apparent lack of other references to the resurrection in 1 John. Smalley and Lieu both take this view:

> The words αἱ χεῖρες ἡμῶν ἐψηλάφησαν, 'and felt with our hands' possibly connect with the tradition behind Luke 24:39 (the risen Jesus says, 'Touch me and see,' using the aorist ψηλαφήσατε, 'touch'), although interestingly the resurrection is not otherwise mentioned in 1 John.[11]

> If it is drawing on resurrection traditions – and the absence of any interest in the resurrection elsewhere makes this entirely hypothetical – it takes the language of sensory experience, on which the proclamation of the message rests, and makes it its own, inviting readers to do likewise.[12]

In the course of this study, and the presentation of its new reading, these three standard reasons are discussed and considered.

The first part outlines and reviews the reading methods used in previous research on 1 John. The first chapter critically reviews previous methods for reading 1 John. The Historical Critical method and its resultant identifications are surveyed before more recent literary approaches are discussed. In light of this discussion, the second chapter outlines the method adopted in this research. This is a historically conditioned intertextual approach.

---

[9] Brown 1982: 163. Although Law (1979: 120) is not commenting on the possible resurrection allusion in 1:1, he still denies reference to the resurrection in 1 John on the basis of his historical reconstruction of the opponents when he states: 'It is sufficiently remarkable that the Resurrection finds no place in the apologetics of the Epistle, although the proofs of its reality are so carefully set forth in the Fourth Gospel. The reason probably is that Cerinthus and his school did not deny the *resurrection of Jesus*' (italics his). Similarly, Painter (1975: 113) argues: '1 John was not written to show that Jesus of Nazareth was divine (against Judaism), but to affirm his real humanity (against Gnosticism) to be the revelation of the character and saving work of God. In this context the importance of the resurrection falls into the background.'
[10] Johnson 1993: 25.   [11] Smalley 2007: 8.   [12] Lieu 2008a: 40.

The second part presents the reading of 1 John, paying particular attention to the introduction, due to its importance in establishing the reader's expectations. The third and fourth chapters contain detailed exegesis of the introduction (1:1–2:11). The third chapter is devoted to 1:1–5 and argues that the verses refer to the author's preaching of his/ her first-hand experiences of Jesus' resurrection appearances. The fourth chapter presents a detailed reading of 1:6–2:11, arguing that these verses comprise the rest of the introduction to 1 John and as such provide a characterisation grid for understanding the situation of the author and readers. It suggests that the 'claims' in those verses could have occurred within first-century Judaism.

With the introduction in mind, the fifth and subsequent chapters explicate the rest of 1 John, paying particular attention to texts that apparently question either the proposed christology or the suggested historical situation ascertained from 1:1–2:11. The fifth chapter examines the verses that discuss the schism (2:15–27). It argues that 1 John can be understood in the context of intra-Jewish disagreement about the identity of Jesus. It provides an extended discussion of the historical evidence that supports such a reconstruction of first-century Judaism. The sixth chapter provides the results of reading 2:28–3:24. The seventh chapter is dedicated to a thorough discussion of the test for discerning if a spirit is from God or from the antichrist (4:2–3). This is because these verses are thought to contain 1 John's clearest affirmation of the incarnation. The eighth chapter outlines the reading of 1 John 4:7–5:21 before a conclusion reviews the reading method and summarises its results.

The reading finds explicit references to Jesus' resurrection in four places (1:1–3; 4:2–3, 5:6–7, 20) and provides some fresh perspectives on other passages. By allowing the introduction to establish the framework for interpreting 1 John, the resurrection is brought to the foreground with the result being a more satisfying reading of 1 John as a whole.

PART I

A Reading Method

1

METHODS OF READING 1 JOHN

This chapter reviews past methods of reading 1 John in order to inform the reading method utilised in this study. Previous methods can be grouped into two main categories – Historical Critical and Literary/Rhetorical. As a result the chapter has two parts. The first critically reviews the Historical Critical method and its resulting identifications of the opponents. The second describes and evaluates the work of four scholars who adopt a Literary/Rhetorical method. The observations that result from this assessment are used to inform the reading method adopted and described in the next chapter.

The Historical Critical method

The Historical Critical method seeks to reconstruct the historical situation that gave rise to 1 John. This involves the key issue of identifying the 'opponents' who have 'gone out' from the community (2:19). Scholars using the Historical Critical method tend to argue that 1 John was written for a polemical purpose in response to false teachers and teaching.[1] Their method has two stages. First, they use a mirror-reading method where the situation behind the text is reconstructed from the text itself. Then second, confirmation of the situation is sought in either a reconstruction of a split within the Johannine community due to internal factors, or identification of external false teachers based on other documents of the time.[2]

The situation behind the text is observed in three sets of passages. First, from 2:19 it is argued that a schism has taken place in which some people

---

[1] For example Brown 1982; Strecker 1996; Painter 2002.

[2] See Barclay 1987 for a description of this type of approach. Although he uses Galatians as the example, he lists the Johannine polemic against 'the Jews' or the schismatics as examples of opponents in the New Testament (1987: 73), and concludes: 'If these cautionary notes and positive suggestions are of any value, they could equally well be applied to … the Johannine letters' (1987: 90).

have left the church. Second, two groups of passages are understood to explicitly reveal the teaching of those who have departed. The passage that contains the description of the schism (2:18–23) also speaks about antichrists who deny that Jesus is the Christ (2:22). This same group of people is again referred to in 4:1–3, where it is indicated that they would not confess that Jesus has come in the flesh (4:2). To these two passages is often added 5:1–8 on the basis of the similarity of language. Even though the vocabulary of antichrists and false prophets is not present, the themes of the identity of Jesus as the Christ (5:1; cf. 2:22), and the Son of God (5:5), and the idea of him 'coming' in blood and water (5:6; cf. 4:2) are cited as evidence that these verses are again describing those who have left. From these verses it is concluded that christology is an area of disagreement. Third, it is argued that some verses record the 'claims' (or sentiments) of the false teachers (1:6, 8, 10; 2:4, 6, 9; 4:20) and John's response. These passages reveal that a disagreement on ethics also contributed to the schism. The mirror-reading first step is circular in that it seeks to understand the text in light of a historical situation that is reconstructed from the text itself.[3]

With this first circular step completed, the majority of scholars start a second step of the process, investigating the first- and second-century milieu for any known people or movements that displayed the same christology and/or ethics opposed in 1 John.[4] This second step is an appeal to history to validate the historical reconstruction made in the first step. It does not prove the reconstruction so much as display that the reconstruction is viable within the first-century context and so supports the reconstruction.

Beyond the general problems associated with mirror reading that Barclay seeks to overcome,[5] there are four main problems with the mirror-reading method when it is applied to 1 John.

First, there is some dispute over which texts should be used in identifying those who have left and their teaching. There is a general consensus that the christological texts (2:22–3; 4:2–3; 5:6–8) reveal something of the opponents' teaching. However, there is disagreement about those used to reconstruct the ethics of the opponents (1:6, 8, 10; 2:4, 6, 9;

---

[3] The observation that the method is 'circular' is not meant to be negative or dismissive. The next chapter will outline a method that argues for the strength of a 'circular' method validated by tangents.

[4] A minority of scholars prefer to construct a source internal to the community as the reason for the schism. See for example Brown 1982; Painter 1986; Klauck 1988; von Wahlde 1990.

[5] Barclay 1987.

4:20). Lieu argues that the ethical texts should not be included because the opponents are not discussed explicitly until 2:18 and then only in relation to the christological question.[6] Edwards contends that the ethical passages are addressed to the author's community and not the opponents, so the passages should not be used in any reconstruction of the opponents.[7] Further, Griffith has argued that the 'claims' formulae ἐὰν εἴπωμεν ὅτι and ὁ λέγων ὅτι are a common rhetorical device used in the first century to transmit teachings and define communities and so should not be used to reconstruct the ethics of the opponents.[8]

Second, there are some problems associated with reconstructing the christological teaching of those who have left. Only the first two christological texts (2:22; 4:2–3) possibly report the position of the opponents and neither of these spells it out in any detail, so caution is warranted in their use as sources for a reconstruction. Further, scholars usually start with 4:2–3 because it is more detailed and then read 2:22 and 5:6–8 in light of it.[9] However, this reverses the natural reading order of the text.

Third, the 'polemical' tone of the language of 1 John poses potential problems for the reconstruction. Perkins warns about identifying the opponents due to the rhetorical nature of 1 John's language in describing them.[10] Further, Burge notes that there does not appear to be any extant record of the opponents' teaching in their own words.[11] So to reconstruct their teaching through the words of others who are in disagreement with them is problematic.[12]

Fourth, there is growing scepticism about the possibility of reconstructing history in general. Schmid, on the basis of a more post-modern epistemology, insists that it is virtually impossible to move from a text to its historical situation.[13]

However, these weaknesses do not negate the value of the method, rather they temper the certainty with which identifications can be made. Identifications of the opponents made solely from the text of 1 John may pass the first two tests of any good hypothesis, that they explain the data and that they are internally self-consistent. Yet, if they lack any

---

[6] Lieu 1981: 211. She concludes: 'it is therefore the christological statements which must bear the full weight of any attempt to define the heresy'.

[7] Edwards 1996: 67.

[8] Griffith 1998: 255–60, although his position is qualified in chapter 4.

[9] For example Thompson 1992: 79; Johnson 1993: 6; Uebele 2001: 119; Thomas 2003: 132.

[10] Perkins 1979: xxi-xxiii.   [11] Burge 1996: 27.

[12] Johnson 1993: 6.

[13] Schmid 2002: 54–8; Schmid 2004a: 30, 33.

substantiating evidence from the first century, they should be adopted with caution. The value of identifications resides not just in their explanation of the details of 1 John, but also in the first-century evidence cited to support the identifications. With these warnings in mind, it is to a review of the identifications that the research now turns.

Historical identifications

The following list of identifications of those who have left is not intended to be exhaustive.[14] Instead, its aim is to outline and critique the main proposals found in the secondary literature. It should be noted at the start of this list that many of the identifications also cite the ethical material as support. This material is not discussed here because it is unclear what role the 'slogans' should play in a reconstruction of the opponents.[15] Further, the differences between the christology of 1 John and that evident in the proposals, are enough to evaluate the identifications' plausibility, without utilising the ethical material.

Opponents within earliest Christianity

The usual place to start possible identifications of the false teachers is with opponents addressed in the other earliest Christian documents.[16] Brown cites four possible alternatives: those addressed by Paul in Colossians, those addressed in the Pastoral Epistles (1 and 2 Timothy, Titus), the groups condemned in the letters of Revelation 2–3, and the sectarian followers of John the Baptist.[17] Though not cited for the sake of identifying the opponents but rather dating 1 John, Robinson notes some parallels between 1 John and the false teachers/teaching in 2 Peter and Jude.[18] This results in possible parallels with eight other early Christian books.

The christological deviations addressed in Colossians are the basis for paralleling the opponents. These deviations seem to be addressed in Colossians 2:8–10 and 16–23. However, even though these deviations involve christology, there are significant differences between those in

---

[14] Lists of identifications can be found in most commentaries but see in particular Brown 1982: 55–68; Beutler 1988: 3774–9; Streett 2011: 5–111.

[15] See Lieu and Griffith's criticisms noted in the last section.

[16] This study limits these documents to the New Testament but does not label the group as such in order to avoid historical anachronism.

[17] Brown 1982: 56–7.   [18] Robinson 1976: 286–7.

Colossians and 1 John. The false teaching in Colossians involves feasts, angels, and rules, none of which are mentioned in 1 John.

Brown groups the Pastoral Epistles together in his analysis of their false teachers. However, they are three different letters to different localities so the opponent in each letter needs to be examined on its own terms.

The false teachers in 1 Timothy have wandered away, devoting themselves to myths and genealogies. They desire to teach the law (1:3–7) but follow evil spirits, denying marriage and certain foods (4:1–3). They are caught up in godless talk and ideas that are falsely called knowledge (6:20–1). This description does not contain the christological errors opposed by John. Likewise, the false teachers described in 2 Timothy also lack correspondence with 1 John. They are recorded as believing that the resurrection has already happened (2:17–18), something not addressed in 1 John. Finally, the false teachers in Titus appear to have a Jewish flavour, being described as 'of the circumcision group' (1:10–11), teaching Jewish myths (1:14) and arguing about genealogies and the law (3:9). This description does not match the portrayal of John's opponents because there are no points of christology at stake.

In the opening chapters of Revelation there are two groups who are condemned as teaching false ideas.[19] The Nicolatians seem to be advocating eating food sacrificed to idols and sexual immorality (2:6, 14–15). The false prophetess Jezebel was also teaching that sexual immorality and eating food sacrificed to idols were acceptable (2:20–3). There appear to be no christological denials in the false teaching in Revelation 2–3.

Brown also noted a possible parallel with the sectarian followers of John the Baptist who may be addressed in John's Gospel.[20] Brown suggests that these followers saw John the Baptist (and not Jesus) as the light sent by God (1:8, 30). However, even Brown acknowledges that so little is known about this group it would be difficult to identify them as the opponents in 1 John.

Robinson noted four similarities between the opponents' teaching in 2 Peter/Jude and 1 John.[21] Both seem to deny Jesus as the Christ/Son of God (1 John 2:22ff.; 4:15; 5:1, 5; cf. Jude 4; 2 Peter 2:1). The promise that believers will share in the divine nature (2 Peter 1:4) is similar to John's teaching that God's children will be made like God when Jesus returns (1 John 3:2). The false teaching in both 2 Peter and 1 John is connected

---

[19] Büchsel 1933 as noted in Brown (1982: 56).
[20] Brown 1982: 57.   [21] Robinson 1976: 286–7.

to a false eschatology (2 Peter 3:4 and 1 John 2:18; 4:3). Finally there is an absence of reference to persecution in the three epistles. These parallels seem much stronger than those discussed above; however, they are not strong enough to compel an identification of the opponents of 1 John with the adversaries of 2 Peter/Jude. First, that there is no reference to persecution is an argument from silence and so should be accepted with caution. It also ignores the strong language of 1 John 3:13ff. where John commands his audience not to be surprised if the world hates them, a hate that is then understood in terms of murder (3:13–15). Second, the false eschatology connected with the teaching in each case is not the same. In 2 Peter it is the doubt that Jesus will return (3:4) while in 1 John the eschatological stress is on the false teachers being present now. There appears to be no doubt about Jesus returning in 1 John (cf. 2:28–3:2). Third, the promises of sharing in the divine nature and being like God do not occur in the context of the false teachers or their teaching. Without occurring in this context there is no control over finding similar teachings and labelling them as revealing the same opponents. Further, the teaching on participation in the divine nature or being like God is not unique to these two letters in the New Testament. For instance it could be said to occur in Colossians 3:1–4, a letter that has already been demonstrated not to have the same opponents as 1 John.

So it appears that there is no strong parallel with opponents found elsewhere in the earliest Christian writings.

Jewish teachers

Some scholars identify Jewish teachers as the opponents addressed in 1 John.[22] They often see a link between John's Gospel and 1 John. John's Gospel was written so that its readers would believe that 'Jesus is the Christ, the Son of God' (20:31). 'The Jews' denied these two titles in John's Gospel (9:22; 10:24, 36; 19:7) and in 1 John the opponents deny that Jesus is the Christ (2:22). They further argue that the audience of 1 John are Jewish Christians who are being tempted to return to the synagogue and deny their faith.

This identification has three weaknesses. First, 2:19 seems to indicate that the false teachers were once part of the group with John, not just non-Christian Jews.[23] Second, Brown argues that 1 John is not in the

[22] Wurm 1903; O'Neill 1966: 29–30; Thyen 1988: 191; Schenke 1997: 206–7; Griffith 2002: 174–9; Witherington 2006: 431; Streett 2011.
[23] Marshall 1978: 17; Brown 1982: 52; Schnackenburg 1992: 18; Lieu 2008a: 105.

style expected for arguing with Jews. There is a lack of Old Testament quotations to support 1 John's argumentation.[24] This is an argument from silence and so must be treated with caution. In response to this objection, Griffith has noted the similarity in style between 1 John and John 14–16, where there is no mention of 'the Jews' and only one Old Testament quotation. Further, John 15:18–16:4 contains the most vivid description of Jewish persecution of Christians, warns against falling away, and talks of being put out of the synagogue/being killed. Yet instead of speaking of 'the Jews' it uses the non-specific word 'world' (15:18–19, 23–5) for those who hate Christians (1 John 3:13).[25] So this difficulty is not enough by itself to refute the identification of the opponents with Jewish teachers. Third, Lieu argues that this 'intriguing' identification, although 'making sense of the scriptural echoes and parallels with other texts usually deemed "Jewish"', fails to explain why the author often describes 'Jesus as the Son of the Father' and regularly places the term 'Christ' in the context of discussion of Jesus' sonship.[26]

Cerinthus

Some scholars have identified the false teachers with Cerinthus or adherents to his teaching.[27] There are two historical reasons for identifying Cerinthus as John's opponent. First, Irenaeus records Polycarp's story that John fled a bathhouse when he found out that Cerinthus 'the enemy of the truth' was within (*Against Heresies* 3.3.4). So it seems that John knew Cerinthus and his teaching. Second, Irenaeus also states that John taught in order to remove the errors of Cerinthus' teaching that were spreading (*Against Heresies* 3.11.1).

Little is known about Cerinthus' teaching as none of his words are in existence today, so what he taught needs to be recovered through his opponents who may or may not have recorded his teaching accurately.[28] It appears that Cerinthus taught that Christ descended on Jesus at his baptism allowing him to teach and perform miracles before departing

[24] Brown 1982: 52; du Rand 1994: 168.
[25] Griffith 1998: 275. For a study of the similarities of style and themes between John 14–16 and 1 John see Yarid 2003.
[26] Lieu 2008a: 105–6.
[27] Brooke 1912: xlv-xlix; Gore 1920: 111–16; Windisch 1930: 127; Ross 1954: 114; Robinson 1962: 134–6; Westcott 1966: xxxiv-xxxvi; Bruce 1979: 17; Law 1979: 36–8; Stott 1988: 50–5; Hengel 1989: 59–60; Womack 1998: 18–22; Akin 2001: 121; and tentatively Wengst 1976: 15–34; Wengst 1988: 3759–60.
[28] Brown (1982: 766–71) has collected what can be known about Cerinthus' teachings from the Church Fathers.

from him before his death (Irenaeus, *Against Heresies* 1.26.1). This teaching could parallel that opposed in 1 John. For example, in 1 John 5:5–8 the stress that Jesus came by water and blood, not just water alone, could be aimed to correct the teaching that the Christ ascended before Jesus died. Further, Cerinthus seems to have taught some doctrines of a Gnostic nature – that there were multiple gods emanating from the original God and that once Christ had left Jesus he ascended back into the Pleroma (Irenaeus, *Against Heresies* 3.11.1).

However, the identification of the opponents with Cerinthian teaching has three weaknesses. First, some elements of the 'heretical' teaching of Cerinthus, as it is reconstructed, are not opposed in 1 John. For example, John does not oppose the distinction between the supreme God and the inferior creator, or the idea that Jesus was the Son of the inferior creator, or even the Gnostic cosmology of a series of aeons evident in Cerinthus' teaching.[29] Further, Brown only finds one idea that is common to both 1 John and the teaching of Cerinthus, the possible idea of the descent of Christ on Jesus at the baptism.[30]

Second, Cerinthus' teaching lacks concepts addressed in 1 John that were apparently part of the false teaching. For example, Cerinthus does not appear to have taught sinlessness or that the spirit was the basis for his teaching.[31] Further, some of Cerinthus' teachings are consistent with 1 John in contrast to the opponents. Both Cerinthus and John argue that Jesus is the righteous example to be followed (Irenaeus, *Against Heresies* 1.26.1; 1 John 2:6; 3:7).[32]

Third, 1 John 2:19 assumes that the antichrists were part of John's community. Even though there is evidence that John knew Cerinthus, the evidence does not go so far as to indicate that they were part of the same community.[33]

Docetism

Another alternative identification is that the opponents are Docetic.[34] Docetism is the theological position that states that Jesus only seemed to be human. It rests on the foundation of Greek thought that sees a separation

---

[29] Marshall 1978: 18; Thompson 1992: 16; Kruse 2000: 21.
[30] Brown 1982: 67.
[31] Marshall 1978: 18; Thompson 1992: 16.
[32] Thompson 1992: 16.   [33] Kruse 2000: 21.
[34] Larsen 1990b: 35; Loader 1992: 66–8; Strecker 1996: 69–76; Uebele 2001: 136–7, 147–52.

between flesh and spirit, between deity and humanity. In Jesus, the second person of the Trinity seemed to be human but was not really flesh.

The main evidence cited for this identification is found in the letters of Ignatius written early in the second century. Three of Ignatius' letters reveal the existence of Docetic beliefs within the early church (*Letter to the Smyrnaeans, Letter to the Magnesians, Letter to the Trallians*). There were some people who said that Jesus' passion was merely semblance and so denied Jesus' death and his resurrection (*Smyrn.* 2:1; 4:1–2; *Trall.* 10:1). Further, these people showed no concern to love others, and abstained from the Lord's Supper and prayer because they denied the reality of Jesus' death for sin (*Smyrn.* 5:1–3; 6:1–7:1; *Trall.* 9:1–2). This caused Ignatius to stress the real humanity of Jesus in his life, death and resurrection (*Smyrn.* 3:1–3; *Magnes.* 11). These beliefs also seem to have been coupled with Jewish practices that Ignatius condemns (*Magnes.* 10:1–3).

This evidence fits neatly with some of the teaching found in 1 John. First, John's stress on the humanity of Jesus (1:1–3; 5:6–8) seems congruent with Ignatius' emphasis. Second, the denial of the real humanity of Jesus apparently made by Ignatius' opponents could have parallels with those addressed by John (4:2; 5:6–8). Third, love is a large theme in 1 John, a theme that could occur because the opponents were not valuing love just as Ignatius' opponents devalued love.

However, there are significant differences between John's opponents and those addressed by Ignatius. Both Marshall and Schnackenburg note that Ignatius' opponents have a Jewish flavour lacking in 1 John.[35] The problem with this critique is that it assumes that Ignatius was writing about the same opponents in each of his three letters. Does every reference to false teachers/teaching in Ignatius refer to the same type of false teaching/teachers? Could not each letter be addressed to a group facing a different background threat?[36] Brown argues that *Philadelphians* and *Magnesians* seem to be against combining Judaism and Christianity (a Jewish Christian problem), while *Smyrnaeans* and *Trallians* seem to affirm Jesus' real humanity in the face of Docetists. If only *Smyrnaeans* and *Trallians* are cited as evidence, then the objection that 1 John lacks a Jewish flavour is removed.[37]

Another difference is that the phrase 'Jesus Christ has come in the flesh' (4:2) affirms Jesus' humanity but it is not clear what form of denial is being addressed. It could be the Docetic teaching that Jesus only 'seemed' to

---

[35] Marshall 1978: 19; Schnackenburg 1992: 23.
[36] Brown 1982: 57–8.   [37] *Ibid.*: 58.

be human but it could also be the total denial of the incarnation.[38] 1 John 'seems concerned with the salvific importance of the flesh and the death of Jesus, not with a defense of the reality of Jesus' humanity'.[39]

These weaknesses result in some scholars acknowledging the differences between the Docetism addressed by Ignatius and 1 John. Yet these scholars maintain a tentative identification of Docetism as the view opposed in 1 John.[40]

Gnosticism

Another identification of John's opponents made in the secondary literature is with Gnosticism.[41] With the discovery of the Nag Hammadi writings, scholars were able to find parallels between the beliefs of Gnostics and 1 John.[42] Both see a dualism between light and darkness, and truth and falsehood (1 John 1:5; *The Paraphrase of Shem* (VII 1–49; NHL 308–8) and *Gospel of Truth* (I 18:17–22; NHL 38 and I 26:19–35; NHL 42)). Both claim union with God that results in sinlessness (1 John 3:9; 5:18; *Gospel of Mary* (BG 8507 7:13–8:4; NHL 471–2)). Both view their adherents as born of God (1 John 2:29; 3:9; 4:7; 5:1, 4, 18; *Discourse on the Eighth and Ninth* (VI 62:33–63:3; NHL 297)). Both see some humans as having a spiritual seed in them (1 John 3:9; *The Gospel of Truth* (I 43:9–16; NHL 49)).[43] Both argue that a special anointing comes from the Father and will teach the believers everything (1 John 2:27; *Hypostasis of the Archons* (II 96:35–97:4; NHL 159), *Pistis Sophia* (II 195; III 292)). Both call their opponents 'children of the devil' moved by a spirit of deceit (1 John 3:10; 4:6; *Apocalypse of Peter* (VII 73:23–6; 77:22–5; NHL 341–2), *Authoritative Teaching* (VI 33:26; 34:28; NHL 282–3)). Both speak of fellowship and perfect love (1 John 1:3, 4:17; *Second Treatise of the Great Seth* (VII 67:15–19; 67:31–68:5; NHL 337)).

However, it is difficult to identify the opponents of 1 John with Gnosticism for several reasons. First and foremost, there were many different gnosticisms in the second and subsequent centuries.[44] To identify

---

[38] Thompson 1992: 17.   [39] Brown 1982: 58–9.

[40] Schnackenburg 1992: 21–3; Kruse 2000: 26.

[41] Dodd 1946: xvi-xxi; Bogart 1977: 115–22. Weiss (1973) discusses the language and thought 1 John shares with later Gnosticism.

[42] These parallels are conveniently reproduced in Brown (1982: 60–3). See also Thompson 1992: 17.

[43] Burge (1996: 32) cites the idea of 'God's seed' echoed in the teaching of Valentinian Gnostics.

[44] Williams 1996.

the opponents with such a broad movement, within which there was diversity, is unsustainable. Further, most of the Gnostic material is dated fifty to two hundred years after 1 John, resulting in possible historical anachronism.[45] Second, Brown notes that since John's Gospel influenced some of the Gnostic writings, apparent parallels with 1 John may really be with John and it would be mistaken to identify the opponents on the basis of these parallels. Further, the ethical accusations made against both the opponents of 1 John and the Gnostics 'are a standard polemic' used in Christian disagreements over the ages. In addition to this, many of the similarities apply as much to what John affirms as to what he attacks.[46] Third, Perkins notes that Gnostics did not deny that Jesus had a body (*Gospel of Truth* even alludes to 1 John 1:1–4, cf: NHL 43).[47] Moreover Perkins states that there 'is no known Gnostic Christology that really fits the slogan' that denies 'Jesus is the Christ' in 2:22.[48]

Some scholars note the similarities but due to these weaknesses, especially the late date of the Gnostic texts, explain the differences on the basis of a trajectory that ends with Gnosticism. As a result they speak of the opponents in 1 John as proto-Gnostics or of John correcting some incipient Gnosticism.[49] However, this identification is so general in character and so insufficient in evidence that it is impossible to evaluate.[50]

Multiple opponents

In the absence of one clearly identified opponent, Smalley argues that John is addressing more than one opponent.[51] Brown notes that this could follow from the exegesis of 2:19 where many antichrists imply more than one position with reference to heretical christology.[52]

Smalley suggests that the preliminary problems in the Johannine community are evident in John's Gospel. There are two groups in the community – Jewish Christians and Hellenistic Christians. The Jewish Christians were committed to Jesus but were loyal to Judaism, resulting in them finding it difficult to accept the divinity of Jesus. They would

---

[45] This assumes a mid to late first-century date for 1 John.
[46] Brown 1982: 63–4.   [47] Perkins 1979: 10.
[48] *Ibid.*: 35.
[49] Haas, Jonge and Swellengrebel 1972: 15–16; Marshall 1978: 15; Palmer 1982: 60–5; Burdick 1985: 49–67; Hiebert 1991: 20–2; Carson 1994: 230–2; Sloyan 1995: 43.
[50] Brown 1982: 59.
[51] Smalley 1980: 337–43; Smalley 1984: xxiii–xxv; Smalley 2007: xxii–xxiv.
[52] Brown 1982: 50.

have looked something like Ebionites. On the other hand, the Hellenistic Christians were converts from a pagan background who found it difficult to break free of the dualistic nature of the Hellenistic systems of salvation. For them, the full humanity of Jesus was hard to accept. They would have looked like what was later called Docetism.

The balanced christology of John's gospel was written to correct the one-sided stress that each group had falsely made in their understanding of Jesus.[53] Yet the community had not paid sufficient attention to John's Gospel but rather had used it to reinforce their own positions. The result was a secession from the community which gave rise to the writing of 1 John.

This means that John is addressing a community split into three groups. First, there were the Christians who were committed to the Gospel. Second, there were the heretics from a Jewish background who stressed the humanity of Jesus. Third, there were the heretics from a Hellenistic and/or pagan background who stressed the divinity of Jesus.[54] There may also have been some eschatological and pneumatological difficulties in both heretical camps.[55]

Smalley further argues that there was a fourth group who had left the community – the secessionists. They were heretically minded and had left the fellowship, even though they never really belonged to it (2:18–19). He suspects that the secessionists came from the Hellenistic–Christian group because of the final Greek worldview that dominated Johannine Christianity.[56]

This identification has the attraction of taking the strengths of previous positions while avoiding the weaknesses by seeing the inconsistencies as representing the other opponent. However, there are two weaknesses with this identification that have resulted in it being a minority position in scholarship.[57]

First, there is no reason from the text to suggest more than one opponent.[58] That many antichrists have come (2:18) does not necessarily mean that they represent many different views. It could mean that the number of people representing the one false view is large. This understanding is suggested by the next verse (2:19) where they all have the common origin of having been with the author.

---

[53] Smalley 1980: x; Smalley 1984: xxiii; Smalley 2007: xxiv.
[54] Smalley 1980: 340.   [55] Smalley 1984: xxiv.
[56] *Ibid.*: xxiv-xxv.   [57] Brown 1982: 50; Burge 1996: 28.
[58] Marshall 1978: 16.

Second, the heresy seems to be something organised. There appears to be a group that are distinct from the audience, having gone out from them (2:19). This group is a threat as they are trying to lead the audience away from what they have heard (2:26).[59]

Internal opposition

In contrast to the previous proposals that scanned the first and second century for external opponents, a minority of scholars prefer to reconstruct the situation with an internal cause for the split.

Brown argues that the schism was due to different interpretations of John's Gospel.[60] The secessionists devalued the salvific value of Jesus' career in the flesh – his life and death. As such, 1 John is written to affirm the teaching of John's Gospel, that Jesus lived and died as a human, a life and death that had salvific significance. The value of Brown's reconstruction is its ability to explain most of the elements in the text of 1 John. However, even with some self-aware methodological statements, Brown reads every christological statement as a polemic against the false teachers, even those that may not occur in the context of a mention of the false teachers. Further, his proposal lacks first-century evidence outside 1 John to substantiate his historical reconstruction. Brown's lack of historical evidence has led some to label his proposal as methodologically suspect. As Childs notes: '[W]ithout solid evidence to support either end of the hypothesis, what purports to be an historical investigation is actually an exercise in creative imagination with very few historical controls.'[61]

Painter also identifies the cause of the split in a misunderstanding of the Gospel of John tradition.[62] He suggests that as Gentiles entered the Johannine community, they interpreted the Johannine tradition without reference to the Jewish conflict that spawned the community. The result was a distortion of the tradition seen in distinguishing between the human Jesus and the divine Christ, in which the human was devalued. Further, the opponents claimed sinlessness due to their participation in the divine through his σπέρμα. Although this view is able to account for the material concerning the opponents in 1 John, it fails to cite historical support from documents other than 1 John. Further, his reconstruction relies on a Gentile audience, a position that some scholars dispute.

---

[59] Brown 1982: 49.
[60] *Ibid.*: 69–86.   [61] Childs 1984: 483. See also Edwards 1996: 64.
[62] Painter 1986; Painter 2002. See also du Rand 1994: 174–6.

Von Wahlde notes in regard to Painter's position: '[T]here are so many parallels between the position of the opponents and Old Testament passages associated with Jewish eschatological hopes that I find it difficult to think of the opponents as coming from anything else than some form of Jewish background.'[63]

Klauck identifies the opponents as wealthy ex-members of the community.[64] He supposes that the opponents had a realised eschatology that found its starting point in their baptism. They focussed on Jesus' baptism as the central christological event. Yet Klauck also adds to the christology the theme of wealth. Klauck's argument is that since the world listened to the opponents (4:5), they were more able to get a hearing from the world. This is understood to imply that the opponents were significant in the world's opinion. Since there is a denunciation of wealth (2:16) and those who do not use wealth to support brothers in need (3:17), Klauck identifies the opponents with wealthy ex-members. This view suffers two weaknesses. It fails to cite evidence of this situation from external documents and thus lacks proper historical controls. Further, it is flawed to base the identification of the opponents as the wealthy on the evidence of 2:16. 1 John 2:16 does not criticise wealth but the boasting (ἡ ἀλαζονεία) in wealth. The verse does not criticise boasting in wealth alone, but also the desires of the flesh and eyes. When 4:5 refers to the world listening to the opponents it does so on the basis that they belong to the world, which should also include the aspects of the desires of the flesh and eyes as described in 2:16. Thus to narrow the identification of the opponents down to the wealthy is to neglect the other descriptions of the world contained in 2:16.

Von Wahlde argues that the opponents stressed the role of the Spirit and viewed the ministry of Jesus as preparing for this outpouring of the Spirit.[65] This accounts for their insistence that they are sinless and require no one to teach them, and their devaluation of the atoning work of Jesus. However, the absence of explicit mention of the Spirit in the context of the first description of the opponents' denial (2:22) indicates this view is problematic. Further, the descriptions of the opponents reveal that they deny Jesus' identity as the Christ (2:22) who came in the flesh (4:2). This is stronger than just stressing the role of the Spirit. It is a denial of Jesus.

[63] von Wahlde 1990: 130.
[64] Klauck 1988: 56–8; Klauck 1991: 32–3. See Witetschek (2004) for a similar view based on a comparison of the characterisation of the opponents and Judas – the lover of money (John 12:6).
[65] von Wahlde 1990: 114–27. Similarly Brown (2003: 237–57) argues that the opponents stressed the Spirit as the present 'broker' in the audience's relationship with God, a view that downplayed the significance of Jesus' death.

These options all have the same fundamental weakness – they lack support from any material secondary to 1 John, thus rendering them conjectural. They may result in a consistent reading of 1 John but fail to cite evidence that moves this reading from possible to probable. In some cases the proposed reconstruction is not even falsifiable since no other evidence exists by which to test the historical situation. This reveals that a reading of 1 John requires some understanding of the historical background demonstrated from first-century documents in order to demonstrate its plausibility.

Other

There are a number of other less popular identifications. Weiss suggests the opponents were teachers of Greek philosophy.[66] However, it is hard to see how these people could be described as 'having gone out from us' (2:19) in that they were never Christians because their teaching is so little like Christianity.[67]

Büchsel argues that there was an uncontrolled outbreak of speaking in tongues and other behaviour similar to that addressed by Paul in 1 Corinthians.[68] The weakness with this position is that there are no references to uncontrolled behaviour or speaking in tongues in 1 John. The false prophets are from the world and speak the language of the world (4:4–6). The error is christological (2:22–23; 4:2–3). The secessionists seem to be unified in an organised group, not in a spiritual frenzy that is fractured.[69]

Haupt proposes that John's opponents had a low christology that recognised Jesus as the Christ yet denied his divinity, something akin to the Ebionites.[70] There are three weaknesses with this identification. First, why would John stress the humanity of Jesus in light of its apparent denial if indeed the Ebionites did not deny it (4:2; 5:6–8)?[71] Second, if the opponents are akin to Ebionites, why does John not spend more time affirming the divinity of Jesus?[72] Third, it seems unlikely that John would describe these people as being with him and then going out if they never believed that Jesus was divine. The stress on the divinity of Jesus

---

[66] Weiss 1967.   [67] Marshall 1978: 21; Brown 1982: 52.
[68] Büchsel 1933 cited in Brown 1982.
[69] Brown 1982: 49.
[70] Haupt 1879. Similarly Goulder 1999: 341–5.
[71] Brown 1982: 53.
[72] Although 1 John 5:20 does contain a disputed reference to Jesus' divinity.

in John's Gospel (1:1–3; 20:28) seems to make it part of the core beliefs that John requires of a believer.

Summary

The Historical Critical method has the main strength of attempting to locate the document in its first-century context. It was observed that any proposed reading that does not provide some description of the historical situation that gave rise to 1 John may explain the details of the text and be internally self-consistent, but without reference to the historical situation lacks a level of plausibility. However, the critical review of the proposed historical situations revealed that none of the suggestions was without difficulty. The result is that current readings may explain the details of the text of 1 John, but they lack plausibility since their historical reconstructions are not viable. This opens up the way to propose a new understanding of 1 John. The understanding would need to explain the details of the text, be internally self-consistent, and describe the historical situation behind 1 John.

Literary/Rhetorical Methods

The weaknesses within the proposed identifications have led some modern scholars to abandon the Historical Critical method and adopt a more Literary/Rhetorical approach. There are four main scholars who have utilised such approaches to 1 John. This section will critically describe each of their contributions.

Judith Lieu

In 1981 Judith Lieu published an important article that started the new literary direction in the study of 1 John.[73] She warned that the 'heresy v. orthodoxy' model, on which the Historical Critical method was based, required caution, and she questioned the evidence for the generally accepted historical reconstruction of Gnostic opponents.[74] Without historical sources providing plausibility to the Historical Critical method, Lieu moved to utilise a more literary method. She paid particular attention to the author's own reasons for writing (1:4; 5:13),[75] noting the

---

[73] She has subsequently published a fuller explanation and defence of her views in Lieu 1991 and Lieu 2008a.
[74] Lieu 1981: 210–11.   [75] *Ibid.*: 212–15.

context of both the christological statements, and the apparent moral debate. The result of her greater attention to context were observations that the christological statements are linked with the antichrists or past members of the community,[76] and that moral debate is seldom linked to the opponents. This means that the moral exhortations are not in response to the opponents but rather aimed to effect change in the audience.[77] In this way, Lieu set out to provide an understanding of 1 John that started with the text of 1 John and not an identification of the opponents.[78]

However, this pastoral understanding of 1 John was not totally divorced from an historical situation. Lieu suggested that 1 John was:

> directed within the community to confirm its members in their assurance and to struggle with those aspects of its theology which some could – and indeed did – develop in a way which led to the schism reflected in ii 18. The task of polemizing [*sic*] against these past members of the community is subordinated to this primary inward concern.[79]

Lieu's arguments have forced scholarship to examine the text of 1 John more carefully, integrating the purpose statements into any proposed reading. They seem to have also resulted in greater caution being taken in the level of confidence that scholars have in applying the 'heresy v. orthodoxy' tool and identifying the opponents with known first- or second-century people/movements. However, they have not stopped the quest for the historical opponents nor the view that 1 John was primarily polemic. This is because the language of 'antichrists, false prophets, spirit of the antichrist' is very strong and seems to indicate a polemical purpose.[80] Lieu's recent commentary is a product of her early work, providing a reading of 1 John that relegates the opponents 'to the shadows'.[81]

Dietmar Neufeld

Neufeld applied a modified version of J. L. Austin's speech-act theory to 1 John in order to ascertain the effect of the christological confessions and exhortations of 1 John.[82] He noted the scarcity of historical reference in 1 John, on which the Historical Critical method placed so much

[76] *Ibid.*: 215–21.   [77] *Ibid.*: 221–4.   [78] Lieu 1991: 16.   [79] Lieu 1981: 212.
[80] Kruse 2000: 16.   [81] Lieu 2008a: 12.   [82] Neufeld 1994.

weight, and the multiple ways these references were pieced together to render many different identifications of the situation. He suggested that it was problematic for the Historical Critical approach to limit the potential meaning of 1 John based on such slim evidence construed in so many different ways.[83] These observations do not rule out the historical enterprise but show that it is a weakness to limit the potential meaning on this basis.

Neufeld's research argues that the author of 1 John uses christological confessions and exhortations to indicate to the readers the boundaries of proper faith and behaviour.[84] Thus references to the opponents are vehicles to achieving the same ends – they personify those who have left the true faith either by denial or false ethics. This in no way denies that the opponents could have existed historically, but argues that their identification is not required in order to ascertain their function in the text and their effect on the reader. In this way the author seeks to affirm the faith and behaviour of the readers so that they will remain true to his teaching.

The strengths in Neufeld's work are his attention to the rhetorical effects of the language and statements in 1 John. He has demonstrated that knowledge of the historical situation is not required in order to understand the text. However, his failure to locate his reading in an historical context results in a possible reading that requires more evidence to be accepted as plausible.

Terry Griffith

The last verse of 1 John is the stimulus for Griffith's reading of 1 John.[85] He uses a literary/thematic approach to 1 John that seeks to make sense of this unusual ending. After discussing the ending (5:21), demarcating the closing section (5:6–21), and discussing the literary notion of closure, Griffith notes that the themes of assurance, sin and apostasy, and christology occur in the closing section of 1 John. Each of these themes in 1 John is then examined so as to reveal how the closing section functions and thus to display the role of the final verse in the book as an ending. Attention is paid to vocabulary usage for each theme and how the themes relate to each other in the closing section.

Griffith's reading has a number of convincing arguments and results. His study of the 'claim' formulae (ἐὰν εἴπωμεν ὅτι and ὁ λέγων) cautions

---

[83] *Ibid.*: 39.   [84] *Ibid.*: 135.   [85] Griffith 2002: 2–4.

against the identification of the 'claims' in 1:6, 8, 10 and 2:4, 6, 9 with the opponents.[86] His study of the theme of sin as it occurs across the letter reveals a logical progression that many scholars had not previously identified.[87] The reading of the christological statements in the order in which John presents them opens up other options with regard to identifying the opponents.[88]

Griffith's work has an understanding of the historical situation behind the text. He argues that 1 John is written to a situation where ethnic Jews had become Christians but were denying that Jesus was the Christ and so were returning to Judaism.[89] However, this situation does not determine the text's meaning. Rather, it reveals the plausibility of his reading.

Yet there is one major weakness in Griffith's argument. There is no detailed exegesis of 1:1–4 in the work. Starting with the last verse of 1 John runs contrary to the reading order of the text. Even though the reading order is given significance in the study of the christological texts, the lack of attention to the start of 1 John is a glaring omission.

Hansjörg Schmid

Schmid is the last of the four scholars under review who utilise a modern literary method.[90] He applies it more radically than either Lieu or Griffith, denying the possibility of the historical reconstruction of the external situation.[91] He argues that Lieu, Neufeld and Griffith are inconsistent in their break from the Historical Critical method. Lieu does not challenge the polemic reading method in terms of hermeneutics and epistemology. As a result there is a question remaining about the viability of historical reconstruction.[92] Neufeld breaks from the method in using speech-act theory but fails to break free of the selection of texts that speak of the opponents. His inclusion of a chapter on the 'claims' of 1:6–2:11 reveals the weakness of not questioning the Historical Critical method's selection of texts.[93] Griffith's identification of the opponents with Jews committing apostasy plays into the hands of the 'method' which sees 1 John as primarily polemic in purpose.[94]

[86] Griffith 1998: 255–60; Griffith 2002: 122–4.
[87] Griffith 2002: 109–48.
[88] Griffith 1998: 267–73; Griffith 2002: 166–88. [89] Griffith 2002: 175.
[90] Schmid 2002; Schmid 2004a.
[91] Schmid 2002: 54–8; Schmid 2004a: 30.
[92] Schmid 2004a: 27. [93] *Ibid.*: 29. [94] *Ibid.*: 28.

Schmid's denial of the possibility of historical reconstruction is due to his application of Niklas Luhmann's system theory. He understands 1 John as part of an intertextual sign system with John's Gospel that aims to strengthen the reader's faith and love.[95] He proposes 'an intertextual model constructed from the implicit reader's perspective which combines elements of intertextuality with reader response criticism'.[96] So meaning is found in the relationship of each element of the system and not in relation to external events. The system is self-referential so that even its descriptions of its environment are from within the system. Within this view, the question is not who the opponents were but why does John create them?

Schmid makes a number of observations in investigating the function of the opponents in 1 John. The opponents are set in an apocalyptic context and function to urge the reader to good deeds.[97] The ethical issues found either side of the opponent texts are cited as supporting evidence.[98] Further, the opponent texts are the basis for ethical behaviour because when the readers move past the opponent texts they are strengthened to resume the ethical teaching. In this regard 1 John 3:23 is a key verse because it speaks of both faith and love and also structures the section that follows.[99] These lead Schmid to conclude: '[T]he main function of the opponents interacting with the reader is to operate as a counter-concept to the community.'[100] The opponents' passages draw the boundaries of the community with regards to faith and love. They demonstrate the consequences of border crossing, hence they are described in the same vocabulary as the ethical breaches in 1:6, 8, 10.[101]

Even though Schmid's argument contains some interesting exegetical insights, the argument as a whole has three weaknesses. First, the gap between the textual world and the external world is suspect. Why should the intertexual system be established in the first place if not to change people's perception of reality – to give them a new perspective on the external world? Further, why would John want to change his readers' perception of the external world unless he thought it was lacking in some way? This observation comes to a head when the opponents are seen as a counter-concept to the community to enforce a boundary. A boundary takes the purpose of the text back into the historical external world.

[95] *Ibid.*: 36–8.
[96] *Ibid.*: 31.   [97] Schmid 2002: 96–101; Schmid 2004a: 34–6.
[98] Doing (2:17, 28–9), loving one another (3:11–24; 4:7).
[99] 4:1–6 are about faith, 4:7ff is about love, especially 4:11.
[100] Schmid 2004a: 38.
[101] ψεύδομαι, ψευδοπροφήτης, ψεῦδος, ψεύστης, πλανάω.

Second, although Schmid's reading makes sense of the text of 1 John and is thus possible, the lack of historical references results in it failing to be viable. It would be more plausible as a reading if a description of the historical situation that gave rise to 1 John was provided. Third, descriptions of the external world are in themselves texts. Schmid has focussed on John's Gospel as the source for establishing his intertextual sign system. However, John's Gospel is only one of a multitude of texts that could have been used. Every reader is exposed to a multitude of texts from which they establish their sign system and the original readers would have been no exception. Further, the attempt to limit the number of texts appears problematic as readers seem to consciously and subconsciously make intertextual links when reading. In fact this thesis will suggest that the more texts a reading can incorporate, the more plausible the reading becomes.

Summary

The application of more literary methods to 1 John acknowledges the weaknesses of the Historical Critical method and the proposed identifications of the opponents, and focusses again on the text. It cautions against an over-dependence on proposed historical situations while not denying the external world entirely (except for Schmid). The resultant readings stress the purpose statements and order of the text as significant in interpretation, along with the role of intertextuality in the process of understanding the meaning of the text. These strengths will be incorporated into this study's approach to reading 1 John.

Conclusion

After surveying previous methods for reading 1 John, this chapter has noted four aspects that should inform the reading method of this research. First, the strength of the Historical Critical method was in locating the text in a first-century context. This appeal to history should result in a reading that explained the text and was consistent, being not just possible but plausible. However, after critically reviewing the proposed identifications, it became evident that none of the historical reconstructions was viable. Thus, previous explanations of 1 John may explain the text and be internally consistent, but they lack evidence to move them from possible to plausible. Second, the method should pay attention to 1 John's explicit purpose statements. Third, the text of 1 John should be read in the order in which it is presented. Fourth, this research should acknowledge the role of intertextuality in the reading process.

The next chapter presents the reading method adopted in this research. Wolfgang Iser's early work is modified in light of the above observations as they relate explicitly to 1 John.

2

CIRCLES AND TANGENTS: A READING STRATEGY

The last chapter critically reviewed two reading methods utilised in previous study of 1 John. This chapter describes the approach this research takes in light of the results of the review. It presents a model for reading 1 John that is likened to a circle and its tangents.

The chapter has five main parts. First, there is a brief explanation of the metaphor of circles and tangents, where the Historical Critical and the Literary/Rhetorical methods are used as illustrative examples. Second, there is a brief review of Wolfgang Iser's early approach to reading that this study develops with respect to 1 John. Third, the understanding of the concept of 'gap' taken by this research is described. Fourth, three devices in 1 John that limit how gaps can be filled are explained. Fifth, the process for filling gaps (intertextuality) is outlined.

Circles, tangents, and reading

A circle is one of the simplest geometric shapes. It is made up of only one line that leads back to itself. Yet the circle has an infinite number of tangents: lines that touch the outer edge of the circle and have one point in common. A circle and its tangents provides a metaphor for describing the reading method utilised in this thesis.[1]

It is obvious that the presuppositions of a reader influence the process of understanding a text and thus the resultant reading. In this way reading is a circular task: presuppositions influence reading that influences presuppositions. Further, the standard two tests of any hypothesis require a reading to be circular – it must be internally self-consistent and able to explain all the elements of the text. This means that the observation

[1] The circle and tangent metaphor is employed in Jensen and Payne (1995: 15–17) to explain the Australian Fellowship of Evangelical Students' doctrinal statement on the Bible.

that a reading is 'circular' should not be understood as a criticism but rather an acknowledgement of its internal consistency. However, since presuppositions are many, there are also a variety of resultant readings. This raises a question about judging between readings: what makes one reading more valid than the next? Once the reading has passed the standard two tests, it is argued that ultimately the reader decides which reading is most plausible or viable.[2]

In terms of the methods reviewed in the last chapter, the Historical Critical method appeals to the tangent of history to demonstrate its viability. However, when each of the historical reconstructions suffers weaknesses, the plausibility of the readings comes into question. Childs' criticism of Brown is an example of this problem: '[W]ithout solid evidence to support either end of the hypothesis, what purports to be an historical investigation is actually an exercise in creative imagination with very few historical controls.'[3] The resultant readings of the Historical Critical method may make sense of the text and be internally consistent. But the weaknesses in the tangents to these circular readings result in the readings only being as plausible as each other.

The Literary/Rhetorical methods attempt to by-pass the problems associated with the Historical Critical approach. However, even they appeal to some tangents to make their readings viable. Although Lieu and Griffith do not allow their understanding of the historical situation to determine their readings, they still propose some form of first-century context. Neufeld uses speech-act theory to demonstrate the plausibility of his reading. Schmid appeals to intertextual connections in order to demonstrate the plausibility of his reading. Each of these is a tangent to the proposed circular readings.

The approach taken in this study is to build on many of the insights of the scholars who apply modern literary methods in understanding 1 John. In this way it is circular. Yet it also aims to present the resultant reading as plausible by appealing to other texts of the period, tangents to the circle. It views the division between the Historical Critical method and modern literary methods as a false dichotomy. This is because the appeal of literary methods to other texts in establishing meaning (intertextuality) should not rule out an appeal to history since history itself is an understanding of a combination of texts.[4] The most common tangents appealed to in this research are the historical documents of the first century and the documents that reveal the theology of the earliest church. These tangents do not determine the circle but demonstrate its

---

[2] Clines 1993.   [3] Childs 1984: 483.   [4] Evans 1997.

viability. In this sense the approach aims to bridge the divide between the Historical Critical method and modern literary methods.

Thus the monograph proposes a method that seeks to understand the text of 1 John using a historically conditioned intertextual approach. It likens the method to a circle and tangents where the circle is the application of a more literary method to the text of 1 John and the tangents are the appeal to texts outside of 1 John to demonstrate the plausibility of the resultant reading.

Wolfgang Iser

This research builds on three of Wolfgang Iser's contributions to literary criticism, all three of which are contained in his famous quote:

> [T]wo people gazing at the night sky may both be looking at the same collection of stars, but one will see the image of a plough, and the other will make out a dipper. The 'stars' in a literary text are fixed; the lines that join them are variable.[5]

First, Iser notes that there are two poles in the reading process, a text and a reader. He argues that meaning is constructed in the interaction of a reader with a text.[6] A text is comprised of sentences, each of which arouses expectations of what is to come. Subsequent sentences affirm, modify or completely change these expectations. So as each sentence is encountered, a reader reviews previous sentences but also anticipates what is to come. Even though a reader is ever changing their expectations, Iser argues that a reader strives to see patterns and order in a text, grouping sentences together in the desire to have a consistent reading.[7]

This means that reading is both linear and circular. It is linear in the sense that the text presents sentences in an order – from start to finish. Since anticipation is generated from the start and then subsequently modified, the start of a text sets the horizon for interpretation, taking on a prominent position. Yet reading is also circular, in the sense that subsequent sentences cause some review of expectations. This is especially the case when gaps are encountered.

This introduces Iser's second contribution: the existence of 'gaps' within a text. Gaps are places where the flow between sentences (or groups of sentences) is interrupted. At these places the reader fills the gap, providing connections between the sentences.[8] In the analogy of the

---

[5] Iser 1972: 287.   [6] *Ibid.*: 274–82.   [7] *Ibid.*: 282–4, 288.   [8] *Ibid.*: 285–7.

stars in the quote, the lines of the plough or the dipper are the connections the reader has formed.

Yet, third, Iser observes that it is not possible to fill the gaps in every conceivable way. The text itself limits the possible connections. This is done through structural components of the text – familiar literary patterns, themes, and devices – along with social and historical contexts.[9] However, it is the reader who fills the gaps and thus the interaction of the reader with the text is how meaning is constructed.

The following reading of 1 John makes use of Iser's observations that reading is circular, that a text contains gaps, and that the text also limits how these gaps can be filled. However, the proposed reading strategy extends Iser's method in four ways. First, Iser's early observations and method are primarily associated with narrative texts. However, his more recent research uses this theory with regards to hermeneutics, applying it not just to narrative texts but also to knowledge in general.[10] In applying a modified version of the method to 1 John, a non-narrative text, this research is extending the application of Iser's method.[11] Second, in addition to Iser's definition of a gap as the place where the flow between sentences is interrupted, the research pays particular attention to two other potential sources of gaps in 1 John (pronouns and 'reader-experienced gaps'). Third, the thesis notes three particular approaches 1 John seems to use to limit the connections possible for filling gaps (the use of γράφω, the vocative, and boundary crossing). Finally, more attention is paid to the role of the reader – in particular the role intertextuality plays in filling gaps, suggesting that intertextual connections are like tangents to Iser's reading circle.[12]

Gaps

In addition to Iser's view that gaps occur when the flow between sentences is interrupted, there are two other potential sources of gaps in 1 John that this research pays particular attention to – one located in the text, the other due to the reader.

First, a potential source of gaps is located in the use of pronouns.[13] Pronouns by their very nature cause a reader to pause in order to identify

---

[9] *Ibid.*: 293.   [10] See Iser 2000.

[11] A recent unpublished thesis that applies Iser's method to produce a reading of 1 John is Baker 2004.

[12] For a defence of Iser's reading method against the critiques of Fish 1981; Eagleton 1983; and Lentricchia 1980; see Baker 2004: 57–67.

[13] von Wahlde (2002: 319) comments: 'Determining the antecedents of pronouns in the First Letter of John is a notorious problem for commentators.'

their referent. The referent can be located in two places – before the pronoun (anaphoric) or after the pronoun (cataphoric).

Anaphoric pronouns do not usually result in a gap because a reader has already experienced their antecedent and so is able to supply it quickly. However, there are two situations where anaphoric references may result in a gap: when it is unclear what the antecedent is or when the antecedent is some distance from the pronoun. Anaphoric pronouns in these situations are discussed because they may cause gaps.

Cataphoric pronouns may constitute a gap because they require a reader to identify their postcedent from the text that follows the pronoun. This process may then require 're-reading' the section in light of what is found. As a result of this search for the postcedent and re-reading, cataphoric references gain a level of prominence in a reading. This understanding of cataphoric pronouns is evident in 1 John. Anderson and Anderson present and evaluate three cataphoric pronominal phrases that occur in 1 John: ἐν τούτῳ, the combination of εἰμί and οὗτος, and τίς.[14] They argue that the phrases give prominence to the statements to which they are attached. The combination of a recursive reading process prompted by cataphora, and prominence caused by cataphora, often results in scholars understanding cataphoric statements as indicating the opening boundaries of paragraphs and sections of a text.

However, it is not always the case that cataphora indicates a boundary in the text. The author may use the prominence function to draw attention to a point in the argument that is dependent on the previous material. An example of this is the phrase ἔστιν αὕτη in 1:5, which is clearly linked to the previous verses both syntactically (καί starts 1:5 and the antecedent of the pronoun αὐτοῦ in 1:5 is from 1:1–4) and lexically (1:5 shares the vocabulary of ἀκούω and the ἀγγελ-word group with 1:1–4).[15]

Second, there are more general gaps that a reader experiences. The reader, as the second pole in the reading process, comes with presuppositions and experiences that can result in the occurrence of gaps. These can occur when the reader's presuppositions are called into question by the text because their immediate intertextual connections fail to plausibly fill a gap, or when the reader's expectations, generated by their experience

---

[14] Anderson and Anderson 1993. See also Larsen 1990a, who argues that of the twelve occurrences of the phrase ἐν τούτῳ without a noun in 1 John, all but one (3:18–19) are probably cataphoric.

[15] Chapter 3 contains fuller exegesis of these verses.

of the text already encountered, are called into question. With respect to the reading proposed in this thesis, the understanding of the christology and historical situation often result in gaps since it is at odds with the majority of the secondary literature. These gaps focus the interaction with secondary literature in the monograph to these two main topics – the christology and historical situation of 1 John.

Limiting devices

There are three devices used in 1 John that limit how gaps can be filled. These are the use of the verb γράφω (I write), the role of the vocative, and boundaries in the text.

The use of γράφω

1 John has an unusually high occurrence of the verb γράφω (I write) – thirteen times in one hundred and five verses (1:4; 2:1, 7, 8, 12, 13 (x2), 14 (x3), 21, 26; 5:13). All are in the first-person singular, except 1:4, that is in the first person plural. The first seven are in the present tense (up to 2:13); thereafter they are all in the aorist (2:14ff). Of the occurrences, three are followed by a purpose clause (ἵνα) indicating the aim in writing (1:4; 2:1; 5:13), seven are followed by a causal clause (ὅτι) revealing the reasons for writing (2:12–14, 21),[16] and the final three describe the content of what is being written (2:7–8, 26).

Since in these statements the writer pauses to self-reflectively comment on the purpose, reason or contents of the text, they address a reader directly and move to a different level of communication, indicating how the text was intended to be understood. Lieu helpfully brought attention to the significance of these statements in her research.[17] The occurrence of this type of statement has parallels in narrative texts where it is known as an 'aside' or the voice of the 'intrusive narrator'. Asides break the narrative sequence, slowing a reader down to give them time to process the episode just read or the extra information provided by the narrator. Thatcher argues that the asides in John's Gospel 'guide the reader's

---

[16] The ὅτι clause that follows γράφω could be understood to be recitative rather than reason; see Noack 1959–1960. Understanding ὅτι as expressing reason is favoured by Bultmann (1973: 31) and Marshall (1978: 136–7). However, even if ὅτι were recitative, it would group with the 'content' category and so still function to limit 'gap filling'.

[17] Lieu 1981: 212–15.

interpretation of and response to events. Asides thus have a rhetorical function.'[18]

The statements in which γράφω occurs in 1 John seem to have the same rhetorical function. Each type of statement limits 'gap filling' as it reveals the intended meaning.

When γράφω is followed by a purpose clause (ἵνα) it limits 'gap filling' by revealing the purpose for writing. For example, in 2:1 the purpose for writing is explicitly outlined – so that the readers might not sin. Sin is the theme of 1:5–2:2 and, coming near the end of this section, this purpose clause indicates why the section was written.[19] It thus limits potential filling of gaps in the section because it signals the theme and the purpose for writing about that theme.

When γράφω is followed by a causal clause (ὅτι) it limits 'gap filling' by revealing the reason for writing. For example, in 2:12 the author states that he writes because the readers' sins have been forgiven on account of Jesus' name. This limits how passages that discuss sin and forgiveness are understood in 1 John (eg: 1:6–2:2; 3:3–9 and 5:16–21), since it indicates that Jesus is where sin is dealt with and forgiveness is found.

When γράφω is not followed by a purpose or a causal clause, 'gap filling' is limited because it reveals the content of the writing. For example, in 2:26 the author states that he is writing περὶ τῶν πλανώντων ὑμᾶς (concerning those leading you astray). This statement is located in the section about antichrists (2:18–27) and so at a minimum is indicating the content of this section. However, the verb πλανάω and its cognate πλάνη are used in four other sections of 1 John (1:8; 2:26; 3:7; 4:6), revealing that this content statement may refer to more than just 2:18–27. The vocabulary associated with false teachers (ἀντίχριστος, ψευδοπροφήτης) is found in two of these sections (2:18–27 and 4:1–6), suggesting that the content of the middle third of the letter could be described as being περὶ τῶν πλανώντων ὑμᾶς.[20] Thus, the statement describes the content of the section (and maybe the middle third of 1 John) and so limits the filling of gaps because it reveals the section's theme and thus gives a background for intertextual connections.

Thus statements that use γράφω in 1 John 'guide this reader's interpretation' of the text. They do this by indicating either the purpose for

---

[18] Thatcher 1994: 430.

[19] That 2:1 is limited to providing the purpose for 1:5–2:2 is evident from the observation that the letter does not speak about sin again in a block of teaching until 3:4, by which time γράφω has been used ten times and the purpose clause of 2:1 is no longer prominent in the reader's mind.

[20] ἀντίχριστος is found in 2:18, 22; 4:3 and ψευδοπροφήτης is found in 4:1.

writing, the result of writing or the content of the writing. Often these statements have the added emphasis of the vocative, thus stressing the content of the text and so limiting its reading.[21]

Vocatives

In Greek, the vocative (or its nominative equivalent) is the case of direct address. It is used when an author speaks directly to the reader/audience.[22] The vocative often reveals the relationship of the speaker and the audience and usually marks the start of units within a text.[23] It signals either the opening boundary of a text (Romans 2:1; 12:1) or the paragraphs within a larger span of text (Ephesians 5:22–6:9; Colossians 3:18–4:1; 1 Peter 3:1–7).[24] This use of the vocative is also evident in 1 John. A vocative occurs at an opening boundary in 2:18 and 28, and could be used to mark paragraphs within a span (the use of ἀγαπητοί in 3:21; 4:1 and 7).[25] Longacre suggests a structure for 1 John based mainly on this understanding of the vocative.[26]

This function of the vocative as indicating the start of a unit within a text is founded on the observation that vocatives are usually located at the start of a sentence and rarely found within a paragraph.[27] However, the vocative can occur at positions other than the start of sentences and the start of accepted paragraphs, questioning the adequacy of this usual understanding to explain all the uses of the vocative. Rogers, after examining the placement of vocatives in paragraphs as determined by the United Bible Society's Greek Text of the Pauline letters, notes that about one third of the vocatives are not in the initial sentence of a paragraph. Some occur in combination with conjunctions that signal the conclusion of an argument and so are not paragraph initial (eg: Romans 7:4; Galatians 4:31; 2 Thessalonians 2:15), while others exist in the middle of paragraphs (eg: Romans 9:20; 1 Corinthians 1:11; 7:16 (x2), 29).[28] Clark

---

[21] Larsen 1991: 52 comes close to this observation.

[22] Clark (2006: 35) suggests that in the New Testament letters, the density of vocatives used indicates the closeness of the relationship between the author and his recipients – the higher the density, the closer the relationship. With respect to 1 John, Clark observes, 'In 1 John no addressees are stated, but both the density and the nature of the vocatives point towards a close relationship between writer and readers.'

[23] Barnwell 1974: 9–10.   [24] Young 1994: 252–3.

[25] Clark (2006: 34) suggests that in 2:12–14 the vocatives mark paragraphs within a span similar to the household code. This however seems unlikely because it would render every sentence a new paragraph.

[26] Longacre 1992.   [27] Young 1994: 253.

[28] For a full list see Rogers 1984: 25–6.

reports that about one third of the vocatives in the New Testament letters occur within a paragraph. Some are very near the end of a letter (Galatians 6:18; 1 Thessalonians 5:25; 1 Timothy 6:20; Hebrews 13:22; James 5:19; 2 Peter 3:17), others near the end of a paragraph (1 Corinthians 11:33; 14:39; 15:58; Philippians 4:1), and others in the middle of a paragraph (Romans 10:1; 12:19; 1 Thessalonians 2:14; 3:7; James 5:9).[29] Some vocatives in 1 John also occur in non-initial positions. For instance, a vocative occurs near the end of the letter in 5:21, near the end of a paragraph in 2:1 and in the middle of a paragraph in 2:7.[30]

The occurrence of vocatives in locations other than the start of sentences and paragraphs leads Clark to conclude that their 'existence may call into question the paragraph divisions in printed editions of the Greek text, and a lot more study is needed before a reliable system of paragraph divisions can be regarded as firmly established'.[31] Rogers takes her conclusion further, suggesting a possible alternative explanation for the function of the vocative: 'In itself, the vocative form cannot be said to signal change in theme ... Perhaps the value of the vocatives for prominence has been neglected in the undue attention given to them as boundary markers.'[32] Following Rogers' suggestion this research understands the rhetorical effect of the vocative (or its nominative equivalent) as one of emphasis or prominence. This seems in keeping with the definition of the vocative as the case of direct address. In one sense the whole of a text is the attempt of an author to speak to an audience, but with a vocative the level of communication is changed. It seems to heighten the proximity of the author to the audience, appealing to them more directly than in the surrounding text and so giving prominence to the statement in which it occurs. On this understanding, a vocative *may* alert a reader to a new section in a text (a boundary indicator) or a new paragraph in a span.[33] However, its rhetorical effect may be used for other purposes as well. It *may* occur in order to draw a reader's attention to a summary statement, a conclusion of a section, a key piece of argumentation, etc.

This understanding of the vocative is evident in 1 John. Larsen argues that the vocatives in 1 John seem to be used primarily for the rhetorical effect of adding emphasis to the verse in question.[34] The verse may start

---

[29] Clark 2006: 43–4.
[30] For the reasons for understanding the vocatives in 2:1 being at the end of a paragraph and 2:7 in the middle of a paragraph, see chapter 4.
[31] Clark 2006: 44.   [32] Rogers 1984: 26.   [33] Barnwell 1974: 10.
[34] Larsen 1991: 50–1.

a new section (2:18) or paragraph within a span. But it may also be used in a conclusion to stress the point of the preceding argument (2:1).[35]

This reading pays particular attention to the vocatives in 1 John. Since they can give prominence to summary statements, conclusions, and boundaries, they are one feature that can limit the way gaps in the text are filled.

Boundaries

Crossing a boundary in the text into a new unit causes a gap between units but also limits how the completed unit (and its gaps) can be understood. In closing a unit, the boundary affords the reader an opportunity to review the unit and the decisions made in filling gaps in their reading. The significance of concluding boundaries for whole works seems an accepted axiom. Griffith's study of 1 John 5:21 and its implications for understanding 1 John is premised on such an understanding of concluding boundaries.[36] Yet it is not just the final boundary of a text that functions this way but also concluding boundaries of units. So this research pays particular attention to boundary crossing as a device that limits the way gaps can be filled.

However, identifying the boundaries of 1 John is difficult, as the multitude of structures proposed for 1 John testifies. There are two main means by which boundaries are usually identified. The first uses the formal features of a text. These can be initial boundary markers such as orienters, vocatives, topic sentences, certain conjunctions, a new setting (in a narrative situation), and final markers such as doxologies, summaries, and tail-head links.[37] A change in grammatical person or verb tense-form can indicate a boundary.[38] The repetition of forms or phrases can indicate boundaries in two ways. On the one hand, a phrase can flag a move into a new topic. An example of this is Brown's understanding of the use of the phrase 'this is the gospel' in 1:5 and 3:11 as indicating two main sections to 1 John.[39] He perceives the phrase as introducing a new section and thus as a boundary marker. On the other hand, a phrase can provide continuity

---

[35] Callow 1999: 401, 403.   [36] Griffith 2002: 2–4.

[37] Larsen 1991: 49–51; Young 1994: 253–4. An example of repetition, especially of apparently redundant material that seems to mark a boundary, is the third line in the seemingly two-line parallelism of 2:11 that repeats the first line of 2:9. This is similar to one of the functions of the tricolon in Hebrew poetry, see Watson 1995: 183.

[38] Porter 1994: 301–2.

[39] Brown 1982: 126. The phrase 'this is the gospel' translates ἔστιν αὕτη ἡ ἀγγελία in 1:5 and αὕτη ἐστὶν ἡ ἀγγελία in 3:11.

to a section, so that its absence after a period reveals that a new topic has begun somewhere in the immediate past. Examples of phrases Brown identifies as giving continuity to sections are ἐὰν εἴπωμεν in 1:6, 8, 10; ὁ λέγων in 2:4, 6, 9; (καὶ) ὑμεῖς in 2:20, 24, 27; πᾶς ὁ in 2:29; 3:3, 4, 6 (x2), 10; and οἴδαμεν in 5:18, 19, and 20.[40] Brown's use of repetition in both ways suggests that more than just repetition as a formal feature is required to justify boundary decisions.

The second way boundaries are identified is through examination of theme. Beekman and Callow argue that the 'basic criterion' for 'a section, or paragraph, [is that it] deals with one theme. If the theme changes, then a new unit has started.'[41] Noting a theme change can then limit 'gap filling' because it can alert the reader to introductions and conclusions to sections. Larsen builds on this understanding and argues that '[f]or nonnarrative material, an introduction states or alludes to the theme which is going to be developed ... a conclusion often repeats in some way what was stated in the introduction'.[42] Using Larsen's suggestion to identify boundaries is appealing except that it fails to indicate how the theme is identified in order to recognise the introduction and conclusion.

This study combines both the formal features and the theme approach in identifying content. First, it associates theme with vocabulary usage so that when there is a sustained occurrence of a word group (or its synonyms) and then an absence of it, a boundary will be assumed.[43] This inductive approach identifies the theme at the end of the unit so that the boundary affords an opportunity to review the unit with the theme in mind. The boundary is then examined for formal features that could add support to the decision to understand it as a boundary. This method thus avoids the pitfall of assuming a formal feature is always being used in the same manner, a problem demonstrated with regards to Brown's use of repetition.

The small unit 2:15–17 provides a good example of this method. That it is a unit is observable due to its repeated use of κόσμος, six times in these three verses. This noun was last used in 2:1 and is not used again until 3:1, thus indicating that it is the theme of this small unit. The unit opens with an asyndetic clause revealing no logical or temporal link to 2:12–14. This disjunction is a formal feature that can often indicate an opening boundary.[44] The closing of the unit contains a contrast between

---

[40] *Ibid.*: 118–19. [41] Beekman and Callow 1974: 279. [42] Larsen 1991: 51.
[43] This is similar to the concept of 'topic' in Callow 1999: 400.
[44] BDF §462–3; Young 1994: 180; Wallace 1996: 658–9.

the world and the person of God. This contrast summarises the content of the unit and acts as a closing statement. This understanding is further supported by an examination of 2:18 that starts with a vocative and an eschatological reference, both of which could indicate the start of a new unit.

Filling gaps: intertextuality

When a reader comes to fill gaps in a text, they trawl (both consciously and subconsciously) through the other texts they have experienced for analogous examples in order to fit the text together in a consistent pattern. This is because meanings of words are described in other words and their meanings. As Barthes states: 'The text is a tissue of quotations drawn from the innumerable centres of culture.'[45] This has often been assumed to result in the death of the author because it is the reader who supplies the links between words and texts.[46] However, the author is involved in the process because the author is also subject to words and their usage in texts. Authors choose to express themselves with particular words as a result of their experience of texts. This process of understanding words and texts in terms of their usage in other texts is known as intertextuality. Intertextuality can be both general (anything the author or reader have ever encountered) through to specific (explicit quotes of other texts in the text being written/read). It is intertextuality that makes communication between author and reader possible because the more texts they share, the more likely their assigning of meaning will be similar.

Intertextuality can occur at five points: the author in their choice of vocabulary and expression, the original reader in the way they fill in the gaps, the text in the sense that only through the text is the real reader able to experience the implied author and implied reader, the real reader as they fill gaps, and the community of interpretation that conditions how present readers fill gaps. This thesis follows Hays in attempting to hold together these five points rather than focussing on one at the expense of the others.[47] As a result it aims to produce a historically conditioned twenty first-century intertextual reading of 1 John. It applies Hays' seven tests for identifying intertextual echoes to 1 John:

1.   An echo must be available to the author and original readers.
2.   An echo is required to have some volume of repetition in words or syntactical pattern.

---

[45] Barthes 1977: 170.   [46] *Ibid.*   [47] Hays 1989: 26–7.

3.   A higher recurrence of the echo in other Johannine literature (John, 2–3 John, Revelation) is used to justify its validity.[48]
4.   An echo must have thematic coherence with the point being made in the text.
5.   The echo is required to be historically plausible in the sense that John and his readers could have understood it in their historical milieu.
6.   Someone else in the history of interpretation of 1 John should have heard the echo.
7.   The echo needs to make sense of the unit of text in which it occurs.[49]

These tests underlie the identification of echoes and will not be explicitly acknowledged with each echo cited.

This process of intertextuality is used throughout previous research on 1 John to justify choices in readings. Until fairly recently scholars did not explicitly acknowledge their method for making intertextual choices nor the basis for their choice of texts in forming the canon for their intertextuality. Yet in their actions they generally appeal to the same arguments that Hays suggests as tests for identifying echoes. The adoption of these tests in previous research is evident because the grounds given for identifying an echo are often repetition of vocabulary and syntactical patterns (no. 2), thematic coherence (no. 4), and that an echo makes sense of the text (no. 7). Moreover, research is generally agreed in its appeal to the other Johannine literature (no. 3) and early Christian documents (nos. 1, 5, 7).[50] So this book will search for intertextual links in the other earliest Christian documents, especially within the other Johannine literature.

Further, scholars generally use as many texts as possible to form the basis of their intertextuality.[51] So it seems that the more texts that can be cited, the stronger the case. Texts cited in filling gaps in 1 John include the Old Testament, the Qumran documents, the rest of the New

---

[48] This study also uses intratextual references (references drawn from elsewhere in 1 John) only after the references have already been discussed. Limiting the use of intratextual references in this way avoids the charge that the research 'begs the question' and allows the introduction to establish the parameters of interpretation since it maintains the reading order of the text. For a defence of Revelation being included in this list of Johannine literature see Smalley 2007: xx.

[49] Hays 1989: 29–32.

[50] The dispute over whether to include Revelation in the Johannine corpus does not affect this point.

[51] There are some specialised studies of links between 1 John and the Old Testament – Kennedy 1916; Malatesta 1978; and between 1 John and the Qumran documents – Brown 1966; O'Neill 1966; Boismard 1972; Hoffman 1978.

Testament (especially the Johannine corpus), Greco-Roman material, Ignatius' letters, and Gnostic texts.

However, recent scholarly debate about intertextual links and 1 John is devoted to the extent of Jewish thought evident in 1 John. In 1988 Carson wrote an article on the use of the Old Testament in John and the Johannine Epistles. In this twenty-page article he spent less than half a page on the Old Testament in the Johannine Epistles and stated: 'The most striking feature relevant to our subject in these epistles is the absence not only of OT quotations but even of many unambiguous allusions to the OT.'[52]

In 1991 Lieu took issue with Carson and suggested that the Old Testament lies behind the thought, language, and many of the images of 1 John.[53] Further, in 1993, Lieu published an article devoted to the issue. She noted that O'Neill's work in citing parallels between 1 John and the Qumran literature 'clearly demonstrate(s) the Jewishness of 1 John'.[54] Then she argued that explicit Old Testament quotation is an inadequate measure of Jewishness. By an exploration of three themes and passages (1:9–2:2; 3:7ff.; 2:11) Lieu demonstrated that 1 John displays patterns of interpretation that have parallels in contemporary Jewish exegesis.[55]

In response to Lieu's work, Carson rethought his original statement, and although holding to its accuracy with regards to the number of explicit quotations, now regards the Old Testament as providing the basis of the author's thought. Lieu's work, along with the work of Kennedy,[56] Boismard,[57] and Malatesta,[58] has resulted in Carson now concluding: 'In 1 John the Old Testament is not so much a source that is quoted as the very matrix of reflection of a Christian who for many years has thought hard about the relation of Christian truth to antecedent revelation.'[59] Since 1 John displays Old Testament influence and Jewishness in its exegetical methods, particular attention is paid to echoes between 1 John and the Old Testament when intertextual connections are used to fill gaps. The reason for focusing on the Old Testament for intertextual connections, and not also citing Jewish intertextual literature and the Qumran documents, is that the Old Testament is the source of Jewish thought. These other documents record historical interpretations of the source documents that were roughly contemporary with 1 John. As such they will be appealed to in the section on tangents to the reading as they

---

[52] Carson 1988: 256.   [53] Lieu 1991: 87.   [54] Lieu 1993: 459. See O'Neill 1966.
[55] Lieu 1993.   [56] Kennedy 1916.   [57] Boismard 1949.   [58] Malatesta 1978.
[59] Carson 2004: 274. For how Carson works this out with regards to the whole of 1 John see Carson 2007.

may reveal evidence of similar contemporary understandings of the source documents.

This model has the strength of combining the best parts of both the Historical Critical and Literary/Rhetorical approaches but also avoiding their pitfalls. The Historical Critical approach seeks to use the situation behind the text and historical sources as the means to fill the gaps, that is, it uses its reconstruction of history as the basis of its intertextual solutions. The literary critical approach makes use of other pieces of literature to fill the gaps – mainly those written in the 'Johannine school'. However, this research does not make intertextual connections on the basis of *either* history *or* literature. Instead it uses both. It uses a form of historically conditioned literary intertextuality that seeks to use as many texts as possible. It understands history as a text but also checks literary texts against their historical plausibility, asking whether the original author and readers would have had access to and understood the connections being suggested.

Conclusion – circles and tangents

The method of reading used in this thesis can be described as circular. Even though 1 John as a text is linear in presentation, being written in a language that moves from left to right, with a start and finish, the strategy is circular.

The approach starts with the text of 1 John and, on encountering a gap, seeks to fill the gap through intertextual similarities with the Old Testament and/or the earliest Christian writings. When another text is cited, it is checked as to its historical viability, its volume, its recurrence and thematic coherence, and its ability to make sense of the text at hand. The text is then re-read in light of the devices that limit the meaning in order to test the intertextual fill. Thus, just as a circle is a self-supporting geometric shape, a line that repeats back on itself, so the reading of the primary text is justified mainly in light of itself. A decision on filling a gap is ultimately justified through its ability to explain the text. In this sense the reading is necessarily circular because the reading produced should be tested by its self-consistency and its ability to explain the most data in the simplest way.

However, just as there are tangents to a circle, lines that touch the circle at points but do not in themselves support the circle, so there is a secondary line of evidence that is appealed to in order to demonstrate the plausibility of the proposed reading. This evidence is another line of intertextuality that supports and informs reading, but does not justify the reading. The primary text justifies the overall reading (circle) and secondary lines of intertextual evidence show the reading's plausibility (tangents).

In summary, the method has two parts with the following steps (Table 1):

Table 1. *The steps in the reading method*

1. The reading circle
   a. Read the text of 1 John under consideration
   b. Identify gaps in the text
      i. Interruptions to sentence flow
      ii. Use of pronouns
      iii. 'Reader experienced'
   c. Identify the limiting devices in the text
      i. Use of γράφω
      ii. Occurrence of vocatives
      iii. Boundary crossing
   d. Ascertain intertextual links that may fill the gap
      i. Old Testament
      ii. Early Christian writings
   e. Re-read the text to test the fill, paying attention to the limiting devices
2. Plausibility tangents
   a. Qumran documents
   b. Church history
      i. Acts
      ii. Apostolic Fathers
      iii. Church Fathers
   c. Earliest Christian theology

The following chapters apply this reading method to 1 John. The method follows the linear presentation of the text, moving systematically from the start to the end of 1 John. This allows the introduction to establish the expectations for the reader and avoids 'begging the question' since texts that are not yet experienced do not limit possible meaning before time.

Since an introduction establishes the expectations of the reader for the text, the next two chapters are a detailed working out of the approach on 1:1–2:11. Thereafter, the chapters record the results of the reading method and focus on texts that question the expectations aroused in the introduction.

PART II

A Reading of 1 John

3

THE RESURRECTED INCARNATE CHRIST: 1 JOHN 1:1–5

The start of a text establishes its framework for interpretation by arousing expectations of what is to come, expectations that are then affirmed, modified or completely changed by the rest of the text.[1] As such, a text's starting point plays a significant role in the interpretation of the rest of a text and the start of 1 John is no exception.[2] This chapter applies the reading method discussed in the last chapter to the opening verses of 1 John in order to understand the expectations that these verses arouse and start constructing the framework for understanding 1 John.

Following the reading method, the chapter has five main parts. First, the limits of 1 John's introduction are proposed. Second, the gaps, limiting devices, and structure of 1 John 1:1–5 are identified and discussed. Third, there is a critical review of how scholarship has 'filled the gap' caused by the ambiguous referent of the opening verses, with the suggestion that it refers to the incarnation. Fourth, an intertextual reading of 1:1–5 is undertaken in which the referent of the verses is understood to be the message of the *resurrected* incarnate Christ. Intertextual evidence is cited from the resurrection narratives of John and Luke, before the 'fill' is tested through a rereading of 1:1–5. Finally, tangents to the reading are provided in order to show its plausibility.

The introduction of 1 John

The first four verses of 1 John are usually considered to be the introduction of 1 John.[3] This research proposes that the introduction of 1 John continues until 2:12–14 because these verses appear to form a

---

[1] Iser 1972: 282–4, 288.

[2] A point made by Francis 1970; Watson 2003: 285–6; Morgen 2005b; even though they all limit the introduction to 1 John 1:1–4.

[3] For example see Gaugler 1964; Malatesta 1973; du Rand 1979; Brown 1982; de Boor 1982; Klauck 1990; Vouga 1990; Sherman and Tuggy 1994; Strecker 1996; Thomas 1998; Wu 1998; Tollefson 1999; Morgen 2005b; Witherington 2006.

transitional unit that signals the end of the introduction and the start of the body of the text.[4] This suggestion runs against the grain of previous studies of 1 John. As Griffith notes: 'No one has advanced a satisfactory explanation of the role of 2.12–14 within the body of 1 John.'[5] However, this reader's attention is drawn to these verses on account of their prominence within the text. In a book where the units are notoriously difficult to ascertain, scholarship has generally accepted that these verses form a unit. Further, they are prominent because they group together two of the limiting devices, vocatives and the use of γράφω, and may have a poetical form that is different from the rest of the book.[6]

1 John 2:12–14 is composed of parallel tristiches (Table 2):

Table 2. *The parallel poetic form of 1 John 2:12–14*

[12] Γράφω ὑμῖν, τεκνία,	[14] ἔγραψα ὑμῖν, παιδία,
ὅτι ἀφέωνται ὑμῖν αἱ ἁμαρτίαι διὰ	ὅτι ἐγνώκατε τὸν πατέρα.
τὸ ὄνομα αὐτοῦ.	
[13] γράφω ὑμῖν, πατέρες,	――― ἔγραψα ὑμῖν, πατέρες,
ὅτι ἐγνώκατε τὸν ἀπ᾿ ἀρχῆς.	――― ὅτι ἐγνώκατε τὸν ἀπ᾿ ἀρχῆς.
γράφω ὑμῖν, νεανίσκοι,	――― ἔγραψα ὑμῖν, νεανίσκοι,
ὅτι	ὅτι ἰσχυροί ἐστε
	καὶ ὁ λόγος τοῦ θεοῦ ἐν ὑμῖν
	μένει
νενικήκατε τὸν πονηρόν.	――― καὶ νενικήκατε τὸν πονηρόν.
[12] I write to you little children,	[14] I write to you little children,
because your sins have been forgiven on	because you know the father.
account of his name.	
[13] I write to you fathers,	I write to you fathers,
because you know the one from the	because you know the one from the
beginning	beginning
I write to you young men	I write to you young men
because	because you are strong
	and the word of God remains in
	you
you have conquered the evil one. ―――	and you have conquered the evil one.

The repetitive formula of γράφω/ἔγραψα ὑμῖν + vocative + ὅτι gives these verses a unity. Yet the change in the tense-form of γράφω reveals two sets of three stiches in parallel. Even though the first and fourth lines

---

[4] Only Grayston (1984: 4) understands 2:12–14 as a transitional unit between the introduction (1:1–2:11) and body of 1 John.

[5] Griffith 2002: 65.

[6] The attempt of du Rand 1979 to break 1 John into poetical units has some basic value in identifying patterns but has not won wide acceptance.

have different vocatives (τεκνία, παιδία), both are drawn from the same semantic domain. The second and fifth statements are identical except for the change in the tense of γράφω. The third and sixth lines address the same audience (νεανίσκοι) and contain the same reason (νενικήκατε τὸν πονηρόν), with the sixth also containing additional reasons. Yet the repetitive structure of these verses also draws attention to differences, inviting the reader to explore these variations.[7]

The most obvious variation is the change in tense-form of γράφω. It caused difficulty for some in the early church, as can be seen in the textual variant in verse 14 that replaces the aorist tense-form with a present tense-form for the sake of consistency.[8] Yet a pattern is observable on closer examination of the use of γράφω in 1 John. Up until 2:14, every occurrence of the verb γράφω is in the present tense-form (1:4; 2:7, 8, 12, 13). From 2:14 until the end of the book, every occurrence of γράφω is in the aorist tense-form (2:14, 21, 26; 5:13). So the change in tense-form in 2:14 marks some sort of turning point or transition in the book.[9]

Following this change in tense-form, and dividing 1 John into two parts either side of the poem, reveals a dominant motif in each part. Brown argues that 1 John has two parts, the first of which has as its central motif 'God is light', a motif introduced straight after the prologue in 1:5.[10] Yet his claim that the first part ends at 3:10 seems flawed if 'light' is indeed the key motif. This is because neither φῶς (light) nor its antonyms σκοτία (darkness)/σκότος (dark) occur after 2:11. However, if 2:12–14 is a transitional unit that ends the first part and starts a second, then 'light' is indeed the dominant motif of the first part. The language of light (φῶς) and darkness (σκοτία/σκότος) forms an inclusion for the part (1:5–7; 2:8–11). Further, it is unique to 1:1–2:11, as the language is not found again in 1 John.

Since the dominant motif of the first part (φῶς, σκοτία/σκότος) was introduced at its start (1:5), it is not surprising that the paragraph that opens the second part also seems to contain its dominant motif (2:15–17).

---

[7] Some scholars understand this invitation as the text posing questions for the reader to answer. For example Watson (1989: 97–8) lists four questions the text raises for the reader. How many groups are represented by the vocatives – one, two or three? Why did the author repeat verses 12 and 13 in verse 14? Why is there a change in the tense-form of γράφω from present to aorist? How does this unit function in its context? Noack (1959–1960) raises a fifth question about how ὅτι should be understood – as causal (giving reasons for writing) or recitative (outlining the content of what is written).

[8] The older more reliable texts favour the harder aorist reading ($\mathfrak{p}^{74\text{vid}}$, ℵ, A, B, C …) while only a few more recent manuscripts contain the present (1175, *Byz* [K], *l* 147 …); see Metzger 1994: 640.

[9] I have no explanation of the reason for the change in tense-form and aspect, but am rather drawing attention to the effect of the change.

[10] Brown 1982: 126.

This first paragraph of the second part is all about the world (κόσμος). The series of imperative verb forms draw particular attention to the world. Κόσμος occurs 23 times in 1 John,[11] more per thousand words than in any other New Testament book, and all but one of the occurrences is in the second part.[12] This seems to mark it as the key motif.[13]

Confirmation that these are key motifs in each part is found in their common description. In the only two occurrences of the verb παράγω in 1 John, both σκοτία/σκότος and κόσμος are described as passing away (2:8, 17). Even though the motifs occur independently of each other, they have the same fate.

This division of 1 John into two parts around the poem of 2:12–14 also makes sense of Lieu's observation that the false teachers are not discussed until 2:19.[14] The first part (1:1–2:11) seems to act as an extended introduction before the historical issue that caused 1 John to be written is introduced and addressed. Thus 1:1–2:11 shapes the expectations of the reader before the text turns to consider the historical reason for writing.

So, 1 John has two parts, one either side of the poem of 2:12–14. The first part (1:1–2:11) has 'light/darkness' as a dominant theme, while the 'world' seems to be the dominant theme in the second part (2:15–5:21). The first part acts as an introduction before the historical situation is presented in the body of the text.[15]

The gaps, limiting devices, and structure of 1:1–5

In keeping with the reading method outlined in chapter 2, this part of the chapter has three sections. The first identifies the gaps in 1 John 1:1–5, the second identifies the limiting devices that occur in these verses, while the last section discusses the structure of the verses.

Gaps

There are three sources of possible gaps in 1 John 1:1–5 – interruptions to the flow of sentences, cataphoric pronouns, and reader-experienced gaps.

---

[11] 2:2, 15 (x3), 16 (x2), 17; 3:1, 13, 17; 4:1, 3, 4, 5 (x3), 9, 14, 17; 5:4 (x2), 5, 19.

[12] Only John's Gospel uses κόσμος more times (78). Yet 1 John's usage per 1,000 words (9.22) is more than twice that in John's Gospel (4.29).

[13] The one occurrence of κόσμος in the first part is in 2:2.   [14] Lieu 1981: 211.

[15] For a fuller discussion of the structure and argument of 1 John see Jensen 2012. A summary can be found in the Appendix: The Structure of 1 John. I have also discussed this structure with regards to the themes of 'Sonship' and 'Victory over Evil' in 1 John in Jensen 2008 and Jensen 2009.

Interruptions to the flow of sentences

The syntax of the opening verses of 1 John is notoriously difficult. As Dodd notes: 'The opening sentence of the Epistle, extending to the end of verse 3, is exceedingly complex. The writer has tried to pack into it more than a single sentence can well contain, at the cost of clarity.'[16] The first paragraph of 1 John consists of four sentences. The first is long and complex spanning the first three verses (1:1–3a). It opens with four relative clauses (1:1), moves to a parenthetical aside (1:2), and resumes the thought of 1:1 with another relative clause before the main verb (ἀπαγγέλλομεν) appears (1:3). The result is a sentence that has lots of interruptions and lacks flow. It requires readers to work hard on their original reading. They are forced to re-read these opening clauses once the main verb is located in order to check their understanding. The whole sentence poses a gap for the readers as they need to establish the object of the verb and its relationship to the relative clauses. The subsequent sentences in the verses all start with καί, so there are no further interruptions to the flow of sentences.

Cataphoric pronouns

There are four different pronouns used a total of twelve times in 1:1–5. Six of these occurrences are 'clear' anaphoric usages resulting in no gap. Of the remaining six occurrences, five are cataphoric and there is one ambiguous usage, all of which require interpretation from the reader.

The clear anaphoric uses have as their antecedents 'eternal life' (ἥτις in 1:2), 'the message of life' (ὃ in 1:3), 'the Father' (αὐτοῦ in 1:3), 'the message' (ἣν in 1:5), 'Jesus Christ' (αὐτοῦ in 1:5),[17] and 'God' (αὐτῷ in 1:5). The first four cataphoric pronouns appear in a series of parallel relative clauses. Since their postcedent (τοῦ λόγου τῆς ζωῆς) follows the last relative clause, there is no syntactical gap. However, it is unclear how these clauses explicate their postcedent – the message of life. The other pronoun being used cataphorically is αὕτη in 1:5. However, its postcedent is ὁ θεὸς ... οὐδεμία, which, due to its relatively close proximity, results in no gap. The one ambiguous use of a pronoun is ταῦτα in 1:4. It is unclear if the referent is the paragraph or the text

---

[16] Dodd 1946: 1.
[17] The antecedent could be 'the Father' in 1:3 but it seems better to understand it as 'Jesus Christ' since this is nominalised at the end of the verse. Either way, the pronoun is anaphoric.

of 1 John as a whole.[18] This does not result in a gap because either the demonstrative refers to the immediate paragraph which the reader has experienced and so can fill any potential gap, or it refers to the whole of 1 John of which the paragraph is a part and so can be used to start filling the potential gap.

So the pronouns themselves do not provide any syntactical gaps. Yet there is a gap in understanding how the relative clauses of 1:1 are related to their postcedent (τοῦ λόγου τῆς ζωῆς). This gap becomes more significant when it is combined with the interruptions in the flow of sentences. What is 'the message of life' which the author has experienced first hand?

First- and second-person personal pronouns also occur in these verses. That both pronouns are used, allows a distinction to be made between the inclusive and exclusive use of the first person. That is, the first person refers to the writer only and not the readers. This implies that the second-person pronouns refer to the readers. If a gap is felt in relation to the identity of the author, any discussion needs to fall within the decisions about the content of the opening verses, especially the claims to be an eyewitness. However, the explicit lack of names suggests that the opening verses do not encourage any identification to be made.[19]

Reader-experienced gaps

The lack of a conventional opening to the document, indicating which genre rules should be used in reading, poses a gap for the reader. It forces the reader to choose how they should read the text. This, in combination with the lack of sentence flow, and the uncertain semantic relationship between the relative clauses of verse 1 and their postcedent, causes a large gap that the reader needs to fill. The reader is required by these opening verses to take a considered examination of the unit and hence very actively build the framework for interpreting 1 John. What is the 'message of life' that the author experienced first hand and announced to the readers which generates the expectation of the reader and forms the framework for interpreting 1 John?

---

[18] The majority of scholars understand it as referring to the letter as a whole. See for example Smalley 2007 14; Plummer 1911: 76; Law 1979: 371; Marshall 1978: 105; Bultmann 1973: 13; Painter 2002: 123; Brown 1982: 172–3; Schnackenburg 1992: 62. For the arguments that it is only the paragraph see Stott 1988: 70.

[19] Lieu 2008a: 48.

Limiting devices

There are no occurrences of vocatives in these verses that limit how gaps can be filled. There is one use of a form of γράφω in 1:4, where the purpose (ἵνα) for writing is outlined. A decision about the extent of what is written is not required with respect to filling gaps in this unit because the gaps are limited by the author's purpose of completing their joy.

Establishing the closing boundary of the introduction's first unit is a difficult task. The general consensus in scholarship understands 1:1–4 as the prologue to 1 John, so it would be natural to take 1:1–4 as the first unit of the introduction. There are three reasons for identifying a boundary at the end of 1:4.

First, a cataphoric statement opens verse 5 (καὶ ἔστιν αὕτη ἡ ἀγγελία). However, justifying the division on the basis of the cataphoric statement has some weaknesses. The cataphoric statement starts with καί, linking it to the previous verses. The antecedent of αὐτός is found in verses 1:1–4. The vocabulary in 1:5 is related to that used in 1:1–4, indicating a continuation of the discussion.[20] The main rhetorical function of cataphora is prominence.[21] This does not exclude that it may be used to mark division in the text; rather, it is used to draw attention to the division in a text, a division that is identified on grounds other than the occurrence of cataphora.

The second reason for identifying a boundary at the end of verse 4 is the vocabulary shared by 1:5 and 1:6–7 (φῶς and σκοτία/σκότος). Yet there are weaknesses in this argument. For instance, 1:6 is asyndetic, meaning that there is no syntactical link to 1:5. Further, even though this vocabulary of light and darkness is repeated, implying some semantic link, to note only the recurrence of that language is to miss the repetition of κοινωνία (1:3b) in 1:6–7. Thus there is also a link between 1:6–7 and 1:3b. The ἐὰν εἴπωμεν ὅτι statement in 1:6 is based on ideas that span the proposed division of 1:4, the ideas of fellowship and the character of God as light (1:3b–5).

The third reason for identifying a boundary at the end of verse 4 is the placement of the γράφω statement in 1:4. However, 1:4 does not break the logical flow so much as function as a parenthetical statement that comments on the motivation of the author in announcing the message of 1:1–3. The purpose statement (1:4) moves to a different level of communication. To read it as a boundary in the text appears to be a mistake that

---

[20] ἀκούω and the ἀγγελ– word group.   [21] See the discussion in chapter 2.

the author acknowledges could be made and is at pains to avoid. The καί that starts 1:5 deliberately links it with the preceding verses, in particular 1:3b. The cataphoric statement ἔστιν αὕτη ἡ ἀγγελία and repetition of related vocabulary draw the reader's attention to the continuation of the previous verses (1:1–3). This seems in keeping with the style of 1 John's author, who used the repetition of vocabulary in 1:3a to signify the end of a parenthetical statement (1:2) and the resumption of the main argument (from 1:1). To put it differently, if 1:4 is deleted there is a consistent flow of logic between 1:3 and 1:5.

These weaknesses suggest that 1:5 should not be understood as the start of a new unit. Instead, 1:5 seems linked to 1:1–4 both syntactically and through vocabulary repetition. This suggests that 1:1–5 should be understood as the first unit. The theme of the unit is the 'message' that the author preached to the readers. So gaps in 1:1–5 are limited to some extent by their ability to be related to the theme of the preached message.

Structure

The first sentence has six main parts. First, a series of four relative clauses (ὃ ἦν ἀπ' ἀρχῆς, ὃ ἀκηκόαμεν, ὃ ἑωράκαμεν τοῖς ὀφθαλμοῖς ἡμῶν, ὃ ἐθεασάμεθα καὶ αἱ χεῖρες ἡμῶν ἐψηλάφησαν) starts the sentence before a prepositional phrase (περὶ τοῦ λόγου τῆς ζωῆς) occurs. These relative clauses have the prepositional phrase as their postcedent. So any decision about how to understand these relative clauses needs to take into account not just the meaning of the prepositional phrase, but also the way that the relative clauses are in apposition to each other. This means that they are describing the same entity and as such any reading needs to account for all of the relative clauses.

Second, the prepositional phrase (περὶ τοῦ λόγου τῆς ζωῆς) is the object of the main verb that is yet to be encountered by the reader. This verb (ἀπαγγέλλομεν) and its cognates are often followed by a περὶ phrase, indicating the content of the proclamation (Luke 7:18; 13:1; Acts 7:52; 28:21; Romans 15:21).[22] Yet on two occasions it precedes the verb (John 16:25; 1 Thessalonians 1:9). So the phrase περὶ τοῦ λόγου τῆς ζωῆς at the end of verse 1 gives the content of the proclamation in view in the main verb. Thus the relative clauses refine the description of the content of the proclamation.

---

[22] BDAG 1a: 797.

Third, between the prepositional phrase and the main verb is a parenthetical description. The description explicates the content of the message, not the words τοῦ λόγου but τῆς ζωῆς. So any proposal for the meaning of the relative pronouns should focus on τῆς ζωῆς rather than τοῦ λόγου.

Fourth, the parenthetical description continues until a relative clause of the same form as those that started the sentence is reintroduced at the start of verse 3 (ὃ ἑωράκαμεν καὶ ἀκηκόαμεν). This relative clause signals a return to the main sentence.

Fifth, the main verb is given (ἀπαγγέλλομεν). This indicates that the verses are a description of the preaching of the author. The relative clauses are neuter because they have the whole prepositional phrase (περὶ τοῦ λόγου τῆς ζωῆς) as their referent.

Finally, the sentence ends with a purpose statement (ἵνα καὶ ὑμεῖς κοινωνίαν ἔχητε μεθ᾽ ἡμῶν). This statement indicates the intention of the author in preaching the word of life to the audience – that they might have fellowship with the author.

The second and subsequent sentences (1:3b–5) are more straightforward. The second sentence (1:3b) amplifies (καί) whom this fellowship is with. The third sentence (1:4) gives the author's purpose for writing (γράφομεν … ἵνα). This sentence acts as an aside in the argument, revealing the intentions of the author. The fourth sentence (1:5) continues (καί) the argument of 1:1–3a. The cataphoric statement (καὶ ἔστιν αὕτη ἡ ἀγγελία) redirects the reader's attention from the aside of 1:4 back to the argument of 1:1–3a and provides the reader with a summary of the message and thus a vehicle to check their understanding of 1:1. That is, the content of the relative clause in describing 'life' must also fit with the description of the message provided in 1:5, that God is light and in him there is no darkness.

Summary

The opening paragraph of 1 John forces the reader to construct the framework for interpreting the text that follows. The first sentence lacks a smooth flow between clauses with the result that there is a gap from the start. Further, the cataphoric relative clauses have an ambiguous semantic relationship to their postcedent further widening the gap. The lack of any genre identifiers results in the entire unit being a gap.

The purpose statement and closing boundary limit the way that this opening paragraph can be understood. The paragraph was written to complete the joy of the author and is about 'the message of life'.

The syntax of the paragraph requires any proposal for understanding the content of 'the message of life' to make sense of all the relative clauses, fit with the parenthetical description of life in 1:2, result in fellowship with God, and be congruent with the summary of the message contained in 1:5.

'The message of life' (1:1) in previous research

The secondary literature reveals a general consensus that 1 John 1:1 refers to the incarnation. A possible allusion to the resurrection is sometimes noted before being rejected. This section outlines and then evaluates the consensus position before analysing the reasons given for rejecting the allusion to the resurrection.

The incarnation

The majority of scholars understand the first verse of 1 John as affirming the incarnation: that the man Jesus was truly God incarnate.[23] The evidence cited to support this proposal is the intertextual links with the prologue of John's Gospel. It is argued that the intertextual affiliations with John 1:1–18 are so numerous that 1 John 1:1–5 cannot be understood apart from the Gospel's prologue. For instance Schnackenburg states: 'In order to understand this prooemium [1 John 1:1–5] we must compare it closely with the Prologue of John ... One may say that the opening of the letter presumes the Gospel Prologue or the Logos hymn embedded in it. It takes up the theme of the Prologue and exploits it for the purposes of

---

[23] For example see Dodd 1946: 1–6; Bultmann 1973: 7–8; Burdick 1985: 99; Hiebert 1991: 35; Schnackenburg 1992: 48–52; Johnson 1993: 25–6; Burge 1996: 52–4; Rensberger 1997: 46–7; Kruse 2000: 51–3; Akin 2001: 51–3; Uebele 2001: 125–8; Painter 2002: 126–40; Morgen 2005b: 65–6; Beeke 2006: 20–1; Smalley 2007: 8–9; Yarbrough 2008: 34–40. There are some differences about whether it is the fact of the incarnation, or the process of the incarnation, or the actual life of Jesus that is being affirmed. But in general, this verse is understood to affirm that the man Jesus was God. De Boer (1991: 328) presents another alternative, that the 'concrete reality of the "eternal life"' is what is on view in these verses, a reality 'so tangible that the author can even speak, in striking rhetorical excess, of having physically touched it'. The problem with this view is that there are no indicators in this verse that the verbs should be read in a metaphorical sense. If they can be understood without appeal to metaphor, then there is no necessity for reading them metaphorically. De Boer's argument that the neuter form of the relative pronoun cautions against identifying the antecedent as the person of Jesus Christ is a fair criticism, but his identification of the antecedent as 'life' also fails to grammatically match the relative pronoun since ἡ ζωή is feminine.

relevant proclamation.'[24] Brown also observes similarities in vocabulary and themes.[25] He lists the following vocabulary similarities (Table 3):

Table 3. *Brown's similarities between John 1:1–18 and 1 John 1:1–4(5)*

John 1:1–18		1 John 1:1–4(5)	
1a	In the beginning was the Word	1a	What was from the beginning
1b	The Word was in God's presence	2de	Eternal life which was in the Father's presence
4a	In him (the Word) was life	1f	The word of life
4b	This life was the light of men	5d	God is light
5ab	The light shines in the darkness, for the darkness did not overcome it	5e	and in Him there is no darkness at all
14a	The Word became flesh	2a	This life was revealed
14b	and made his dwelling among us	2f	and was revealed to us
14c	and we looked at his glory	1d	what we looked at
16ab	Of his fullness we have all received	3de	The communion we have with
17a	through Jesus Christ		The Father and with His Son,
18b	God the only Son		Jesus Christ

Brown further notes the following similarities in themes:

- The theme of divine reality (which was in/from the beginning) starts both prologues (John 1:1; 1 John 1:1).
- The theme of life appears partway through both prologues (John 1.4; 1 John 1:1).
- A double interruption breaks the grammatical connections within each prologue (John 1:6–9, 15, and 12–13; 1 John 1:1f and 2).
- The theme/vocabulary of witness (μαρτυρέω) only occurs in the parenthetical interruptions.
- A visual reaction of the author ('we') is recorded in both (John 1:14; 1 John 1:1, 2, 3).
- Each refers to the results of the manifestation of the divine reality as a participation with God (John 1:16; 1 John 1:4).

---

[24] Schnackenburg 1992: 50.
[25] Brown 1982: 179. See also Weir 1975: 119; Painter 2002: 127, 131–2; Scholtissek 2004: 154–5; Heckel 2004: 434–6. Klauck (1991: 56–8) notes both similarities and differences.

These similarities of 1 John 1:1–4(5) with John 1:1–18 result in the opening verses of 1 John being read as about the incarnation, since the prologue of John is about the incarnation of the Word in the man Jesus.

When it is understood that the incarnation is on view in the relative clauses of verse 1, support is then claimed from two elements in the following verses. First, the prepositional phrase περὶ τοῦ λόγου τῆς ζωῆς contains the key word λόγος that is central to John 1:1–18. Further, its combination with life (ζωή) is cited as confirmation of the incarnation since in the incarnation the pre-existent second person of the Trinity enters into human life. Second, the description of the Word of life in the parenthetical verse 2 is that it appeared from the Father. Given the context of John 1:1–18, the pre-existent Word was with the Father and, in becoming human, appeared on earth. The verb φανερόω refers to the incarnation because the location of the 'to us' (ἡμῖν) is earth while the point of origin is from the position of being with the Father (πρὸς τὸν πατέρα). The similarity between πρὸς τὸν πατέρα (1 John 1:2) and πρὸς τὸν θεόν (John 1:2), in their use of the unusual associative sense of πρός, is noted as additional support for this understanding.

Critique of the incarnation understanding

The main strength of understanding the opening verses of 1 John as referring to the incarnation is the support for the reading given by the number of intertextual connections observed with the prologue of John's Gospel. These intertextual connections make a strong case for understanding these opening verses as referring to the incarnation. However, there are also weaknesses in the consensus view because of the weaknesses in the intertextual evidence cited.

Although there are numerous intertextual connections between the prologues of John's Gospel and 1 John, they are not necessarily as similar as some exponents claim. Even though similar vocabulary occurs in both prologues, there are formal divergences in expression. Schnackenburg lists the following formal divergences (Table 4):[26]

These divergences temper Brown's noted similarities. As a result, some scholars question the weight that these intertextual connections bear in justifying reading the two prologues together. They suggest that the parallels rest on general impressions rather than on lexical or syntactical accuracy. It is not that the prologues are not similar, just that they

---

[26] Schnackenburg 1992: 50.

Table 4. *Schnackenburg's divergences between John 1 and 1 John 1*

John 1		1 John 1	
ἐν ἀρχῇ	v. 1	ἀπ' ἀρχῆς	v. 1
ἐν αὐτῷ ζωὴ ἦν	v. 4	τοῦ λόγου τῆς ζωῆς	v. 1
ἦν πρὸς τὸν θεόν	vv. 1, 2	ἦν πρὸς τὸν πατέρα	v. 2
ὁ λόγος σὰρξ ἐγένετο	v. 14	ἡ ζωὴ ἐφανερώθη	v. 2
ἐθεασάμεθα τὴν δόξαν αὐτοῦ	v. 14	ὃ ἐθεασάμεθα	v. 1
		or: ἑωράκαμεν ... τὴν ζωὴν τὴν αἰώνιον	v. 2

are not as similar as suggested, and therefore not as determinative for ascertaining meaning. For instance:

> The differences show that only a few concepts correspond; even the same words are used differently. Thus not only is the absolute ὁ λόγος missing from 1 John, but there is a difference between ἀπ' ἀρχῆς (1 John 1:1) and ἐν ἀρχῇ (John 1:1): the incarnation is predicated in 1 John not of the Logos, who 'became flesh' and 'tented' among us, but of ζωή. In addition, the object of seeing is not the *doxa* of the Incarnate One, but eternal life (v. 2b). Beyond this, it is clear from the comparison that not even the sequence of the Logos hymn reappears in 1 John. It follows that the author of 1 John is not referring to the prologue of John ... rather, this author is employing the independent language and world of ideas of the Johannine school, which is also used – even though in a sharply divergent manner – in John 1:1–14.[27]

> [O]ther scholars remain sceptical about allusions to the Fourth Gospel's Prologue as the exegetical key to 1 Jn 1,1–4. 1 John shows no trace of Jewish Wisdom traditions of cosmology and dwelling in the souls of the righteous which provide the poetic framework to the Prologue. Scattered words rather than concepts or poetic phrases are the only pegs on which to hang the association between 1 John and the gospel Prologue.[28]

So even though there are similarities between the prologues of 1 John and John's Gospel, to have these as solely determinative when filling the

---

[27] Strecker 1996: 9–10.   [28] Perkins 2005: 250.

gap of the first verse seems problematic. They should contribute to filling the gap but other factors may also be involved.

The resurrection

Some scholars recognise a possible allusion to the resurrection of Jesus in 1 John 1:1 when the author says 'that which … our hands touched' (αἱ χεῖρες ἡμῶν ἐψηλάφησαν).[29] For example:

> 'Handled' seems to be a direct reference to the test demanded by S.Thomas (John xx. 27) and offered to the other disciples (Luke xxiv. 39, where the same verb is used as here).[30]

> [T]he most relevant passage for this verse is found in [John] 20.27, where Jesus instructs Thomas to place his hand in Jesus' side. Such a reference suggests that the readers of 1 John would most likely think of this resurrection story. That reference is made to the resurrection might also be supported by the use of the term for handle (ψηλαφάω) in Lk. 24.39, one of its four New Testament occurrences, where Jesus seeks to demonstrate to the startled and frightened disciples that he is alive.[31]

However, even when this link is acknowledged, the allusion is rejected:[32]

> [Ψ]ηλαφάω ('touch') can refer in this context only to the historical figure of Jesus (the 'incarnated one') and not to the resurrected one, as in Luke 24:39; cf. Jn 20:24ff.[33]

> Although this recalls Lk. xxiv 39 and Jn. xx 27, the resurrection of Jesus and its reality are not in mind here.[34]

There are three reasons for this rejection – historical, intertextual, and thematic.[35]

---

[29] Haupt 1879: 7, 11; Gore 1920: 59; Ross 1954: 135; Richter 1977: 141; Bruce 1979: 36; Barker 1981: 307; Stott 1988: 65; Klauck 1991: 61–4; Beutler 2000: 37; Heckel 2004: 436–8; Kinlaw 2005: 99, 106; Morgen 2005a: 50–3; Yarbrough 2008: 38; Jones 2009: 21.

[30] Plummer 1911: 73.   [31] Thomas 2003: 65.

[32] Brooke 1912: 4; Gaugler 1964: 37–8; Grayston 1984: 38–9; Burdick 1985: 99; Vouga 1990: 25; Hiebert 1991: 39–40; Uebele 2001: 126; Smalley 2007: 8.

[33] Bultmann 1973: 9.   [34] Lieu 1981: 214.

[35] Schnackenburg (1992: 52) could provide a fourth reason with his argument that seeing an allusion to the resurrection narrows the understanding of the verse unduly. However, according to Yarbrough (2008: 38) this reason 'seems arbitrary'.

The historical reason for rejecting the possible allusion is a result of the dominance of interpreting 1 John in light of a proposed reconstruction of the events behind the letter. On the basis of 1 John 4:2, the opponents are often identified as denying the incarnation. So the opening verses of 1 John are understood to affirm the incarnation.[36] For example, Marshall states:

> A reference to touching Jesus is to be found in John 20:24–29, and the same verb ψηλαφίζω occurs in Luke 24:39, again in the context of demonstrating the reality of the resurrection. The reference here, *however*, is broader, and there is possibly *a polemical point against the Docetists*, who denied the real physical incarnation of the Son of God.[37]

However, the review of the reconstructions of the historical situation behind 1 John conducted in chapter 1 demonstrated that none of the proposed identifications of the opponents was plausible. So it seems invalid to reject the possible allusion to the resurrection on these grounds.

The intertextual reason for ignoring the resurrection allusion is based on the observation of numerous links between the prologue of John and the opening verses of 1 John. These links were cited as support for using John 1:1–18 as the key for interpreting 1 John 1:1–5. However, the discussion above has called attention to the deficiencies in this view. There are links between the two texts, but to rule out the resurrection allusion on the basis of the links may be giving too determinative a role to the similarities than can be warranted.

The final reason for disregarding the possible allusion to the resurrection is on the grounds of an apparent lack of reference to the resurrection in the rest of 1 John.[38] So Lieu states: 'If it [1:1] is drawing on resurrection traditions ... the absence of any interest in the resurrection elsewhere makes this entirely hypothetical.'[39] However, this reason is contrary to the reading order of 1 John. It presumes something that the reader has not yet experienced.[40] Further, the original readers probably would have experienced some teaching about the resurrection, because

[36] Painter 1975: 113; Law 1979: 120; Brown 1982: 163.

[37] Marshall 1978: 101 (italics added).

[38] Smalley 2007: 8.   [39] Lieu 2008a: 40.

[40] One of the objectives of reading the whole of 1 John is to ascertain if this reason is valid. Even if it were the case that there were no other references, this does not rule out the possibility here. However, as will be argued in the rest of the thesis, there are three other explicit references to the resurrection, all noted as a result of reading 1 John in the order in which it is written and in light of the resurrection reference in 1:1.

as Painter states: 'The complete absence of reference to the resurrection of Jesus in 1 John has to be seen over against the strong emphasis on this event in the Gospel of John.'[41] Thus to disregard the allusion on thematic (or lack of thematic) grounds is a weakness. The fact that the resurrection is emphasised in the Gospel of John is suggestive that the relative clauses may have been understood by the original readers as referring to the resurrection

An intertextual reading of 1 John 1:1–5

Given the weaknesses both in understanding the relative clauses as referring to the incarnation, and in the reasons for rejecting an allusion to the resurrection, this thesis proposes that 'the *resurrected* incarnate Christ' 'fills' the gap as the referent of the relative clauses in 1 John 1:1 and thus the 'message of life'.[42]

This section has two main parts. First, intertextual links with the resurrection narratives of Luke 24 and John 20–1 are cited to suggest that the referent of the 'message of life' is the message of the resurrection of the incarnate Christ. Second, with this proposal in mind, a reading of 1:1–5 is undertaken in order to test if the proposed 'fill' for this gap makes sense of the verses. The reading pays attention to the limiting devices of the purpose statement (1:4), and the unit's boundary (1:5).

Intertextual links

The descriptions in these relative clauses include intertextual echoes from both John 1:1–18 *and* the resurrection narratives of Luke 24 and John 20–1.[43] The similarities with the opening verses of John's Gospel have been presented earlier, so will not be presented again. There are a number of intertextual connections with the resurrection narratives.

First, the verb ψηλαφάω (1:1) is a rare verb in the New Testament only occurring three other times (Luke 24:39; Acts 17:27; Hebrews 12:18). The rarity of this verb, combined with the observation that the

[41] Painter 1975: 113.

[42] Freyne (2002: 61) links the prologue of John with the resurrection narratives, suggesting that they together address a denial of Jesus' physicality as the Christ. Further, he understands 1 John 1:1–4 in light of John 1:1–18; however, he does not identify the referent of the relative clauses of 1 John 1:1 with the resurrected incarnate Christ.

[43] Hills (1989: 304–6) suggests some parallels with passages in Isaiah 40–8. However, Hills admits that these parallels do not include the key clause αἱ χεῖρες ἡμῶν ἐψηλάφησαν which 'resists being conformed to the Isaianic model'.

only other occurrence of its use in relation to Jesus is his request for the disciples to touch his resurrected body (Luke 24:39), results in a strong intertextual link. This link is widely noted in the secondary literature, even if it is dismissed.[44]

Second, the verbs of perception with their corresponding sense organs (1:1) are reminiscent of the resurrection narratives. The vocabulary occurs in combination in Jesus' post-resurrection appearances to Thomas in John 20:24–7 (where ὁράω and χείρ are used repeatedly),[45] and to the disciples in Luke 24:39–40 (where ψηλαφάω, χείρ, and θεωρέω, the cognate of θεάομαι, all occur).[46]

Third, the verb φανερόω (1:2) is used to describe Jesus' resurrection appearances to his disciples in John 21:1 and 14.[47] Throughout the rest of the New Testament the verb φανερόω is used to refer to Jesus' incarnation (1 Timothy 3:16),[48] his resurrection life (2 Corinthians 4:10–11; 2 Timothy 1:10; Hebrews 9:26), and his return to judge (Colossians 3:4; 1 Peter 5:4).[49] However, the occurrence of the verb is another intertextual link with the resurrection narrative of John.[50]

Fourth, the phrase πρὸς τὸν πατέρα (1:2) occurs ten times in John and refers to the place where the Father exists. On all but one occasion, Jesus uses it to refer to his returning to the Father after his death and resurrection (13:1; 14:6, 12, 28; 16:10, 17, 28; 20:17 twice). The last two uses of πρὸς τὸν πατέρα occur in 20:17, forming another intertextual link between the prologue and the resurrection narrative of John. Although the sense of the preposition πρός in these verses can be directional rather

---

[44] Haupt 1879: 7, 11; Plummer 1911: 73; Brooke 1912: 4; Gore 1920: 59; Ross 1954: 135; Bultmann 1973: 9; Painter 1975: 113; Marshall 1978: 101; Bruce 1979: 36; Law 1979: 120; Barker 1981: 307; Lieu 1981: 214; Brown 1982: 163; Grayston 1984: 38–9; Burdick 1985: 99; Stott 1988: 65; Hiebert 1991: 39–40; Schnackenburg 1992: 52; Thomas 2003: 65; Smalley 2007: 8; Lieu 2008a: 40; Yarbrough 2008: 38; Jones 2009: 21.

[45] Yarbrough (2008: 37) notes that the first-person plural form of ὁράω only appears five times in the New Testament – three times here in 1 John 1:1–3, once in John 3:11 and once in the resurrection account of John 20:25.

[46] Schnackenburg (1992: 12) notes the intertextual link with John 20:24–9 on the basis of the verbs of perception but denies that it is on view.

[47] There are also two occurrences of φανερόω in relation to post-resurrection appearances of Jesus in the longer ending of Mark (16:12, 14).

[48] This is the only possible occasion in the New Testament and is open to another interpretation, that it refers to the resurrection, see Collins 2002: 108–9.

[49] Bockmuehl 1988.

[50] Bockmuehl (*Ibid.*: 91–2) notes the substantial links between φανερόω in John 21:1, 14 and the resurrection narratives in John 20:18, 20, 25, 27 and 29. Yet he fails to interpret the occurrence of the verb in 1 John 1:2 as anything other than a reference to the incarnation. Thomas (2003: 66–7) notes the occurrences of φανερόω in John 21:1 and 14, and continues to understand 1 John 1:2 to be about the incarnation. However, he also concludes: 'that there is a growing emphasis upon the resurrection of Jesus'.

than locative, it reveals that Jesus had to go to the Father before he could appear as the resurrected incarnate Christ to the apostles (John 20:19ff). The one occasion where the phrase does not refer to Jesus returning to his Father, it refers to Jesus' future position beside the Father (5:45). That is, πρὸς τὸν πατέρα is the place that Jesus goes to before he appears to his disciples in his post-resurrection body.[51]

On the basis of these intertextual links, both to John 1 and the resurrection narratives of Luke 24 and John 20–1, it is proposed that the referent of the relative clauses in 1 John 1:1 is the resurrected incarnate Christ. This does not deny the language that sounds like it is referring to the incarnation, but rather expands the referent to include the resurrection. The events that the relative clauses are referring to are the resurrection appearances of the incarnate Christ after his crucifixion.

Expanding the referent to the resurrected incarnate Christ seems to account for the intertextual echoes used in the descriptions in the relative clauses of 1:1. Further, this understanding seems truer to John's Gospel. Like any good narrative, John 1:1–18 was written to introduce the reader to the themes that find their culmination in John 20–1. For instance, the prologue of John's Gospel introduces the theme of Jesus' divinity (1:1–3) that is affirmed explicitly at the climax by Thomas (20:8). The parallels in 1 John 1:1–5 with John 1:1–18 do affirm the incarnation. However, the incarnation is assumed in the climax of John's Gospel, in chapters 20–1, and is not repeated with the same vocabulary. The reference to touching Jesus in the resurrection narratives stresses Jesus' identity as the resurrected incarnate Christ. Thus the relative clauses of 1 John 1:1 span the whole of the narrative of John's Gospel and not just the prologue. The content of the preaching referred to in 1 John 1:1 is the whole of John's Gospel and not just the prologue.

These intertextual links fulfil some of Hays' criteria for identifying an intertextual echo. The echo was available to the author and original readers because of its existence in the gospel tradition as recorded in John and Luke. The echo has a repetition of words drawn from another Johannine source, in this case John's Gospel. The echo is historically plausible because both the author and his readers could have understood it in their historical milieu since it is drawn from the gospel tradition. The echo is heard in present commentaries. Hays' other criteria, whether the echo has thematic coherence with the surrounding text and whether the echo makes sense of the unit of text in which it occurs, are tested in

---

[51] Harris 1983: 50.

the following reading. The final section, 'tangents', will demonstrate that a similar understanding was current in the early church.

Understanding the referent as the resurrected incarnate Christ in this way does not deny the connections with John 1:1–18, but incorporates them, thus enhancing the reading of 1 John.

Intertexual test reading

The resurrected incarnate Christ and 1 John 1:1–5

From the syntactical observations made earlier in this chapter, for this reading to be consistent with the syntax of the verses it must make sense of all the relative clauses, be describing 'life', fit with the parenthetical description of life in 1:2, be clear how it results in fellowship with God, and be congruent with the summary of the message contained in 1:5. Since 1:1–5 is made up of four ideas – the message preached (1:1–3a), the resultant fellowship (1:3b), the motivation for preaching (1:4), and the message restated – God is light (1:5), these ideas are the basis of the headings under which the reading is performed.

The message preached (1:1–3a)

The four relative clauses have as their postcedent the prepositional phrase περὶ τοῦ λόγου τῆς ζωῆς. The first relative clause sounds like the start of John's Gospel but it also has some differences. It does not refer to the absolute start of all things like John 1:1 (ἐν ἀρχῇ). Rather it seems to refer to another start, this being the effect of the preposition ἀπό.[52] It says that ὁ λόγος τῆς ζωῆς was there from the beginning. That is, the message of the resurrected incarnate Christ was there from the beginning of Christianity. The resurrected incarnate Christ was heard and seen with the eyes and looked at and touched with the hands. The intertextual links of these statements with Luke 24 and John 20 were given above. Thus each relative clause describes an element of the resurrected incarnate Christ.

The change in tense-forms receives attention in much of the secondary literature.[53] The changes in tense-form across these verses can be explained through reference to verbal aspect and support understanding

---

[52] Bruce 1979: 35; Johnson 1993: 26.

[53] See for instance Louw 1975: 98–101; Strecker 1996: 12–13. Brown (1982: 153) comments on this: 'there is a puzzling alternation of tenses in the many "we" verbal forms, especially of the aorist and the perfect. Commentators debate whether it is a purely stylistic feature or connotes subtle distinctions of meaning.'

the resurrection appearances as the content of the relative clauses. When the present and perfect are understood as imperfective in aspect, with the tense-forms semantically encoding proximity and heightened proximity respectively,[54] then the opening verses present an emphatic declaration of an event that the author affirms as if it was still happening right in front of him. The use of the aorist tense-form allows this event to be identified as the resurrection appearances of the incarnate Christ. This is because the aorist tense-form in the perfective aspect provides a summary of the event being spoken about.[55] The verbs in the aorist (θεωρέω, ψηλαφάω) that summarise the event are those that occur in the resurrection appearance narratives, indicating that the content of the relative clauses is the event of Jesus' resurrection appearances.[56]

The phrase περὶ τοῦ λόγου τῆς ζωῆς gives the content of the announcement referred to by the main verb ἀπαγγέλλω. The 'word of life' that the author has announced to the audience is the message of the resurrected incarnate Christ. The noun λόγος should not be understood in a figurative sense as a reference to Jesus, as it is in John 1, but rather with its normal sense of message or word. This is because the parenthetical comment that follows in verse 2 explicates not τοῦ λόγου but τῆς ζωῆς. The content of the message is the focus of this phrase. Since the relative clauses prepare the reader for this phrase and since they were references to the resurrection appearances, it follows that 'life' is the emphasis of the phrase.[57] The parenthetical statement of 1:2 discusses this 'life' further, explaining that it has appeared from 'with the Father' to the author, and that it is eternal.

The first parenthetic description of the life is that it appeared (ἐφανερώθη). The consensus reading understands this to be a reference to the incarnation.[58] However, it is better understood as a reference to the resurrection appearances. The fact that φανερόω is in the aorist tense-form on both occasions in 1:2 directs the reader back to the aorist tense-forms in 1:1 that summarised the events of the resurrection appearances. This supports the proposal that the resurrection appearances are the referent of φανερόω, rather than the incarnation. This understanding is corroborated when the location from which

---

[54] Campbell 2007: 241–4.   [55] Campbell 2008b: 34.

[56] See Haupt 1879: 11; Thomas 2003: 65. Louw's conclusion that the aorist has the same semantic value as the perfects is problematic since they are in different aspects (1975: 101).

[57] The themes of 'resurrection' and 'life' occur together in John 11:25 where Jesus says that he is 'the resurrection and the life'.

[58] See for example Ross 1954: 137.

the 'appearing' happens is taken into account. As was evident in the intertextual links section above, the phrase πρὸς τὸν πατέρα refers to the place that Jesus went to after his death. So the appearing in this verse refers to his appearing after his going to the Father. Further, the one other use of πρὸς τὸν πατέρα in 1 John occurs in a description of the present place of Jesus – in heaven with the Father (2:1). Although the reader has not yet encountered this verse, it occurs in the introduction of 1 John and confirms the suggested reading. So it seems that the appearances referred to here are the resurrection appearances Jesus made after going to the Father.[59]

The second parenthetic element describes the life as eternal (τὴν ζωὴν τὴν αἰώνιον). Eternal life was an expectation of some Jews of Jesus' time, based on the apocalyptic expectations of God ushering in a new age with the resurrection of the dead (Daniel 12:2; Mark 10:30; Luke 18:30). In John's Gospel, this expectation is linked with the lifting up (ὑψόω), or glorification, of the apocalyptic figure 'the Son of Man' (3:14–15).[60] Belief in this figure results in eternal life for an individual and avoidance of God's wrath at the final judgement (John 3:36; 5:24). John presents Jesus as the 'Son of Man' who is glorified in his death and resurrection (John 12:30–6).[61] So this third description of life seems to further support the understanding that the resurrected incarnate Christ is on view in the relative clauses of 1:1.

The announcement of the resurrected incarnate Christ results (ἵνα) in fellowship (κοινωνία). Κοινωνία is not a word that occurs often in Johannine literature – here in 1:3 and only again in 1:6–7. Yet the result of the first proclamation of the resurrection of the incarnate Jesus in Acts 2 was fellowship – fellowship between those who accepted the message and the apostles (Acts 2:42). The author testified to the resurrection of the incarnate Jesus in order that he would have fellowship with the audience.

[59] Harris 1983: 50.

[60] Carson (1991: 434) notes that the term 'glorification' in John's Gospel incorporates both Jesus' death and his resurrection. In commenting on John 12:16 Carson states: 'This verse closely resembles John's remark about what the disciples did not understand when Jesus talked about destroying the temple and raising it in three days … (2:22). There, the crucial turning point in their understanding took place "after he was raised from the dead"; here, it is after Jesus was glorified. But this amounts to virtually the same thing. Jesus' death marked the turning point. It was part of the movement that led on to his resurrection and exaltation, i.e. his glorification, and the bestowal of the Spirit that was conditioned by it (7:39; 16:7).'

[61] Peter twice uses ὑψόω in Acts to describe the ascension of Jesus to the right hand of God (2:33; 5:31) after his death and resurrection. This is similar to John's portrayal of Jesus.

The resultant fellowship (1:3b)

The fellowship that the audience shares is not just with the author but also with the Father and with his Son Jesus Christ. This is the first explicit mention of Jesus in 1 John. The relative clauses allude to his resurrection but in this verse Jesus is described with the title Χριστός. Since Ἰησοῦ is in apposition to τοῦ υἱοῦ αὐτοῦ, it seems that Χριστοῦ is also in apposition and is not being used as a surname but a title.

The motivation for preaching (1:4)

The paragraph is disrupted with the limiting device of a purpose statement. The author explains the purpose (ἵνα) for writing – ἵνα ἡ χαρὰ ἡμῶν ᾖ πεπληρωμένη. The two words χαρά and πληρόω are used in combination six times in John's Gospel. The first occurrence is on the lips of John the Baptist when referring to his joy at Jesus' arrival (3:29). All of the other occurrences are on the lips of Jesus (15:11; 16:20, 21, 22, 24; 17:13) when he is preparing the disciples for his return to the Father after his death and resurrection (13:1; cf: 12:23–36). This reinforces the proposal that the referent of 1 John 1:1 is the resurrected incarnate Christ.

When the references in John 16:20–4 are investigated more closely the proposition is strengthened further. In these verses, Jesus' death and resurrection are on view – his death will mean that his disciples do not see him for a while and will result in their grief, and his resurrection will lead to the disciples seeing Jesus again and result in their complete joy. John 16:24 is of special interest in this case because it is the exact same form as the variant reading of 1:4 (ἵνα ἡ χαρὰ ἡμῶν ᾖ πεπληρωμένη).[62] This variant could be the result of an error of hearing and the difference reflects the decision made on the first textual variant in the verse. However, since this is the exact form of 16:24 it may have been made under the influence of 16:24.[63] If this is the case, then the variant reveals that 1:4 was explicitly understood against the background of John 16:24 and that very early scribes understood 1:1–5 to be about the resurrection of the incarnate Christ.

The message restated – God is light (1:5)

This last sentence is linked to the message of 1:1–3a through the repetition of vocabulary (ἀκούω – 1:1 and 3, ἀπαγγέλλω a cognate of

---

[62] The variant is found in A C^{2vid} K P 33 81 614 1739.

[63] Metzger 1994: 639.

ἀναγγέλλω – 1:2 and 3). Its cataphoric opening (ἔστιν αὕτη ἡ ἀγγελία) is resumptive of the announcing verbs and redirects the reader's attention to ἀγγελία.[64] It causes the reader to look for a clause that will outline the content of the message, a content similar to the resurrected incarnate Christ of 1:1–3. Yet the summary is expressed in slightly different language from a different angle – God is light (φῶς) and in him there is no darkness (σκοτία) at all.

In John's Gospel, light and darkness are used metaphorically to describe life and death respectively. Jesus is described as the light of life (1:4) who came into the world (3:19) and whose followers will have the light of life (8:12). On the other hand, the world is in a state of darkness (1:5) that needs life (20:31). It is belief in Jesus that moves someone from darkness to light, from death to eternal life (12:46, 50). So describing God here as light is depicting him as life and not death, as alive and the life-giver.[65] This is congruent with understanding 1 John 1:1–3 being about the resurrected incarnate Christ because it is through Jesus' resurrection that life is achieved (20:31).

Yet the portrayal of God as light and thus life also has a moral element. Life and death should be understood in a broad sense. Life is more than just having a pulse and breathing, just as death is more than just the cessation of these physical indicators. Life and death are states or modes of existence that have physical, social, and relational aspects.[66] In John's Gospel, the world needs life (20:31) because it exists in a state of death (5:24). The darkness of death is evident in men's evil deeds and their hatred of the truth (3:19–21). This is consistent with the general teaching of the New Testament. Paul describes unbelieving humanity in Ephesians as dead (2:1, 5; 5:8) while still 'living', and believing humanity as 'alive' in Christ (2:5). Matthew quotes Isaiah 9:1–2 in depicting the world that Jesus entered (4:14–16). The Isaiah quote parallels darkness and death, while leaving the parallel of light up to the reader to complete. Thus life and death are broader than just

---

[64] That it is resumptive of 1:1–3a is evident from the observation that if 1:3b–4 were deleted, 1:5 would flow directly from 1:3a.

[65] Baylis 1992: 219–220.

[66] I take it that the curses of Genesis 3 are God fulfilling his promise that Adam and Eve would die 'on the day' that they ate the fruit (Genesis 2:17; 3:4). The curses describe the state of 'death'. I agree with Wenham (1987: 89) that 'The very way the story is told forces the reader to ask again what God meant by "dying" and what the serpent meant, and what the significance was of their "eyes being opened" and "becoming like God".' But I fail to understand why he and other scholars do not see the curses as 'death'. In their narrowing of the meaning of 'death' to only include the cessation of physical life, they have not allowed the text of the curses to inform the meaning of 'death'.

the cessation of vital signs, they include the mode of existence of an individual.

Given that this description of God is a summary of the message of life from 1:1–3, it is not surprising that God is described as light.[67] Yet this description entails more than just that God raised Jesus. It includes moral aspects – a mode of existence in the light. It is this fact that provides the basis of much New Testament ethics. Since believers have been raised with Christ, they should live a resurrection life (Romans 6:11) as children of the light (Ephesians 5:8). It is this moral implication of the incarnate Christ's resurrection that is new and forms the basis of the next unit (1:6ff.).

Further context

Some scholars who understand the incarnation as the referent of 1 John 1:1–5 feel a change in christological understanding occurs between the prologue (high christology – that Jesus is God) and the claims of 1:6–2:2 (low christology – that Jesus is human). In this regard O'Neill states: 'This first section [1:5–10] begins with the assertion of a low Christology; surprisingly so, after the Prologue.'[68] However, the christological references that immediately follow this prologue fit well with the suggestion that the resurrected incarnate Christ is the content of the proclaimed message. This is because the incarnate Christ was resurrected after his crucifixion. The body that the disciples looked at and touched was the resurrected crucified body of Jesus. Thus it is natural for the author to speak about the death of Jesus (1:7, 9; 2:2) and his present heavenly session (2:1) since the resurrected Jesus they saw, heard, and touched was the crucified Jesus who appeared to them from heaven where he is seated at the Father's right hand.[69]

Summary

When the interpretation of the first verse of 1 John is broadened to include the intertextual links to both the incarnation and the resurrection,

---

[67] It should be noted that in Acts, all the descriptions of Paul's conversion on the road to Damascus describe the glorified Jesus in terms of light (9:3; 22:6, 9, 11; 26:13). The link between the glorified Jesus and light is not novel to John.

[68] O'Neill 1966: 8.

[69] The appropriateness of this reference also corresponds to the Johannine category of glorification where Jesus' death and resurrection are understood as one event. Sometimes this study uses the Johannine category of glorification as shorthand for Jesus' death and resurrection.

a reading results that is consistent with the rest of the unit. The message that the author has preached to the audience is the resurrection of the incarnate Christ.

Plausibility tangents

There are three tangents that indicate the plausibility of understanding the content of the preaching in 1 John 1:1–3 with the referent of the resurrected incarnate Christ.

First, the author describes his actions in terms of speech – testifying (μαρτυρέω) and announcing (ἀπαγγέλλω) to the audience 'the life'. These verbs are reminiscent of the actions of the apostles as a result of their experience of the resurrection. According to Acts, the risen Jesus commissioned the apostles to be his witnesses (1:8), witnesses of everything Jesus said and did, and in particular, witnesses to his resurrection (1:21–22).[70] Peter's first speech in Acts 2:14–36 is a prototype of the apostles' witness. In this speech, Peter presents the resurrected incarnate Christ and the implications of this. Jesus was glorified (2:32–3) in the resurrection and ascension of his physical body (2:26, 31).

Second, the use of the verb ψηλαφάω to refer to the resurrection narratives has an early precedent. Ignatius in *Smyrnaeans* 3:1–3 uses ψηλαφάω when affirming the resurrection of the incarnate Christ. This indicates that the original audience could have understood the use of ψηλαφάω to refer to the resurrection, fulfilling one of Hays' requirements for intertextual echoes.

Third, some in the early church understood 1 John 1:1 to refer to the resurrection. Didymus the Blind (*c*. 313–*c*. 398) lists it as one way the text was understood, even though he himself does not agree. In commenting on 1 John 1:1 he says:

> Many think that these words apply to the postresurrection appearances of Jesus and say that John is speaking of himself and the other disciples who first of all heard that the Lord had risen and afterwards saw him with their own eyes, to the point where they touched his feet, his hands and his side and felt the imprint of the nails.[71]

---

[70] The cognate μάρτυς occurs in relation to the apostles' task to testify to Jesus in Luke 24:48 and Acts 1:8, 22; 2:32; 3:15; 4:33; 5:32; 10:39, 41; 13:31.
[71] *Patrologia Graeca* 39:1775–1776 cited in Bray 2000: 166.

This reference indicates that Hays' criterion, that someone else in the history of interpretation hears the echo, is fulfilled and very early in the church's history.

Conclusion

This chapter examined the opening verses of 1 John. It did this because of the significance of an introduction in shaping the expectations of a reader for a document. Before examining the opening verses, it was suggested that the introduction of 1 John continues until 2:12–14. The chapter then turned to consider the gap in 1:1–5, the content of the 'message of life' in 1:1. It critically reviewed the consensus 'fill' that understood the incarnation as the referent of the 'message of life', arguing that the intertextual reason on which the view is based is not as strong as claimed. Further, it noted that the other two reasons for rejecting an allusion to the resurrection, historical and thematic, both suffer weaknesses.

Instead, the chapter proposed that a better understanding of the referent of the relative clauses is the resurrected incarnate Christ. To the intertextual links with John 1 were added links with the resurrection narratives (Luke 24; John 20–1), suggesting this identification. This proposal was then tested through a reading of the first five verses before tangents were identified in order to show the plausibility of the suggestion.

The next chapter will continue the reading of the introduction of 1 John (1:6–2:11), paying particular attention to the descriptions of the claimants.

4

THE CLAIMANTS: 1 JOHN 1:6–2:11

The second part of the introduction (1:6–2:11) continues to construct a framework to help the reader understand 1 John. The application of the reading method results in this chapter having four sections. The first section identifies areas of uncertainty encountered by the reader (gaps) and devices used to limit possible meanings, and briefly reviews the structure of 1:6–2:11. The second section describes and then critiques how previous research has understood ('filled') the identity of the claimants. The third section presents the reading of 1:6–2:11, arguing that the claims could be Jewish, that the negative behaviour could be associated with faithless Judaism, and that the desired behaviour and results could be for faithful Israel. The fourth section provides some tangents to demonstrate the plausibility of the reading. The conclusion outlines a resultant reading grid established for the reader to use in interpreting the rest of 1 John.

The gaps, limiting devices, and structure of 1:6–2:11

This section identifies the areas of uncertainty experienced by this reader (gaps) and the limiting devices in 1:6–2:11, before briefly reviewing the structure of 1:6–2:11.

Gaps

There are three possible sources of gaps for a reader when encountering the text of 1 John – an interruption to the flow of sentences, the cataphoric use of pronouns, and those that the reader experiences.

Interruptions to the flow of sentences

There are two main interruptions to the flow of sentences in 1:6–2:11. At first glance, the asyndetic ἐὰν εἴπωμεν ὅτι seems to be an interruption to the flow of sentences. However, repetition of the clause at the start of 1:8 and 10 indicates that it is a structuring device used to introduce three 'claims'. These 'claims' are presented in a highly structured style of contrasting conditional sentences.[1] When this is observed, an interruption to this flow is detected at 2:1, where the expected contrasting conditional sentence is not encountered but a vocative and γράφω purpose statement are inserted. This is the first interruption to the flow of sentences in 1:6–2:11.

A minor interruption is experienced in 2:3, where a cataphoric pronominal phrase starts the verse (καὶ ἐν τούτῳ). However, the occurrence of καί seems to link it to the preceding verses. The asyndesis of 2:4 could again signal an interruption to the flow of sentences. However, its starting phrase (ὁ λέγων) occurs again at the start of 2:6 and 9, indicating that it is a structuring device used to introduce 'claims'. These claims start following the same contrasting sentence pattern used in 1 John 1. The pattern is broken in 2:7–8, where the anticipated contrasting sentence is replaced with a vocative and γράφω content statement. This is the second interruption to the flow of sentences in 1:6–2:11.

However, neither of these main interruptions cause a gap. This is because both contain the text limiting devices of the use of γράφω and a vocative, the significance of which is discussed later in this chapter.

Cataphoric pronouns

There are ten different pronouns used a total of forty-five times in 1:6–2:11. Forty-one of these occurrences are 'clear' anaphoric usages resulting in no gap. Of the remaining four occurrences, three are cataphoric and there is one ambiguous anaphoric usage, all of which require interpretation from the reader.

The clear anaphoric uses have as their antecedents God (αὐτός in 1:6, 7, 10), the author and audience (ἀλλήλων in 1:7; ἡμεῖς in 1:7, 8, 9, 10 and 2:2; ἑαυτοῦ in 1:8), the author (ἐγώ in 2:1), the audience (ὑμεῖς in 2:1, 7, 8), Jesus (αὐτός in 2:2, 3, 4, 5, 6, 8; ἐκεῖνος in 2:6), the inconsistent claimant (οὗτος in 2:4, 10; αὐτός in 2:11), the consistent claimant (οὗτος in 2:5; αὐτός in 2:10), the action of being consistent (οὗτος in 2:5), the claimant (αὐτός in 2:6, 9, 10, 11), and relative pronouns that refer to the old command in 2:7, the word in 2:7, and the new command in 2:8. Two things should be noted at this stage from this analysis of the clear anaphoric pronouns. First, the author and audience are identified with the claimant in the pronouns used in 1:8. Second, the distinctions

---

[1] See Callow 1999 for an extended discussion of the structure of 1:6–2:2.

made in the list between types of claimant reflect where the pronoun is used in the logic of the verse in question. When the pronoun refers to the behaviour of the claimant the antecedent is listed as the claimant. When the pronoun is used in the result of the description of the behaviour, then it is listed as either consistent or inconsistent.

The three cataphoric uses occur in 2:1 (τις), 2:3 (οὗτος), and 2:5 (ὅς), however none of these results in uncertainty for the reader. The indefinite τις in 2:1 is in the apodosis of a conditional statement that is expounding a general principle. It is the subject of the verb that immediately follows (ἐάν τις ἁμάρτῃ) and as such does not require a referent to be supplied. Thus it does not constitute a gap. The οὗτος in 2:3 is found in the often cataphoric formula ἐν τούτῳ γινώσκομεν ὅτι. The postcedent is ἐὰν τὰς ἐντολὰς αὐτοῦ τηρῶμεν that follows almost immediately. The close proximity of the pronoun to the postcedent prevents this being a gap. The ὅς in 2:5 also does not constitute a gap because, like the τις in 2:1, it is being used in an indefinite way to expound a general principle. It is the subject of the immediately following verb (ὅς δ' ἂν τηρῇ) and does not require an identification of its referent.

The one ambiguous anaphoric use of a pronoun is οὗτος in 2:1. The pronoun clearly refers to what is written. The ambiguity in the pronoun is the extent of the text to which it refers. Given that the things the author is writing about are so that the readers do not sin (ἵνα μὴ ἁμάρτητε), and given that the vocabulary of sin occurs from 1:7–2:2, it appears that the extent of the text referred to is the immediately preceding verses. This does not constitute a gap of any significance.

Reader-experienced gaps

This reader is uncertain of two things in these verses. First, the identity of the claimant is difficult to locate. It is unclear if the claimant is the author and the audience, as the first-person plural of 1:6, 8, 10, and the pronouns of 1:8 would seem to imply. If so, should the claims then be understood in a historical or literary sense? On the other hand, the claims seem to report actual speech in 1:6, 8, 10 and possibly 2:4. So are they more than a literary device and reflect the situation behind 1 John? This difficulty is not confined to this reader, but is evident in the research on these verses.[2]

---

[2] Scholarship also reveals a gap in determining the difference between the claims of 1:8 and 1:10. However, this reader does not experience this gap since the verses are understood to be parallel statements, hence there is no need for them to be different. They are stylistic variations on the theme.

The second problem is in 2:7–8, where the command is described as old and new at the same time. This apparent contradiction across two sentences is a complication that requires resolving. However, since the context for this resolution is the claims, discussion of this complication is subsumed under the larger first difficulty of the identity of the claimants.

Limiting devices

There are three devices that limit the way these gaps can be interpreted – the use of γράφω, the role of the vocative, and boundary crossing.

There are three occurrences of γράφω in this section, 2:1, 7 and 8 . As noted above, each of these verses breaks the flow of the sentences and appears to form a gap. However, in keeping with the understanding of the use of γράφω outlined in chapter 2, these verses function as asides that explain the author's purpose in writing (2:1) and content of writing (2:7–8) . In this way, they do not constitute gaps, but rather elucidate the immediate text and limit the way the gaps can be filled. That the only two occurrences of vocatives also occur at the start of these asides (2:1, 7), suggests that the vocatives give prominence to these statements, more prominence than just the apparent break in the flow of the sentences themselves. The vocatives draw the readers' attention to these statements and hence their qualities in shaping interpretation.

The minor interruption in the flow of sentences experienced at 2:3 signals a boundary.[3] However, this boundary is only minor, marking a change in the theme. That the two units are one section is evident because the verb λέγω forms a backbone that runs through the first part, giving it unity, while a change in tense-form demarcates different units.[4] The near absence of the verb from the second part of 1 John adds further support to the idea of 1 John having two parts.[5] The threefold repetition of ἐὰν εἴπωμεν ὅτι (1:6, 8, 10) structures 1:6–2:2 and has as its theme 'sin'. After the opening verse (1:6), ἁμαρτία or a cognate is found in every verse until the unit's end in 2:2.[6] This vocabulary is absent from the rest of the introduction (2:3–11) . The vocative and γράφω purpose statement in 2:1 together give heightened prominence to the theme of

---

[3] Brown 1982: Kruse 2000: Painter 2002.

[4] This is similar to 2:12–14 where γράφω occurs six times yet in two groups of three, indicated through a change in tense-form.

[5] There are two occurrences of λέγω in the second part. The first is in 4:20 and even though it is similar in form to the aorist uses in 1:6–2:2, it does not seem to have the same structural usage. The second is in 5:16 and bears no similarities to the present tense-form uses in 2:3–11.

[6] Callow (1999: 400–1) identifies 'sin' as the theme of 1:5–2:2.

sin. The three occurrences of ὁ λέγων in 2:4, 6 and 9 structure the second unit of 2:4–11. Its theme is 'love', again evident in the frequent repetition of the vocabulary (ἀγαπάω, ἀγάπη, and μισέω) that is absent from the rest of the introduction (1:1–2:2). The combination of the vocative and γράφω in 2:7–8 further supports the observation that 'love' is the key concern of the writer in this unit. Thus the boundary at 2:3 limits the way gaps can be filled, as it signals a thematic move from 'sin' to 'love'. Therefore gaps in 1:6–2:2 should be filled with reference to sin, and those in 2:3–11 with reference to love.

The structure of 1:6–2:11

In overview, the introduction of 1 John has three units: 1:1–5, 1:6–2:2 and 2:3–11. The first unit describes the message proclaimed (1:1–3a – the resurrected incarnate Christ) and its results (1:3b–5 – fellowship and joy). The second unit takes the results of the proclaimed message (1:3b–5) and presents three case studies about how to live with these results when people sin (1:6–2:2). The vocabulary connections between 1:3b–5 and 1:6–7 were discussed in the last chapter, and the logic of the connection is outlined in Table 5:

Table 5. *The connections between 1:3–5 and 6–7*

Premise 1:	We have fellowship (κοινωνία) with God	(1:3b)
Premise 2:	God is light (φῶς) and without darkness (σκοτία)	(1:5)
Situation 1:	Claim to have fellowship (κοινωνία) but live in darkness (σκοτία)	(1:6a)
Result 1:	We are liars not doing the truth	(1:6b)
Situation 2:	If we walk in the light (φῶς)	(1:7a)
Result 2:	We have fellowship (κοινωνία) and Jesus' blood cleanses us of sin	(1:7b)

The opening verse of the third unit (2:3) is similar in function to 1:3b–5. The καί that starts the verse indicates that it is linked with something earlier, the message proclaimed in 1:1–3a. This is evident in the way the units in 1:6–2:2 and 2:4–11 are parallel. Both units have a three-fold repetition of the verb λέγω. Further, the first line of each case study is similar in form and almost identical in outcome (see Table 6).[7]

---

[7] Brown 1982: 282.

Table 6. *The parallels between 1:6 and 2:4*

	1:6	2:4
a	Ἐὰν εἴπωμεν ὅτι	ὁ λέγων ὅτι
b	κοινωνίαν ἔχομεν μετ' αὐτοῦ	ἔγνωκα αὐτόν
c	καὶ ἐν τῷ σκότει περιπατῶμεν,	καὶ τὰς ἐντολὰς αὐτοῦ μὴ τηρῶν,
d	ψευδόμεθα	ψεύστης ἐστίν
e	καὶ οὐ ποιοῦμεν τὴν ἀλήθειαν	καὶ ἐν τούτῳ ἡ ἀλήθεια οὐκ ἔστιν

Each verse is asyndetic, has the same structure, and repeats vocabulary inside this structure – they are 'liars' in clause d and not in the 'truth' in clause e.

If these observations about the parallel of 1:6 and 2:4 are followed, then it becomes more evident that 1:3b–5 and 2:3 are parallel. The concept of fellowship in 1:6b is similar to knowing God in 2:4b. In addition to this, the concepts of φῶς/σκότος introduced in 1:5 are parallel with τὰς ἐντολὰς αὐτοῦ τηρῶμεν in 2:3, evident in their location in the third line (c) in the Table 6.

Thus 2:3 assumes the concepts from 1:3–5 but it extends the argument.[8] The concepts in 2:3 are extended because the context of their discussion in the second unit is assurance, or as 2:3 puts it, ἐν τούτῳ γινώσκομεν ὅτι ἐγνώκαμεν αὐτόν. So 2:3 flows from the preached message of 1:1–3a but expresses the concepts of 1:3b–5 in different vocabulary in a slightly different situation, that of assurance. This means that the introduction (1:1–2:11) has the following structure (Table 7):

Table 7. *The structure of 1 John 1:1–2:11*

1:1–3a The preached message – the resurrected incarnate Christ	
1:3b–5 Fellowship and light	2:3 Knowledge and the commands
1:6–2:2 Three case studies	2:4–11 Three case studies
1:6–7 ἐὰν εἴπωμεν ὅτι	2:4–5 ὁ λέγων
1:8–9 ἐὰν εἴπωμεν ὅτι	2:6–8 ὁ λέγων
1:10–2:2 ἐὰν εἴπωμεν ὅτι	2:7–8 Vocative purpose statement
2:1 Vocative purpose statement	2:9–11 ὁ λέγων

---

[8] The resumption of the light and darkness vocabulary in 2:9–11 furthers the impression that the units are a parallel.

Summary

There are two gaps in 1:6–2:11. The first is the identity of the claimant. This question pervades the entire section of text to be investigated. As a result, the second gap, the meaning of 2:7–8 with the new and old commands is subsumed and controlled by the answer to how the first gap is resolved. So the next section describes and then critiques how previous research has understood the identity of the claimants.

The 'claims' in previous research

In line with the two methods of interpreting 1 John, there are two main ways that the 'claims' or 'slogans' are understood and the identity of the claimants apprehended.

The opponents/secessionists' claims

The Historical Critical school understands the claims to reflect the sentiments of the opponents (or secessionists) and as such uses them to reconstruct their ethical teaching.[9] However, the level to which the claims reflect the opponents' teaching is disputed within this school.

Brown argues that the clause ἐὰν εἴπωμεν indicates that the claim is not a quotation but the author's summary of the secessionists' teaching. The conditional form of the clause indicates that it represents the opponents' words rather than quoting them. Further, the first-person plural subject includes the author and readers in the claim. This would not be the case if it was a direct quotation of the opponents' false teaching.[10] On the other hand, since the phrase ὁ λέγων is not conditional and does not necessarily include the author and audience, Brown argues that it signals direct quotations of the secessionist teaching. Brown concludes: 'The false statements here [ch.2] may approach being exact quotations from the secessionists, while those in ch.1 may have been secessionist-inspired but rephrased in the author's wording.'[11]

However, Painter disagrees with Brown's reasoning and conclusions. Painter argues that the use of ὅτι following the formulae indicates whether the speech is a direct quotation or indirect speech. He acknowledges that ὅτι can be used to introduce indirect speech but also points

---

[9] Marshall 1978; Brown 1982; Painter 1986; Schnackenburg 1992; Kruse 2000; Akin 2001; Painter 2002; Smalley 2007.
[10] Brown 1982: 197, 232.   [11] *Ibid.*: 253.

out that this happens only when the verb contained in the speech is in the third person. Since it is in the first person in 1:6, 8, 10, and 2:4, they are all direct speech. Since 2:6 and 9 do not use ὅτι and the speech is not in the first person, they are indirect speech and not a direct quotation of the claimant. So he reverses Brown's conclusions about the level of reflection of the opponents' words.[12]

Smalley and Kruse both agree with Painter's conclusions. Smalley understands those holding Gnostic views are quoted in 1:6, 8, and 10.[13] On the other hand, the claims of 2:4, 6, and 9 may be made by any Christian, because these claims 'are positive assurances that may be adopted by the true believer' and are in the third person.[14] Kruse maintains that the slogans of chapter 1 'reflect the author's understanding of the claims of the secessionists'.[15] The claims of chapter 2 reflect 'directly or indirectly, what the author believed the secessionists falsely claimed'.[16]

Yet this uncertainty with regard to how accurately the opponents' teaching is reflected in the claims does not stop Historical Critical scholars from using these claims as a basis for reconstructing the opponents' teaching. This is because, as Painter points out, if the claims as recorded did not bear some similarity to the actual teaching of the opponents, it would have been obvious to the audience and would not have achieved the aim of refuting their teaching.[17]

The claims are literary devices

Moved by the deficiencies in the Historical Critical school's identifications of the opponents, the literary school does not seek to understand these claims as historical. It is primarily concerned with the literary and rhetorical effect of the claims. So for instance Neufeld states: 'The numerous and varied depictions of the identity and beliefs of the opponents, however, suggest that the interpretations of the antithetical statements should not be restricted to a reconstructed historical context.'[18] This does not rule out some possible referent in the historical situation, but rather seeks to understand it primarily in literary categories. So Neufeld also states: 'The language of these boasts, however, need not be taken as a formal delineation of theological beliefs in response to a

---

[12] Painter 2002: 143–4. See also Painter 1986.
[13] Smalley 2007: 19.   [14] *Ibid*.: 43.
[15] Kruse 2000: 62.   [16] *Ibid*.: 77.
[17] Painter 1986: 50–1.   [18] Neufeld 1994: 84.

threat (although it may include that).'[19] Since Neufeld applies speech-act theory to 1 John, he argues that the claims are hypothetical speech-acts that 'reveal what in the author's opinion constitutes improper speech and conduct – thus notifying the readers that they must not speak and act in accord with them'.[20] He concludes: Our speech act analysis shows that these slogans may be taken as hypothetical acts of speech that make plain the attitudes and beliefs of the author.'[21] This builds on the first-person forms that introduce the claims and identifies the author and the audience as people who make the hypothetical claims. Even though this attempts to avoid identifying the claimants, in effect it identifies them as the author and audience.

Griffith starts his discussion of the claims noting that there 'is nothing in 1.6–2.2 to indicate that John is concerned about issues or threats that come from outside the community'.[22] Specific historical referents external to the community do not occur until 2:18–19, with references to the antichrists and the schism.[23] He argues that it is the influence of reading 1 John with an assumption of a polemical purpose that leads scholars to identify the 'claims' with the opponents.[24] Instead, he suggests that the slogans reflect issues that have arisen from the community's theology and concerns, and are 'conducted without reference to the particular issues raised in the schism'.[25] This suggestion involves understanding the plural 'we' as the *pluralis sociativus* associating the writer with the reader (BDF §280), functioning as a rhetorical device 'that reinforces commonly held beliefs and values'. As such the 'statements that they contain do not represent views held by real or imagined interlocutors or opponents. They make perfectly good sense as they stand, as pastoral teaching on the Christian experience of sin and the maintenance of community.'[26] To support this identification Griffith notes examples of the clause ἐὰν εἴπωμεν introducing statements in *Commentaria in Aristotelem Graeca* and other Greek texts.[27] From this he concludes that it was used to advance the speaker's argument in a non-polemical way. The occurrences in the Old Testament and New Testament are in a polemical context which leads to them being interpreted polemically (4 Kingdoms 7:4; Matthew 21:25–26;

[19] *Ibid.*: 94.   [20] *Ibid.*: 84.
[21] *Ibid.*: 94–5.   [22] Griffith 2002: 117.
[23] *Ibid.*: 118.   [24] *Ibid.*: 118.
[25] *Ibid.*: 119.   [26] *Ibid.*: 121.
[27] Alexander Aphrodisiensis, *CAG*, II.2, 539.2–5; Ammonius, *CAG*, IV.3, 44.19–22; IV.4, 7.2–17; Elias, *CAG*, XVIII.1, 7.6–11; Philoponus, *CAG*, XIII.3, 170.23–24; 246.26–7; David, *CAG*, XVIII.2, 12.7–9; 19:30–2; 20.11–13; Themistius, *CAG*, XXIII.3, 19.18–19.

Mark 11:31; Luke 20:5–6). Without this context, there is no reason to read them polemically.[28] He also cites evidence that the same is true of ὁ λέγων, and the formula ἐάν τις εἴπῃ (cf. 4:20).[29] On the basis of this evidence Griffith concludes: '[T]hose statements that are labeled by the vast majority of scholars as the heretical "slogans" or "boasts" of schismatics, fit very well with forms of discussion that occur in communities that debate and transmit their founding traditions. They do not represent the views held by real or imagined interlocutors or opponents.'[30]

Lieu also understands the claims as rhetorical and not necessarily containing historical referent. She argues that the first-person plural in 1:6–2:2 is mainly used in order to debate.[31] The lack of the emphatic first-person plural nominative results in the readers viewing the statements objectively and thus as a mode of debate. However, Lieu admits that the first-person plural is 'at least implicitly inclusive', and so the writer and audience cannot be completely separated from the statements.[32] The debating technique is only effective if the audience can identify with the statements.

Thus the literary school understands the claims as a literary device used to convince the readers of the author's opinion with regards to sin and speech. The claims may (Neufeld) or may not (Griffith) contain historical referent.

Critique

From the foregoing description, analysing the 'claims' requires decisions on three issues – the significance of the grammatical number of the person the formulae use to introduce the 'claim', whether ὅτι is used in the formulae, and the grammatical person of the 'claim' itself.

---

[28] Griffith 2002: 122.

[29] For ὁ λέγων see Alexander Aphrodisiensis, *CAG*, I, 372.2–7, 650.20–37; II.1, 404.27–9; II.2, 178.27; Ammonius, *CAG*, IV.4, 66.27–67.2; IV.5, 93.28–30, 187.30, 208.9, 219.25; Philoponus, *CAG*, XIII.1, 45.16–20; XIII.3, 69; David, *CAG*, XVIII.2, 28.3–6; Themistius, *CAG*, XXIII.3, 130.33–4, 131.21–30; Plato, *Charmides*, 161d; Aristotle, *Metaphysics*, 1011ab, 1047a, 1062a, 1090a; Philo, *Leg. All.* 1.49; 3.198. For ἐάν τις εἴπῃ see Alexander Aphrodisiensis, *CAG*, I, 349.10, 372.7; II.1, 364.3; II.2, 482.13–14; Ammonius, *CAG*, IV.4, 34.16–18; Olympiodorus, *CAG*, XII.1, 44.19; Philoponus, *CAG*, XIII.1, 45.16–20; XIII.3, 409.12–13; David, *CAG*, XVIII.2, 112.14–16; Themistius, *CAG*, XXIII.3, 6.26–27; Aristotle, *Posterior Analytics*, 91b; *Topica*, 126a; Plato, *Fifth Epistle*, 322d; Philo, *Sacr.* 70.

[30] Griffith 2002: 124.

[31] Lieu (2008b: 817) notes one occasion when it is used as an expression of confidence (2:1).

[32] *Ibid.*: 817.

The first-person plural form ἐὰν εἴπωμεν seems to include the author and audience in the claim. However, the Historical Critical school is uneasy with identifying the author and audience with the claims since they are understood to have negative connotations. This motivated Brown to see the claims as indirect speech rather than a quotation. However, Painter, Smalley, and Kruse understand them as quotations and argue that the first person indicates that this is the author's quotation, thus reflecting his/her understanding of the opponents. The literary school acknowledges that the first-person plural includes the author and audience, explaining it as a literary device – the *pluralis sociativus*. The claims are views that the author and audience could hold and not necessarily those of others external to the community. The evidence cited for this view is the use of this clause to introduce claims elsewhere in Greek literature.

It seems the most straightforward way to understand the use of this formula is to see it as reflecting the claims of the author and audience. Griffith's observation that there are no references to external opposition until 2:18–19 again reflects the historical school's weakness of reversing the reading order of the text. Further, to suggest that the claims reflect the author's understanding of the opponents is not the simplest solution. Granted, it is motivated by the desire not to attribute negative statements to the author and audience, but if that is what the text contains, then there may be other ways to explain it. The literary school's explanation seems stronger, yet the evidence provided for the solution has some deficiencies. Griffith's quoting of fifth-century documents (CAG) to explain a first-century document's apparent rhetorical device is historically anachronistic. His point that the occurrences in the Biblical documents are only read polemically due to context, and do not in themselves involve a polemical tone, is stronger. Yet this evidence does not rule out that the 'claims' happened historically. Griffith provides evidence that the 'claim' formulae could be a literary device, but this evidence does not exclude the possibility that these verses also contain a historical referent. When the general combination of ἐὰν λέγω is investigated, without regard for the grammatical person, it reveals that it is a formula used throughout the LXX and New Testament documents to introduce a quotation (direct and indirect).[33] The first-person form of the quotation may be

---

[33] Genesis 21:12; 34:11; 41:55; Exodus 12:26; Numbers 22:17, 35; 24:13; Deuteronomy 5:27; Judges 7:4; Ruth 3:5, 11; 1 Samuel 16:3; 20:21; 28:8; 2 Samuel 15:26; 1 Kings 5:20; 2 Kings 4:24; 7:4; 10:5; 2 Chronicles 18:13; Esther 2:13; Isaiah 8:12, 19; 10:8; Jeremiah 13:12, 22; 15:2; Ezekiel 21:12; 1 Esdras 4:3, 4, 7; Matthew 12:32; 21:24, 25; 23:3; Mark 7:11; 11:31; Luke 20:5; John 3:12; 1 Corinthians 12:15, 16.

nothing more than reporting the author and audience's own words. Thus the occurrences in 1 John could reflect the actual words of the author and audience. The observation that the pronouns in 1:8 identify the claimant with the author and audience would support this proposition. So, applying Ockham's razor, it would appear that this formula reports claims of the author and audience. If this proves untenable, then another more complicated solution may be required.

The third-person form ὁ λέγων leaves the identity of the claimant unspecified. It does not necessarily include the author and audience and so the claims can be taken more easily to reflect the opponents. However, Smalley's observation that they can be made by any Christian plays against the trend to attribute them to the opponents. Further, the parallel nature of the two parts (1:6–2:2 and 2:3–11) seems to indicate that the formula is just a stylistic change, and the natural subject of the quotes continues to be the author and audience. This is confirmed by 2:7–8, in which the audience is referred to in the pronouns, and which are about the commands, the subject of 2:3–6. This evidence refutes the Historical Critical school's use of these verses to describe the opponents. The literary school wishes to understand these claims as a rhetorical device in line with their understanding of ἐὰν εἴπωμεν. However, Griffith once more provides fifth-century examples, again resulting in a somewhat anachronistic historical observation. His material from Philo is stronger but it does not limit understanding ὁ λέγων to having to be a literary device only. The exact phrase occurs throughout the LXX and New Testament documents introducing speech (direct and indirect).[34] It could have a historical referent in the author and audience, and given the context, this seems the simplest way to understand the phrase.

Painter's arguments about the use of ὅτι in introducing the claim are compelling.[35] This indicates that the first four claims are direct quotations. This argues against the literary school's limiting of the claims to having no historical referent.[36] When this is partnered with the analysis of the formulae just provided, it suggests that the first four claims are direct quotations of the author and audience. The last two appear to be indirect quotations. The significance of this change from direct to indirect quotations seems minimal due to the repetition of the formula in 2:6 and 9.

---

[34] Deuteronomy 33:9; Job 9:7; 34:18, 31; Micah 2:7; Habakkuk 2:19; Isaiah 41:13; 42:22; 44:26, 27, 28; 45:10; Matthew 7:21; Romans 2:22; 2 John 11.

[35] Painter 2002: 143–4.

[36] Though to be fair to Neufeld it must be noted that he does not deny the historical angle but downplays its significance.

Finally, the grammatical person in each 'claim' seems to confirm the critique above. The first-person forms in 1:6, 8, 10, and 2:4 seem to report the speech of the author and audience.[37] The grammatical change to the singular in 2:4 matches the stylistic change to ὁ λέγων. This again suggests that the literary school's minimising of the historical context is flawed. The infinitive forms in 2:6 and 9 are indirect speech, but given the parallel patterns in the sections, they suggest that the author and audience could have spoken them.

Summary

The Historical Critical school uses the claims to describe the opponents. It takes the quotation form seriously, yet downplays the first-person plural form of the formula ἐὰν εἴπωμεν, disregarding the option that they are the words of the author and audience. The literary school acknowledges the first-person form of the formula ἐὰν εἴπωμεν used to introduce the claims and as a result prefers to understand them as a rhetorical device. However, the evidence cited to support such a view does not rule out that there could also be a historic referent. When the use of ὅτι, signalling that four of the claims are most likely quotations, is factored into the debate, the historical referent question again comes to the fore. Given the first-person form used in ἐὰν εἴπωμεν, and the parallel nature of 1:6–2:2 and 2:4–11, it appears that the simplest way to understand these claims is that the author and audience made them.

An intertextual reading of 1:6–2:11

Given the problems associated with both the Historical Critical and literary schools' interpretation of the claims, this research proposes a reading of the claims that understands them as made by the author and audience with a historical referent. It suggests that the common feature that allows the use of the first-person plural is Christianity's early understanding of itself as the True Israel, so that the claims could flow from a Jewish self-identity.

In accord with the reading method, this section has two main parts. The first outlines the intertextual evidence used in filling the gap concerning the identity of the claimants. The second section then tests this understanding by performing a reading of 1:6–2:11, paying special attention to the limiting devices.

---

[37] Curtis 1992: 28–30.

Intertextual links

In these verses there are intertextual links in the claims, the descriptions of the behaviour, and the results of the behaviour.

The claims

The six claims, though they are expressed differently, have three topics as their content. First, 1:6; 2:4 and 2:6 are claims of special relationship to God – to have fellowship with God (1:6), to know God (2:4), and to remain in God (2:6). Second, 1:8 and 10 are claims relating to sin – to have no sin (1:8), and to not have sinned (1:10). Third, 2:9 is a claim about lifestyle – to walk in the light. These claims overlap, as the relationship to God is seen in lifestyle and in the view of sin. The content of the claims are ways that first-century Jewish people could have described themselves. That is, there is intertexual evidence from the first century that Jewish people understood themselves to have a special relationship to God, to not have sin, and to walk in the light.

First, evidence of Jewish people thinking of themselves as having a special relationship with God is found in both John's Gospel and Romans. The conflict between Jesus and 'the Jews' in John's Gospel is often about the claim of a special relationship to God based on knowledge. Jesus' responses to the Jews are predicated on their claim to a special relationship to God based on the law. One of the clearest examples of this is John 8:54–5:[38]

> [54] Jesus replied, 'If I glorify myself, my glory means nothing. My Father, whom you claim as your God, is the one who glorifies me. [55] Though you do not know him, I know him. If I said I did not, I would be a liar like you, but I do know him and keep his word.'

The Jews claim to know God, but Jesus denies that they do because they do not know Jesus. This theme runs through the conflict with the Jews in John's Gospel. The Jews claim that God is their father (8:41) and so they are able to judge that Jesus is not from God. However, Jesus states that they do not know God (7:28; 16:3) because if they had known God they would recognise Jesus (8:19). They search the law (5:37–47) but fail to see Jesus, revealing that they do not know or love the Father.

In Romans 2:17–20 Paul describes the first-century Jew's understanding of themselves:

---

[38] Unless otherwise indicated, the English translations in this 'Intertextual Links' section are taken from the NIV.

¹⁷ Now you, if you call yourself a Jew; if you rely on the law and brag about your relationship to God; ¹⁸ if you know his will and approve of what is superior because you are instructed by the law; ¹⁹ if you are convinced that you are a guide for the blind, a light for those who are in the dark, ²⁰ an instructor of the foolish, a teacher of infants, because you have in the law the embodiment of knowledge and truth –

Paul describes first-century Jews as considering themselves to have a special relationship to God (2:17), just like the claim of fellowship with God in 1 John 1:6.³⁹ This special relationship is based on their possession and knowledge of the law (2:18, 20), just like the claim to know God in 1 John 2:4. The overlapping nature of the third claim (1 John 2:9) is also evident in these verses, since in Romans 2:19 the Jew thinks, because of his special relationship based on knowledge of the law, that he is a light. This is similar to 1 John 2:9, where the claim is to walk in the light. Further, Paul reveals his understanding of the Jewish people in Romans 9:4–5. He argues that they have a special relationship with God because God adopted them as sons and gave them the covenant, law, and promises, and a means to worship Himself.⁴⁰ So the first-century Jews thought of themselves as possessing a special relationship with God and Jews could have made the claims of 1:6; 2:4 and 6.

Second, that Jews thought of themselves as having no sin is evident in four places in the New Testament. In John 15:22 and 24, Jesus uses the exact same phrase as the claim of 1 John 1:8 (ἁμαρτίαν οὐκ ἔχομεν) to describe the situation of the world without his words or works:

> ²² If I had not come and spoken to them, they would not be guilty of sin [ἁμαρτίαν οὐκ ἔχομεν]. Now, however, they have no excuse for their sin. ²³ He who hates me hates my Father as well. ²⁴ If I had not done among them what no one else did, they would not be guilty of sin [ἁμαρτίαν οὐκ ἔχομεν]. But now they have seen these miracles, and yet they have hated both me and my Father.

When Jesus speaks in John 13–16, he uses the 'world' to refer to the 'Jews'.⁴¹ Jesus states twice that the Jews would have no sin except for his

---

³⁹ The NIV includes the word 'relationship' in 2:17 even though the Greek says καὶ καυχᾶσαι ἐν θεῷ.

⁴⁰ See also Romans 11:28–30.   ⁴¹ Griffith 2002: 207.

coming to speak and act.[42] This understanding of having no sin is also reflected in the Pharisees' dismissal of the man born blind. In John 9:34 they refuse to listen to the man since he was born in sin. The implication of this is a contrast between the man and the Pharisees – he was sinful and they were not.

That Jewish people thought of themselves as having no sin is also evident in 'the rich young ruler' who comes to Jesus and claims to have kept the law (Matthew 19:20; Mark 10:20; Luke 18:21). Again, Paul describes his pre-conversion understanding of himself as righteous and blameless with regard to the law (Philippians 3:6).[43] These examples reveal that Jews could think of themselves as not having sin. If they followed the rules of the temple, offering the sacrifices for sin, then they could expect God to have forgiven them. This does not rule out that they sin, rather it affirms that they have no sin left in them once the sacrifices are made. There is ample evidence of Jews acknowledging that they have sinned (Ezra 9:6–15; Nehemiah 9:5–37; Psalm 51; Daniel 9:4–19). The issue in the second claim (1:8) is that they *have sin*.

The third claim, to not sin (1:10), takes the whole argument one step further. It would result from overstressing the elective purposes of God and forgiveness to the point where it does not matter what someone does.[44] Again, it seems possible that some Jews went this far, since Paul devotes the whole of Romans 2 to an argument designed to show Jews that they sin. This chapter would not be required if Jews knew they sinned and were not making the claim of sinlessness.

So first-century Jews could have made the claims in 1 John 1:6–2:11, since they apparently thought of themselves in those terms. This is because the content of the claims has its origins in the Old Testament. A key Old Testament passage that describes Israel and that contains most of the elements of the claims is Jeremiah 31:33–4:

> [33] 'This is the covenant I will make with the house of Israel after that time,' declares the LORD. 'I will put my law in their minds and write it on their hearts. I will be their God, and they will be my people. [34] No longer will a man teach his neighbour, or a man his brother, saying, "Know the LORD," because they will all know me, from the least of them to the greatest,' declares the

---

[42] See also John 9:41.

[43] Other examples include Zechariah (Luke 1:6) and Nathanael (John 1:47). Further, Paul's contrast of those born Jewish to Gentile 'sinners' (Galatians 2:15), seems to also imply the same understanding.

[44] The apparent Jewish (Christian?) argument James seeks to correct in James 2:14–26.

LORD. 'For I will forgive their wickedness and will remember their sins no more.'

The claim of fellowship with God (1:6) is reflected in Jeremiah 31:33, where God will be their God and they will be his people.[45] The claim to know God (2:4) picks up the language of Jeremiah 31:34, where God promises that they will all know him.[46] The claim to remain in God (2:6) sounds like a result of having God's law in their minds and on their hearts (Jeremiah 31:33).[47] The claim to have no sin (1:8) is the result of God forgiving their wickedness and remembering their sins no more (Jeremiah 31:34).[48]

The particular claims to have no sin (1:8) and to not sin (1:10) are evident in the Old Testament as a result of God's forgiveness. So for example, Jeremiah 50:20 states:

> 'In those days,' at that time, declares the LORD, 'search will be made for Israel's guilt, but there will be none, and for the sins of Judah, but none will be found, for I will forgive the remnant I spare.'

God removes sins from his sight, putting them behind his back (Isaiah 38:17), out of his mind (Isaiah 43:25), sweeping them away (Isaiah 44:22). The result is that Israel is described as holy (Isaiah 4:3) and righteous (Isaiah 26:2; 45:25; 60:21). They will do no wrong, nor speak lies (Zephaniah 3:13). This goes some way towards a basis for the claim that Jews do not sin (1:10). Faithless Israel even claims not to have sinned in Jeremiah 2:35:

> You say, 'I am innocent; he is not angry with me.' But I will pass judgment on you because you say, 'I have not sinned (חָטָאתִי ἥμαρτον).'

The claim of 2:9, to be in the light, is found as an image of Israel living with God in Micah 7:9, Isaiah 42:16, and 60:1, 19–20. From these people, light will emanate to the nations (Isaiah 42:6; 60:3).

So, first-century Jews thought about themselves in the categories of the claims in 1 John 1:6–2:11 because the Old Testament described them in these terms.

---

[45] See also Exodus 6:7; Leviticus 26:12; Deuteronomy 28:17–18; Ezekiel 11:20; 36:28; Hosea 1:9–10; 2:23; Zechariah 8:8; 13:9.

[46] See also Isaiah 54:13.

[47] See also Deuteronomy 6:6; 11:18; 30:14; 32:46; Isaiah 51:7; Ezekiel 11:19; 36:26–7.

[48] See also Psalms 85:2; 130:4; Isaiah 33:24; 38:17; Jeremiah 33:8; Ezekiel 33:16; Micah 7:18–19; Zechariah 3:4, 9.

The behaviour

Even though these descriptions are applied to Israel in the Old Testament and can be seen as the basis of this self-understanding, it is more than just the claims that have Jewish echoes. The description of the negative behaviour has echoes with how faithless Israel is described in the Old Testament. So 'walking in the darkness' (ἐν τῷ σκότει περιπατῶμεν) in 1:6 sounds like the descriptions of faithless Israel.[49] Psalm 82:5 describes faithless Israel:

> They know nothing, they understand nothing. They walk about in darkness; all the foundations of the earth are shaken.

Or Lamentations 3:2:

> [1]I am the man who has seen affliction by the rod of his wrath. [2] He has driven me away and made me walk in darkness rather than light; [3] indeed, he has turned his hand against me again and again, all day long.[50]

The second description of inconsistent behaviour in 2:4, 'not keeping God's commands' (τὰς ἐντολὰς αὐτοῦ μὴ τηρῶν), also sounds like the descriptions of faithless Israel. Moses promises the curses of God on Israel if she does not keep his commands (Deuteronomy 28:25 and 45). Saul did not keep God's commands and so his descendants did not become the dynastical line of Israel (1 Samuel 13:13). God promises Solomon that if he or his descendants do not keep God's commands, Israel will be removed from the land and the temple rejected (1 Kings 9:6–7). When the exile of Israel is discussed in 2 Kings 17:18–20, it is in terms of not keeping God's commands and hints at Judah's ensuing fate:

> [18] So the LORD was very angry with Israel and removed them from his presence. Only the tribe of Judah was left, [19] and even Judah did not keep the commands of the LORD their God. They followed the practices Israel had introduced. [20] Therefore the LORD rejected all the people of Israel; he afflicted them and gave them into the hands of plunderers, until he thrust them from his presence.

---

[49] Even though the exact phrase is not used in the LXX, the combination of the Hebrew verb הָלַךְ (walk) with the noun חֹשֶׁךְ (darkness) reveals the image is applied to faithless Israel.

[50] See also Proverbs 2:13; Ecclesiastes 2:14; Isaiah 9:2; 50:10; 59:9.

Finally, before Nehemiah returns from the exile he confesses Israel's sins to God (Nehemiah 1:7) in terms of them not keeping his commands:

> We have acted very wickedly toward you. We have not obeyed the commands, decrees and laws you gave your servant Moses.[51]

The last description of inconsistent behaviour is 'hating one's brother' (τὸν ἀδελφὸν αὐτοῦ μισῶν) in 2:9 and 11. Again, this description is used in the Old Testament to depict the faithless within Israel. So in Leviticus 19:17–18 the Israelites are commanded not to hate their brother but love him:

> Do not hate your brother in your heart. Rebuke your neighbour frankly so you will not share in his guilt. Do not seek revenge or bear a grudge against one of your people, but love your neighbour as yourself. I am the LORD.

This reference is probably on the author's mind because he echoes the positive line 'love your brother' in 2:10. Further, in Isaiah 66:5, God describes the faithless Israelites as hating their brothers:

> Hear the word of the LORD, you who tremble at his word: 'Your brothers who hate you, and exclude you because of my name, have said, "Let the LORD be glorified, that we may see your joy!" Yet they will be put to shame.'

So the behaviour inconsistent with the claims also seems to be Jewish, applied in the Old Testament to faithless Israel.

The echoes with Judaism are not finished at this point. They continue in the descriptions of the behaviour consistent with the claims. So 'walking in the light' (ἐν τῷ φωτὶ περιπατῶμεν) in 1:7 is the way the faithful of Israel are described in Isaiah 2:5:

> Come, O house of Jacob, let us walk in the light of the LORD.[52]

'Confessing sins' (ὁμολογῶμεν τὰς ἁμαρτίας) in 1:9 is one of the actions of faithful Jews described in Psalm 32:5 and Proverbs 28:13. The desire not to sin (μὴ ἁμάρτητε) in 2:1 is expressed by true Jews in Psalms 4:4; 39:1; and 119:11. 'Keeping the commandments' (τηρῇ αὐτοῦ τὸν λόγον) in 2:5 is used to describe one of the characteristics of God's faithful people in the Decalogue with reference to idolatry – Exodus 20:6; and

---

[51] See 1 Kings 11:10; 13:21; Psalm 89:31 for further examples.

[52] See further Psalm 89:15; Isaiah 9:2; 60:1–3.

Deuteronomy 5:10.[53] Walking in the ways (2:6) of the Lord describes the faithful in Isaiah 2:5; Hosea 14:9; and Micah 4:2. So the descriptions of the people whose behaviour is consistent with the claims have echoes with how the faithful of Israel are described.

Results of the behaviour

Even the results of both behaviours find echoes in Judaism. First, the results of inconsistent behaviours are found describing faithless Israel. They are described variously as liars (1:6; 2:4), self-deceived (1:8), those who do not live by (1:6) or contain (1:8, 10; 2:4) the truth, but make God out to be a liar (1:10). These descriptions are used of faithless Israel in passages like Jeremiah 9:3–6:

> [3]'They make ready their tongue like a bow, to shoot lies; it is not by truth that they triumph in the land. They go from one sin to another; they do not acknowledge me,' declares the LORD. [4] 'Beware of your friends; do not trust your brothers. For every brother is a deceiver, and every friend a slanderer. [5] Friend deceives friend, and no one speaks the truth. They have taught their tongues to lie; they weary themselves with sinning. [6] You live in the midst of deception; in their deceit they refuse to acknowledge me,' declares the LORD.[54]

These people live in the dark (2:9, 11), where they stumble due to their blindness (2:11). These concepts are used to depict faithless Israel in passages like Isaiah 59:9–10:

> [9]So justice is far from us, and righteousness does not reach us. We look for light, but all is darkness; for brightness, but we walk in deep shadows. [10] Like the blind we grope along the wall, feeling our way like men without eyes. At midday we stumble as if it were twilight; among the strong, we are like the dead.[55]

So the results of inconsistent behaviour are described in terms used to depict the state of faithless Israel.

Second, the results of consistent behaviours are found describing faithful Israel. They will have fellowship (1:7) and be cleansed from their sin and unrighteousness (1:7, 9). They will be forgiven (1:9) and have

---

[53] See also Ecclesiastes 12:13.
[54] See also Isaiah 59:14–15; Jeremiah 5:27; 7:28.
[55] See also Isaiah 6:9–10 and Lieu 1993: 472–5.

an advocate with the Father, an advocate who is the propitiation for sin (2:1–2). The love of God will be made complete in them (2:5) and they will not stumble (2:10). These results are based on the Old Testament texts that formed the basis of the claims. So Jeremiah 31:33–4 indicates that the people will have fellowship with God and have their sins forgiven. The means for forgiveness is described in images drawn from the sacrificial system (eg: Leviticus 4:20; 5:6; 7:11; 19:22).[56] Finally, the description of not stumbling is how faithful Jews who are under God's care are described (Psalms 56:13; 116:8; 119:165). So the results of behaviour consistent with the claims are similar to how faithful Israel is described in the Old Testament.

Summary

These verses have a large number of echoes with the Old Testament, which determined how Jews in the first century understood themselves. So the claims have been shown to be how first-century Jews could have thought about themselves. On closer investigation of the descriptions used of the two types of behaviour, it has become apparent that behaviour inconsistent with the claims was depicted in language and thought used to describe faithless Israel. On the other hand, behaviour that was consistent with the claims was depicted in language and thought that was used to describe faithful Israel. Even the results of the two types of behaviour were presented the same way.

This suggests that the first-person plural could be based on a common identification of the author and audience as Jewish. They could make the claims because the claims are Jewish ones based on Old Testament expectations. However, the behaviour reveals what type of Jew a person is – faithless or faithful. That is, when the author and audience make these claims, they might think they are part of Israel, but their behaviour indicates whether they are part of faithless Israel or members of the True Israel.

One possible objection to the notion that the 'we' could be based on shared Judaism requires answering. The first-person plural is used throughout 1:1–2:2, yet in 1:1–5 it seems to refer to the apostles and so does not rest on a shared Jewish heritage. This observation is valid but does not undercut the position adopted here. This is because there seems to be a

---

[56] Morgen (2004: 490–6) notes that 1:6–2:2 refers to Leviticus 16 but denies a sacrifical reading of the verses.

shift in the first-person plural from the exclusive sense (author only) in 1:1–5 to an inclusive sense (author and audience) in 1:6–2:2.[57] This shift is evident in two ways. First, there is a near absence of second-person pronouns in 1:6–2:2 dividing the author from the audience. The only occurrence is in 2:1, where the author interrupts the third pair of conditional sentences with a vocative and purpose statement. Since vocatives and purpose statements seem to function at a different level of communication with the audience, the verse and its pronoun should be acknowledged as different from the rest of the section. Second, the section is a series of case studies of those living in fellowship with a God who is light. This is not restricted to the author but includes the readers (1:3). This inclusive sense confirms understanding these verses as containing the sentiments of the author and audience.[58] So this shift in sense allows that the first-person plural could be based on shared Jewish heritage.

Intertextual test reading

Since these verses have two units of three claims, the reading to test this intertextual fill for the gap of the identity of the claimants is in two sections. It will pay specific attention to the limiting devices in 2:1 and 2:7–8 as they are encountered in the reading.

1 John 1:6–2:2

The first claim (1:6) is a direct quotation (ὅτι) and is contained in a conditional sentence (ἐάν). It expresses the general Jewish view that they had a special relationship (κοινωνία) with God. The protasis continues, describing behaviour that is contrary to the claim in terms similar to the faithless in the Old Testament (καὶ ἐν τῷ σκότει περιπατῶμεν). Both the claim and the description use the concepts of the premises outlined in 1:1–5, as evident in their repeated vocabulary (κοινωνία, σκότος). The antecedent of αὐτοῦ in the claim appears to be ὁ θεός, who is light (1:5) and with whom fellowship is shared (1:3).[59] Since the lifestyle described is contrary to the nature of God, with whom fellowship is claimed, the apodosis outlines two logical results. First, those making the claim are lying (ψευδόμεθα) and second, they are not doing the truth (οὐ ποιοῦμεν τὴν ἀλήθειαν).

---

[57] Schmid (2004b: 505) and Lieu (2008a: 53) both note the change in the use of the first-person plural between 1:1–5 and 1:6–2:2.

[58] It also rules out that the claims report the speech of the opponents.

[59] ὁ θεός refers to πατρὸς in 1:3 since the following personal pronoun αὐτοῦ has πατρὸς as its antecedent.

These two results seem directly linked to the claim and descriptions – the claim is a lie and the described lifestyle is not doing what is true. Again, this description is how faithless Israel is depicted in the Old Testament.

In contrast (δέ) to the lifestyle described in verse 6, a second conditional statement describes the results of a lifestyle that is in accordance with God's character. This lifestyle is described in terms similar to how faithful Israel is depicted. The apodosis describes the two results for those who make the claim and whose lifestyle is consistent with God's character – fellowship and cleansing. The first result picks up the theme of fellowship (κοινωνία) from 1:3. Just as in 1:3 the description of fellowship started with the author, here fellowship is pictured as being with one another (μετ' ἀλλήλων). Living a lifestyle consistent with God's character brings close association with others who share this lifestyle: the author and other Jews. The second result is a cleansing from all sin (καθαρίζει ἡμᾶς ἀπὸ πάσης ἁμαρτίας) achieved through the blood of Jesus (καὶ τὸ αἷμα Ἰησοῦ τοῦ υἱοῦ αὐτοῦ). Under the Old Testament law, sin required sacrifice in order for cleansing to occur (Leviticus 4:17). This verse understands Jesus' death as a sacrifice for sin – blood (αἷμα) referring to sacrifice. This reference to Jesus' death supports the understanding that John is affirming the glorification of Jesus in 1:1–3a, because just as the message of Jesus' resurrection brought fellowship, so here the death of Jesus brings cleansing from sin.

The second claim (1:8) is again a direct quotation (ὅτι) in a conditional statement (ἐάν). It also expresses a general Jewish view about not having sin (ἁμαρτίαν οὐκ ἔχομεν). This claim is not followed by a portrayal of any behaviour, like the first claim in 1:6. Rather, the apodosis relates the result of the claim immediately – the self-deception of the people (ἑαυτοὺς πλανῶμεν) and a lack of truth within them (καὶ ἡ ἀλήθεια οὐκ ἔστιν ἐν ἡμῖν). These are again descriptions consistent with the picture of faithless Israel in the Old Testament.

In contrast to this claim, a second conditional statement (ἐάν) starts its protasis with the idea of confession. If the author and his audience, rather than claiming to have no sin, confess their sins (ὁμολογῶμεν τὰς ἁμαρτίας ἡμῶν) as faithful Israel did, then the apodosis lists two results. First, their sins are forgiven (ἀφῇ ἡμῖν τὰς ἁμαρτίας) and second, they are cleansed from unrighteousness (καὶ καθαρίσῃ ἡμᾶς ἀπὸ πάσης ἀδικίας).[60] These two results flow from God's character – his faithfulness

---

[60] That forgiveness and cleansing are two results of the confession is evident from the syntax that sees both of them in the subjunctive coordinated by the ἵνα that introduces the result clause.

and righteousness (πιστός ἐστιν καὶ δίκαιος) – and are promised to the faithful in Israel.

The third claim (1:10) also contains a direct quotation (ὅτι) embedded in a conditional statement (ἐάν). It is similar to the second, but a slightly different claim, not to have sinned (οὐχ ἡμαρτήκαμεν). It again appears in the Old Testament (Jeremiah 2:35 – οὐχ ἥμαρτον) and could be evident in first-century Judaism. There is no description of behaviour, and the results of the claim are very similar to those in 1:7 – making God a liar (ψεύστην ποιοῦμεν αὐτὸν) and not having his word in them (καὶ ὁ λόγος αὐτοῦ οὐκ ἔστιν ἐν ἡμῖν). Making the claim not to have sinned calls God a liar (understanding ὁ θεός as the antecedent of αὐτόν in this clause and αὐτοῦ in the next), and denies his word in the audience's lives.[61]

A vocative and purpose statement break the observed pattern of contrasting conditional statements. The vocative introduces a summary statement that occurs towards the end of the unit. This is the second purpose statement in 1 John, indicating the reason (ἵνα) for the author's writing – that you might not sin (μὴ ἁμάρτητε). The main theme of this unit is sin, and here the author wishes to indicate why he has been writing about sin, in order that the readers do not sin. It would appear that claiming to be Jewish requires behaviour that is consistent with the claim. Just as in the Old Testament there were those who were descended from Abraham but were faithless to the covenant, so there were also those in the author's day who claimed to be members of Israel but whose behaviour was at odds with their claims. They were not members of the faithful or True Israel but rather were faithless. So the author wishes the audience would not sin by claiming to be Jewish but continuing to be faithless.

Once the purpose of the unit is given, the author resumes the usual pattern of contrasting conditional statements. The protasis describes the situation – someone sins (τις ἁμάρτῃ). Given the context of the history of Israel, it seems inevitable that all Jews sin. Given the context of the last two claims, the author has affirmed that all Israel has sinned and requires forgiveness and cleansing from sin. In this way, all Israel is faithless. The apodosis locates the answer to sin in the resurrected Jesus, because it affirms that readers have a defender with the Father – Jesus Christ the righteous (παράκλητον ἔχομεν πρὸς τὸν πατέρα Ἰησοῦν

---

[61] Paul understands God to have testified in the Old Testament that all people sin – in the Law (Romans 5:12–14), the Psalms and the Prophets (cf. Romans 3:9–18). The irony is that some Jewish people claimed the law set them apart from the Gentile world (Romans 2:17–19) yet because they did not obey it, it was not in them.

Χριστὸν δίκαιον).⁶² It should be noted at this point that the exact same
location phrase (πρὸς τὸν πατέρα) was used in 1:2 to describe where
Jesus appeared from and that it is assumed that he is now in this location.
Further, the picture of Jesus in heaven assumes the resurrection affirmed
in 1:1–3a. The description of the basis of this defence and its significance
are then given. Jesus is the propitiation for sin (ἱλασμός), not just for the
Jewish people but for the whole world (περὶ ὅλου τοῦ κόσμου).⁶³ The
resurrected Jesus is the answer to the expectations of Israel as his death
brings forgiveness for faithlessness and restores people to God's covenant people.

In summary, 1:6–2:2 contains three test cases of claims that could
have been made within Jewish circles in the first century. The subsequent
descriptions of behaviour and its results demonstrate whether someone is
a member of faithless Judaism or authentic Israel. The death and resurrection of the incarnate Jesus is the means of forgiveness and cleansing
so that someone can rejoin Israel.

1 John 2:3–11

The opening verse of this new unit (2:3) discusses a result of the message of the resurrected incarnate Christ (1:1–3a), paralleling 1:3b–5. The
result is assurance that the author and readers know Jesus.⁶⁴ Given that
Jesus' resurrection is the means of restoration to Israel, the natural question is how the readers can be confident that they have fellowship with
Jesus.⁶⁵ The answer is given in the form of a test – that they keep Jesus'
commands (ἐὰν τὰς ἐντολὰς αὐτοῦ τηρῶμεν).⁶⁶

The first case study of assurance (2:4–5) based on obedience to Jesus'
commands again flows from a direct quotation (ὅτι). The change in person appears to be stylistic, reflecting a second set of three statements.
However, it also marks a slight twist to the Old Testament allusions that
are made. Even though the claims have links with the teaching of the

---

⁶² For the view that παράκλητος is not a legal term but refers to a 'sponsor', representative or defender see Grayston 1981: 79–80.

⁶³ On ἱλασμός meaning propitiation see Morris 1965: 205–8.

⁶⁴ The antecedent of αὐτόν is Ἰησοῦν Χριστὸν from 2:1. This is the last person spoken
of who then is the antecedent of the personal pronoun αὐτός in 2:2.

⁶⁵ The second occurrence of γινώσκω is relational rather than cognitive, as is evident
from the parallel γινώσκω and the concept of κοινωνία in 1:3b.

⁶⁶ Since Jesus is the antecedent of the last personal pronoun, and since no nominal form
has occurred since, Jesus is understood as the antecedent of αὐτοῦ. Discussion of the content of Jesus' commands is deferred until the discussion of 2:7–8, where the issue explicitly
arises.

Old Testament, they are applied to Jesus. He is the subject of many of the pronominal uses of αὐτός. This twist is based on the affirmation in 1:1–3a of the resurrection of the *incarnate* Christ. When first-century Jews made these claims, they should have been made in light of the resurrection of the incarnate Christ. That is, first-century Jews should have recognised that Jesus was God and understood the commands in light of him. So the claim to know Jesus (ἔγνωκα αὐτόν) builds on the Old Testament claim to know God, but builds into the claim the concept of the resurrection of the incarnate Christ. The following description of their failure to keep the commandments (καὶ τὰς ἐντολὰς αὐτοῦ μὴ τηρῶν) reveals inconsistency between the claim and the behaviour, and is put in terms similar to depictions of faithless Israel – that the person is a liar (ψεύστης ἐστίν) and that the truth is not in them (καὶ ἐν τούτῳ ἡ ἀλήθεια οὐκ ἔστιν).

In contrast (δ᾽) to this is the person who keeps Jesus' (αὐτοῦ) word.[67] Faithful Israel kept God's commands (Exodus 20:6; Deuteronomy 5:10). This contrasting behaviour has a different result – God's love being perfected. This linking of love and Jesus' word starts to hint at the particular word or command on view, but no direct identification is available yet. The result is that God's love is made complete in those who keep Jesus' word. The last clause of this verse returns to the idea of assurance, noting that the person who obediently walks in Jesus' words can be assured of their knowing Jesus.

The second case study (2:6) again opens with the phrase ὁ λέγων and again the claim is to have a personal relationship with Jesus (ἐν αὐτῷ μένειν). However this time the claim is not in the form of a direct quotation but appears to be an indirect quotation. It builds on the Jewish claim to know God, applying it again to Jesus, an application possible because he is the resurrected incarnate Christ. The verb μένω is used this time to speak of the relationship. Unlike the first case study, the description that follows is not of a lifestyle inconsistent with the claim, but instead a prescription of the behaviour of someone making the claim. The main verb ὀφείλω has its infinitive complement in the last phrase (καὶ αὐτὸς [οὕτως] περιπατεῖν) and so prescribes how the subject, the one making the claim, ought to walk (περιπατεῖν). In between the main verb and its infinitive complement is placed a simile – καθὼς ἐκεῖνος περιεπάτησεν. The antecedent of ἐκεῖνος is Jesus, so the phrase indicates that the lifestyle of the one making the claim should be the same as that of Jesus.

---

[67] The similarity of this description to the claim in 2:4 suggests that his commands (τὰς ἐντολὰς) and word (τὸν λόγον) are synonymous.

The αὐτός in the infinitival phrase is a renominalisation of the subject, required due to the interruption of the sequence of thought with the insertion of the simile. The interruption gives prominence to Jesus' life as the example that should be followed.

The expected pattern is broken with the vocative and content statements of the next two verses (2:7–8). The vocative and content statements focus on the command (2:3–4) or word (2:5). Instead of reference to the command or word as the way someone should live, 2:6 substitutes the model of Jesus' life. This reveals that Jesus' life was consistent with his command/word but does not explicitly reveal the content of the command. The content statements of verses 7–8 start to address this issue.

The command is described in verse 7 as not new (καινός), but old (παλαιός). The reason for this description is given in the subsequent relative clause and following sentence – it is part of the message the audience heard from the beginning (ἣν εἴχετε ἀπ' ἀρχῆς). The phrase ἀπ' ἀρχῆς could have a few referents – the beginning of the world, the beginning of the resurrection era (the last days), the beginning of the readers' faith.[68] The phrase does not seem to refer to the absolute beginning of everything, i.e. creation, because it is describing a command. Rather, it seems to describe their understanding of the Jewish faith – a command that they have heard from the beginning of their experience as Jews. This command was there at the beginning of the resurrection era because the resurrection was the fulfilment of the Jewish faith. Reading it as referring to the start of a new separate religion called Christianity falsely divides the two. So the phrase seems to refer to both the reader's faith and the beginning of the resurrection age, because they are so closely linked.[69] So the command is not some new teaching – rather it existed from of old and was contained in the first proclamation of the message of life. The next sentence supports this understanding of the relative clause. It describes the old command as the message (ὁ λόγος) that the readers heard (ὃν ἠκούσατε). The combination of λόγος and ἀκούω continues the echo of 1:1–3 started with the phrase ἀπ' ἀρχῆς. That is, the old command is part of the message of life that the readers heard and was fulfilled in the resurrection of the incarnate Christ. Given the understanding that the message of life has moral implications (see the exegesis of 1:5), it is understandable that it can be described as a command (ἐντολή) in these verses.

The next verse (2:8) starts with πάλιν, indicating a restatement of the substance of the last verse. However, this new verse affirms that the

---

[68] Kruse 2000: 57.   [69] This fits in with the usage of the phrase in 1:1.

author is writing a new command (ἐντολὴν καινὴν γράφω), seemingly at odds with the last verse. How can the writer be speaking of a command that is both old and new? Again, the subsequent relative clause and sentence fill this gap. The new command is said to be true or genuine in Jesus and in the readers (ὅ ἐστιν ἀληθὲς ἐν αὐτῷ καὶ ἐν ὑμῖν). The reason (ὅτι) is given as the author returns to the language of light and dark. This continues the links of these verses to the message of life (1:1–5). The moral implications of the message (the command) are new in the sense that before the fulfilment of Judaism in the resurrection of the incarnate Christ, there was only darkness, a darkness that the readers lived in and Jesus entered at his incarnation.[70] As a result of Jesus' resurrection, the darkness is passing and the light is starting to shine. This light is seen in the changed moral lives of the readers as they 'live' genuinely as a result of Jesus' resurrection, as a result of the message of life. So the command is an element of Judaism that finds its fulfilment in Jesus' resurrection. A specific identification will have to wait until 2:9–11.

Thus there is no contradiction between verses 7 and 8. The πάλιν links the ideas that the command is both old – in the sense that it is the moral imperative of the message of life that the readers heard from the beginning of the preaching – and new – because in Jesus' resurrection and in their present lives, the moral implications of the message are being lived out, a morality that did not exist before the resurrection of Jesus.

The third claim in 2:9 returns to the theme that started the case studies in 1:6 – to be in the light (ἐν τῷ φωτὶ εἶναι). This claim again finds its origins in the Old Testament but is now applied to Jesus. It is a claim to live out the implications of the resurrected Jesus.[71] Yet hate of one's brother (τὸν ἀδελφὸν αὐτοῦ μισῶν) is the behaviour accompanying the claim. This is again a description used to depict faithless Israel. The result is that the one making the claim is not in the light but rather in the darkness (ἐν τῇ σκοτίᾳ ἐστίν) – that is, in the state of death.[72]

On the other hand, the person who loves his brother (ὁ ἀγαπῶν τὸν ἀδελφὸν αὐτοῦ) is in the light – that is, he is 'living' as a result of the resurrection of Jesus in a new moral sphere that has as a chief component love. This contrast of love and hate of one's brother suggests, in the context of light and darkness, that the command this section refers to is Leviticus 19:17–18, which Jesus fulfils and sets as a way of life for his disciples in John 13:34:[73]

---

[70] This has already been argued for in 1:8–2:2.
[71] See discussion on 1:5.   [72] Baylis 1992: 219–22.
[73] In the synoptics, Jesus calls the love command of Leviticus 19:18 the second command on which all the Law and the Prophets hang (Matthew 22:29–40), of which there

> Do not hate your brother in your heart. Rebuke your neighbour
> frankly so you will not share in his guilt. Do not seek revenge or
> bear a grudge against one of your people, but love your neigh-
> bour as yourself. I am the LORD.   (Leviticus 19:17–18)

> A new command I give you: Love one another. As I have loved
> you, so you must love one another.   (John 13:34)

Jesus' command is *not* new, as it is a restatement of Leviticus 19:18.
However, it *is* new because Jesus has done it, enabling him to set a model
for the disciples to follow (2:6). Unlike the rest of Israel, he was not
faithless but faithful to the commands of God and thus fulfilled the Old
Testament expectation. Jesus was the light of life who came into the
world so that people could walk in the light (John 8:12). A second result
(καί) of loving the brother is that there is nothing in the person (ἐν αὐτῷ)
that will cause them to stumble or sin (σκάνδαλον).

In contrast to 2:10 (δέ), the one hating his brother is in the dark (ἐν τῇ
σκοτίᾳ ἐστίν), walks in the dark (ἐν τῇ σκοτίᾳ περιπατεῖ), and does not
know where he is going. The contrast is not just in the actions of hating
and loving, but also in the results – not stumbling (2:10) as opposed to
walking in darkness and not knowing where he is going. The reason that
the darkness results in aimless wandering is because (ὅτι) the darkness
has blinded his eyes. This metaphor is the opposite of what one might
expect (usually bright light is understood to blind), but it is understandable. Without light, the eyes are blind to the surroundings. In terms of
the moral sphere, without the light of life, death and darkness result in
hate.

This unit (2:3–11) contains three claims about knowing God, claims
that first-century Jews made. However, the claims have a christological
twist to them, assuming that Jesus as the incarnate resurrected Christ
replaces God in the Old Testament echo. Inconsistent behaviour to the
claims and its results are depicted in images used in the Old Testament
for faithless Israel. Behaviour that is consistent with the claims and the
results of such behaviour are described in terms that are used in the Old
Testament for the True Israel. Each claim should result in a life of love
towards one's brother in fulfilment of Leviticus 19:7–8, and Jesus' own
example and command (John 13:34). This is because God is light, and
knowing him through the resurrection of the incarnate Christ has moral

---

is no greater command (Mark 12:31). See also Luke 10:27. In both Romans 13:9 and
Galatians 5:14, Paul argues that the love command of Leviticus 19:18 is a summary of the
Law. James labels the love command the royal law (James 2:8).

consequences. Instead, hate is the moral result of living in the darkness of death.

Summary

The claims of 1:6–2:11 are those that first-century Jews could have made about themselves. The descriptions of the behaviour that is inconsistent with the claims and its results, are similar to depictions of faithless Israel in the Old Testament, while the descriptions of behaviour that is consistent with the claims (and its results) have similarities to the depictions of the True Israel. Under this influence the claimants could be identified as first-century Jews in general – both the earliest Christians who thought of themselves as the True Israel, and ethnic Jews. The subsequent reading has parallels with the outlook of material from Qumran, especially that contained at the start of the Manual of Discipline.

Plausibility tangents

Filling the gaps of the identity of the claimants as Jews and the new/old command as referring to Jesus' fulfilment of the love command in Leviticus 19:18 produces a reading that accounts for the text and is internally consistent. The main tangent to this circular reading that demonstrates its plausibility is found in the writings of the Qumran community. These writings exhibit a similar outlook to that presented in the reading.[74]

The Manual of Discipline (1QS) contains a large number of parallels with 1 John 1:6–2:11. These parallels reveal a consistency of self-understanding between the Qumran community and the reading proposed above. The Manual starts with a discussion of the community's identity (1:1–18a), before outlining instructions for an annual entry into the community (1:19–3:12), and a description of the Two Spirits that motivate people (3:13–4:26).[75] So the Manual starts with a presupposition that all Israel is welcome into the covenant community. Yet, those who join the community are the True Israel who have the covenant (1:7), the sons of light (1:10). Those Jews who do not enter the covenant are likened to faithless Israel (1:22–23). They are children of darkness and walk in darkness (1:10; 3:20). The sons of light walk in the light (3:13, 24, 25). Truth and justice mark the sons of light, while the sons of darkness

---

[74] O'Neill (1966: 10) states that 1:6–10 'contains a well-marked theology, which fits in with what we know of Jewish sectarian teaching'.

[75] Bockmuehl 2001: 387–8.

are associated with lies and deceit (3:17–19) . The sons of light form a community of humility, love, and good intent towards one another (2:25). Confession of the sin of being faithless to the covenant is a requirement of entry into the community (1:23–26). Purification and cleansing of sin is understood in terms of atonement (3:4).

So the Manual contains a similar understanding to the proposed reading. All Israel can enter the community, but some are sons of darkness who are marked by lies and deceit. They are like the faithless Israel of the Old Testament. On the other hand, those who confess their sin and enter the community through the atonement are sons of light, walk in the light, and have lives marked by love and truth.

Conclusion

An introduction to a text establishes a framework or grid for interpreting the text that follows. The first five verses of the introduction (1:1–5) presented an understanding of Jesus as the resurrected incarnate Christ. This christological understanding colours the interpretation of all subsequent discussion of Jesus. It was argued that the claimants could be identified as Jews, whose actions reveal whether or not they belong to True Israel. To further test this proposal, references to actions and identity in the rest of 1 John are interpreted against this identification. The result is that 1 John is interpreted as being written to an audience who know of the resurrection of the incarnate Christ and who claim to be members of the True Israel. The consistency of their actions with their claims demonstrates their membership.

The rest of this thesis provides a reading of 1 John in light of this framework. The next chapter is less detailed in the level of its comment as it presents the results of the reading method instead of outlining the particulars of the reading process. The chapter focuses on the 'gaps' that question this understanding of the introduction, that is those that question either the christology or the proposed historical situation.

5

THE HISTORICAL SITUATION:
1 JOHN 2:15–27

This chapter provides a reading of 1 John 2:15–27 using the method described in chapter 2. The reading is made within the framework of the introduction (1:1–2:11). The two particular aspects of the framework that inform and are tested in this reading are the affirmation of the resurrected incarnate Christ (1:1–3), and the audience's view of themselves as the True Israel.

There are three main parts to this chapter. The first two parts provide readings of 2:15–17 and 2:18–27. The level of detail in each part is less than in the previous two chapters as a consequence of changing the focus from describing the reading method in detail to outlining the resultant reading. The third part of the chapter is a discussion of the tangents to the understanding of 2:18–27. This discussion is lengthier than that found elsewhere in the research because the proposed understanding of the single historical reference in 1 John (2:19) is unique. The thesis continues to test the identification of the 'claimants' with Jews and proposes that the common feature that allows the use of the first-person plural pronoun in 2:19 is a shared heritage in Judaism.

The setting: 1 John 2:15–17

The poem of 2:12–14 is followed by a short asyndetic paragraph (2:15–17) that contains the first imperative in the book (μὴ ἀγαπᾶτε). All occurrences of the noun κόσμος but one occur in 2:15–5:21, and given that this paragraph contains an extended description of the world, it appears that 2:15–17 sets the backdrop for the rest of 1 John. In this way it acts as the topic paragraph for the body of 1 John.

The paragraph contains no interruptions to flow of sentences, cataphoric use of pronouns, or reader-experienced gaps. Neither are the limiting devices of γράφω or vocatives used. The unit boundary at the end of 2:17 is observable because κόσμος ceases to be used in the following verses (not reappearing until 3:1), and 2:18 starts with a vocative (παιδία) combined with an eschatological statement (ἐσχάτη ὥρα ἐστίν) and the use of the adverb νῦν, which together seem to indicate a new section.[1] The sustained use of κόσμος in 2:15–17, six times in three verses, gives the paragraph a unity. Even though there are no gaps in the paragraph, it is still necessary to provide an intertextual reading of these verses because they form the topic paragraph for the body of the book.

An intertextual reading

The audience is commanded not to love the world or the things in the world. The world is described in moral terms – ἡ ἐπιθυμία τῆς σαρκὸς καὶ ἡ ἐπιθυμία τῶν ὀφθαλμῶν καὶ ἡ ἀλαζονεία τοῦ βίου. This description narrows the referent of κόσμος from all of creation to the attitudes found within humans. These desires do not originate with God but the world. Both the world and its desires will pass away in contrast to the eternal life given to the one who does the will of God.

This topic paragraph seems to appeal to the audience's understanding of themselves as the True Israel, confirming this research's understanding of the introduction. The summary description of the person who does not love the world (ὁ δὲ ποιῶν τὸ θέλημα τοῦ θεοῦ – 2:17) occurs in the LXX, where it is used in the Psalms to describe the desire of the faithful Israelite:

> I want to do your will, my God (τοῦ ποιῆσαι τὸ θέλημά σου ὁ θεός), and your law is in the middle of my being. (Psalm 39:9)
>
> Teach me to do your will (τοῦ ποιεῖν τὸ θέλημά σου), because you are my God, your good Spirit will lead me on level land. (Psalm 142:10)[2]

The duality of either loving the world and its desires or doing God's will, calls to mind the Old Testament themes of the two desires, spirits or ways.[3] Malatesta comments on 2:15–17 that: 'O[ld] T[estament] texts provide the origins for all these themes which were subsequently developed in apocalyptic, Qumranic and rabbinic literature, and found their way into early Christian paraenesis and then into the mainstream of Christian Tradition.'[4] Malatesta then notes in particular that the theme

---

[1] Jensen 2008: 199. [2] See also Psalm 102:21.
[3] See Lazure 1969 for an in-depth examination of the moral terms used in 2:16 against the background of the Old Testament, Hellenistic Literature, Philo and Judaism.
[4] Malatesta 1978: 175.

of 'two ways' features in Deuteronomy 30:15–20. This speech of Moses defines what it means to be a faithful Israelite, challenging the people not to follow their hearts if it turns them away from the Lord to worship other gods (30:17), but rather to remain faithful to the Lord (30:20).[5] The consequence of faithlessness is described as death, while the result of faithfulness is life (30:15).[6]

This appeal occurs in the context of the first description in 1 John of the audience's situation. The audience is in the world, which contains desires that do not originate with God and will pass away. This negative sense of world (κόσμος) is prominent in John's Gospel, throughout the Johannine Epistles, and elsewhere in the New Testament (eg: 1 Corinthians 2:12; 7:31; James 1:27; 4:4).[7] Given that the appeal is cast in Old Testament terms, the world's desires are presented as attitudes that lead the people away from being faithful Israelites. This is not without parallel, as the LXX sometimes uses ἐπιθυμία when portraying faithless Israel (Numbers 11:4; Psalm 9:24; 77:29–30; 105:14; 111:10; 139:9; Jeremiah 2:24).[8] The description of the destiny of the world and its desires as passing away (παράγεται) continues the introduction of apocalyptic themes. The themes started in 2:8, with the darkness passing away (παράγεται) due to the changed moral lives of the readers as a result of their hearing of the resurrection of the incarnate Christ, and gained further prominence in 2:13–14 with the affirmation of the audience's victory over the evil one (νενικήκατε τὸν πονηρόν). These themes come to full bloom in 2:18ff with the mention of the last hour (ἐσχάτη ὥρα) and antichrists (ἀντίχριστοι).[9]

Thus the topic paragraph may continue the identification of the audience with True Israel and draw its imperative from the claims of the introduction – do not love the world and so be a member of faithless Israel. The world is the situation the audience finds itself within, a world that contains desires that if followed would cause apostasy. It is within this broad context that the body of 1 John is to be read.

---

[5] See also Deuteronomy 11:26–8.

[6] This is the backdrop for the statements found in 1 John 3:14 and builds on the understanding of 'light' and 'dark' proposed in my reading of 1:5ff.

[7] Cassem (1972: 91) argues that κόσμος is positive in the first half of John's Gospel. However, Salier (1997: 107) notes that even the positive uses of κόσμος in the first half of John's Gospel seem to imply a negative sense since κόσμος is the object of God/the Son's positive action. This observation is also true of the first occurrence of κόσμος in 1 John 2:2. The only 'positive' use of κόσμος in 1 John is in 3:17.

[8] It also uses ἐπιθυμία of faithful Israel (see for instance Psalm 9:38; 20:3). It is the origin of the desires in the world that makes them negative.

[9] Schmid 2002: 96–101; Streett 2011: 142–3.

Tangents

This understanding of the topic paragraph gains plausibility from four lines of evidence. First, the theme of 'two ways', as a way of challenging a Jewish audience to be faithful, is evident at Qumran (1QS 3:13–4:26) and was used by Jesus (Matthew 6:24; Luke 16:13).[10] Second, Jesus outlines dangers that are similar to the world's desires of 2:16 in the parable of the soils (Matthew 13:22; Mark 4:19; Luke 8:14). These dangers lead someone away from being a faithful Jew to unfruitfulness. Third, James describes love of the world as apostasy. So James 4:4 calls its Jewish (Christian) audience adulterous (μοιχαλίδες) when they love the world, because it makes them enemies of God. The language of adultery is drawn from the Old Testament prophets who describe Israel as an adulterous wife (see for instance Hosea 1–3; 9:1).[11] Fourth, the Book of Hebrews uses the phrase τοῦ ποιῆσαι ὁ θεὸς τὸ θέλημά σου, drawn from Psalm 40:8 (39:9 LXX) to describe both the ideal Israelite – Jesus (10:9) – and his followers (10:36).[12] Thus this phrase (τοῦ ποιῆσαι ὁ θεὸς τὸ θέλημά σου) was used in a range of early Christian literature to describe the faithful Israelite, the one who believed that Jesus was the Christ.

The schism: 1 John 2:18–27

These verses outline the first aspect of living in the world – the existence of antichrists (2:18–27). The opening of the unit has three elements that indicate that it is a boundary – a vocative (παιδία) combined with an eschatological statement (ἐσχάτη ὥρα ἐστίν) and the use of the adverb νῦν.

Gaps

There are three places where the flow of the sentences is interrupted, causing a gap (2:20, 24, 27). However, in each case, the gap is easily filled from the immediate context. It appears that the first two verses (2:18–19) sketch the historical situation. The first gap of 2:20 is experienced because the reader expects a contrast between those who have left and the original audience, yet καί is used to link the verses.[13] This results

---

[10] Malatesta 1978: 175–7.   [11] Davids 1982: 160.
[12] See also Mark 3:35 where the audience appears to be Jewish.
[13] Persson 1990: 20–1.

in a minor gap, but an adversative use of καί is not without precedent (cf. Matthew 6:26).[14] The second gap is the movement from verse 23 to verse 24. Here the asyndetic start to 24 and the change in subject matter appear to form a gap. However, ὑμεῖς is redundant, indicating that more is going on in its usage. Given that the last gap occurred in proximity to a use of ὑμεῖς (v20), it appears that this is not a gap but a device used to recall the reader to the main point after a short digression. This understanding is confirmed with the third occurrence of ὑμεῖς in verse 27, where it performs the same function of returning the argument to the readers' possession of the χρῖσμα.[15] There are two results of this use of ὑμεῖς. First, it breaks the unit into three paragraphs. Second, it signals that one theme of the unit is the readers' possession of the χρῖσμα in contrast to the antichrists.

There are three cataphoric uses of pronouns in this unit. The first two occurrences are in 2:22, where τίς is used referring to ὁ ἀρνούμενος ὅτι Ἰησοῦς οὐκ ἔστιν ὁ Χριστός, and οὗτός has as its postcedent ὁ ἀρνούμενος τὸν πατέρα καὶ τὸν υἱόν. Since the postcedents are located so close to the pronouns, no real gap is experienced. However, the closeness of the two cataphoric pronouns to each other results in prominence being given to the description of the antichrists as deniers, indicating its significance in the text. The third cataphoric use of a pronoun is in 2:25, where the postcedent of αὕτη is τὴν ζωὴν τὴν αἰώνιον. Again, this is not a gap of any significance due to the close proximity of the postcedent to the pronoun.

There are two reader-experienced gaps in this unit. First, how should the antichrists be understood – with a historical referent or as a literary device? Answering this question is difficult because these verses contain the first extant use of the term ἀντίχριστος,[16] and there is a scarcity of historical information in the direct context. Yet the first-person plural pronouns in 2:19 seem to indicate that they are more than just a literary creation. Second, the meaning of χρῖσμα is unclear in this unit. Does it refer to the Spirit of God or to the Word of God?[17]

This reading of 2:18–27 will focus on filling the first gap for two reasons. First, the reading suggested so far, that affirms the resurrection

---

[14] BDF §442.1 contra Persson (1990: 21) who argues that καί links 2:20 to 2:18 yet acknowledges that there is still a contrast between verses 19 and 20.

[15] Note the similarity in the starts of 2:20 (καὶ ὑμεῖς χρῖσμα) and 2:27 (καὶ ὑμεῖς τὸ χρῖσμα).

[16] Jenks 1991: 328; Schnackenburg 1992: 135; Peerbolte 1996: 3.

[17] Most scholars opt for the Spirit of God, however de la Potterie (1971: 114–15) and Brown (2003: 240–1) argue for the Word of God. For a summary and critique of Potterie, see Kruse 2000: 109–10.

of the incarnate Christ in the historical situation of an intra-Jewish disagreement over the identity of Jesus, requires careful explanation of these verses since they are the basis of the historical reconstructions and identification of the antichrists throughout the secondary literature. Second, the first gap (2:18–19, 22–23) provides the immediate literary context for filling the second gap (2:20ff). So attention will be given to filling the first gap and the implications for the second gap will be outlined at the relevant place in the reading.

Limiting devices

There are two occurrences of γράφω in these verses. The first, in 2:21, indicates the reason for writing (ὅτι) – to assure the audience that they know the truth and that no lie comes from the truth. The second occurrence of γράφω, in 2:26, reveals the content of the unit. The author is writing about people who are trying to lead the readers astray (περὶ τῶν πλανώντων ὑμᾶς). These two occurrences indicate that the unit is about people who are questioning if the readers have the truth and so leading them astray.

There is only one vocative in the unit (παιδία), occurring at its start and giving prominence to this unit as one aspect of the world described in the topic paragraph (2:15–17). The unit extends until 2:27, since 2:28 starts with the same three elements that occurred in 2:18 (namely a vocative, an eschatological reference, and the adverb νῦν). The new unit beginning at 2:28 describes a different aspect of the world, as the content changes from the antichrists and the readers' possession of χρῖσμα, to the readers' identity as the children of God.

Understanding the antichrists in previous scholarship

Following the two main schools for interpreting 1 John, there are two main ways that the antichrists are understood in the secondary literature.

Identifying the antichrists

The Historical Critical school seeks to identify the antichrists with people or movements within the late first or early second century. The proposed identifications were reviewed in detail in chapter 1 so will not be repeated here.[18] One area of uncertainty that caused differences in the

---

[18] For a recent critical review of the secondary literature on 1 John 2:18–27 see the discussion in Streett 2011: 133–41.

proposals was the nature of the denial recorded in 2:22 – ὅτι Ἰησοῦς οὐκ ἔστιν ὁ Χριστός. This clause is syntactically difficult since it is unclear which noun is the subject of the verb, and which is the complement. That is, does the clause say 'Jesus is not the Christ',[19] or 'the Christ is not Jesus'?[20] Or to put it differently, is the clause answering the question 'who is Jesus' or 'who is the Christ'?

Those who identify the antichrists with a Gentile situation read the clause with Jesus as the subject.[21] It is unlikely that Gentiles would have the category of 'Christ' in their thinking but more conceivable that they would be answering the question about the identity of Jesus. A minority of scholars think the subject is 'the Christ', indicating a more Jewish question.[22] That is, a first-century Jew had in mind the category of 'Christ' and was denying that Jesus fitted this category. This second alternative is usually rejected under the influence of the first-person plural pronouns in 2:19 that unite the author and audience with the antichrists in some way – usually understood to be Christian faith or church membership.[23]

A third option suggests that the syntactical argument does not matter. Since ὁ Χριστός is articular, it is being used as a title.[24] This observation avoids over-reading the syntax in an attempt to identify the audience while still placing the emphasis on the significance of Jesus' identification with the title. This research will follow this third option.

The literary function of the antichrists

The literary school of interpretation pays less attention to identifying the antichrists. Lieu does not want to deny their importance, but understands their significance as engendering 'a debate within the framework of the author's or community's theology'. As a result she prefers to interpret 1 John in light of the theology it contains, without identifying the antichrists.[25]

---

[19] McGaughy 1972: 51–2; Fee 1992: 2205; Wallace 1996: 44–6; Culy 2004: 55.

[20] Goetchius 1976: 148; Carson 1987: 644–6; Akin 2001: 55; Carson 2005.

[21] For example Bultmann 1973: 38–9; Marshall 1978: 157–8. Westcott (1966: 75) notes the similarity of this denial with the confession of the early church, but due to adopting a late date for 1 John favours understanding the denial as revealing a 'Gnostic' opposition.

[22] For example Griffith 2002: 170–3.

[23] Painter (2002: 200) admits the syntax favours taking ὁ Χριστός as the subject but denies it reveals a rejection of the messiahship of Jesus because 2:23 and 4:2 indicate that the issue is the denial that the human Jesus could be divine.

[24] Griffith 2002: 171–3; Streett 2011: 157–9.

[25] Lieu 1991: 16.

In his speech-act analysis of 1 John, Neufeld also resists identifying the antichrists. He argues that the antichrists are 'imagined as real within an apocalyptic speech act circumstance' but 'are not required to be historical'. He continues:

> Even if the antichrists were real figures historicized in the false teachers, the author is probably referring to false teachers who were generally about and not to one, specific group who originated from the Johannine congregation. The general language of this section and the earlier part of 1 John intimate a phenomenon which is present or might be present in many places.[26]

This leads Neufeld to understand the warning of the antichrists as a means by which the author 'invites his readers to consider his worldview, evaluate it, and allow it to transform their perceptions about who Jesus is and the unity of the Father and son'.[27] They are not necessarily a literary fiction, but are being used as an antagonist so that the audience may better appreciate the author's own position. As such it is not necessary to identify the antichrists, but simply to appreciate how the author is using them for his persuasive ends.

Schmid argues that it is nearly impossible to trace the links between the historical situation and the text as it stands.[28] Instead, under the influence of systems theory, Schmid prefers to understand the opponents as creations of the author, representing 'one of several strategies of self-definition and delimitation with the "Johannine system"'.[29] The result is that:

> [T]he main function of the opponents interacting with the reader is to operate as a counter-concept to the community. The opponents are what the reader should never become, but what he or she will become if he or she does not follow the basic commandments and lines of the Johannine system. As a personification of denial and border-crossing they illustrate the way of departure.[30]

Thus the literary school does not seek to historically identify the antichrists, but prefers to understand them in relation to their function within

---

[26] Neufeld 1994: 101.   [27] *Ibid.*: 111.
[28] Schmid 2002: 54–8.   [29] Schmid 2004a: 34.
[30] *Ibid.*: 38–9.

the argument of 1 John.[31] Within this school, only Schmid denies any historical link and possible significance.

Critique

As discussed in chapter 2, the method of this study does not seek to drive a wedge between these two schools but aims to use the strengths of each.

Since 1 John is a text, this reading follows the insight of the literary school that the antichrists function as a warning to the readers. However, this does not rule out that the text functions as a warning because of a real historical situation, the knowledge of which may further elucidate the text.

The literary school seems fair in its criticism of the Historical Critical school's multiple identifications of the antichrists based on a scarcity of evidence. However, that there is a scarcity of historical material resulting in multiple identifications does not invalidate the desire to reconstruct the historical situation.[32] The lack of information should caution against affirming the situation too strongly and making the exegesis dependant on the reconstruction, but it does not invalidate the Historical Critical enterprise.

As noted previously, the historical question is a tangent to the circle. Building as accurate a picture of the antichrists as possible from the text precedes any identification of the antichrists with historical persons. From the text, then, it is clear that the antichrists were once part of the author and audience's group but have left (2:18–19). The only other concrete reference to the antichrists in this part of 1 John is a description of their denial in 2:22. This thesis will follow the observation that the definite article, at a minimum, indicates that ὁ Χριστός should be understood in a titular sense,[33] and so avoids the syntactical debate.[34] This implies

---

[31] Griffith (2002: 174–9) does make an identification of sorts but attempts to avoid basing his exegetical decisions and argumentation on his historical identification.

[32] The more radical scepticism of Schmid was addressed in chapter 1.

[33] Streett 2011: 157–9; Griffith 2002: 171–3.

[34] The debate boils down to those who identify the subject by the use of the article (e.g. Carson 2005: 711–14 following Goetchius 1976 – both of whom argue that this would make McGaughy's work more consistent) and those who suggest word order is the determining feature (e.g. Wallace 1996: 44–6). However, Wallace (1996: 45) assumes that the 1 John texts are clear passages because he understands 1 John to be written to Gentiles on the basis of 5:21. This assumption 'begs the question' and reverses the reading order of 1 John. Further, Griffith 2002 has demonstrated that 5:21 should be understood as a command to Jews. Carson (2005) also discusses a verse with similar syntax (John 5:15 – ὅτι

that the antichrists are denying that Jesus is the Christ, the long-awaited Messiah of Jewish expectation. When these two points are combined, it suggests that the antichrists were people who were once part of the author and audience's group but have now denied that Jesus is the Christ and have left the group.

Intertextual links

This reading suggests that the antichrists should be identified as first-century faithless Jews, as defined by the author. This suggestion is made under the influence of the introduction (1:6–2:11), where the claims were understood as coming from a Jewish background.[35] The faithless Jew would not be able to live up to the claim, while the True Israelite would live consistently with the claim on the basis of the resurrected Jesus. The understanding of the first-person plural in these claims is continued in the interpretation of 2:19, suggesting that the 'us' of 2:19 refers to Israel. Those who have left Israel are those who claim to be Jews but are living faithless lives. The ultimate act of faithlessness is to deny that Jesus is the Christ, to deny that he fulfils the Old Testament prophecies about Israel, resulting in the denier leaving Israel.

Identifying the antichrists as faithless Jews finds support in three places. First, the message of the apostles to the Jews is summarised in Acts as 'Jesus is the Christ'. So in Acts 5:42, the apostles preach 'Jesus is the Christ' (τὸν χριστόν Ἰησοῦν).[36] In Acts 18:5 the Jews oppose Paul because he is preaching that 'Jesus is the Christ' (εἶναι τὸν χριστὸν Ἰησοῦν). Again, in Acts 18:28 Paul's preaching to the Jews is summarised as 'Jesus is the Christ' (εἶναι τὸν χριστὸν Ἰησοῦν). Each of these summaries occurs in the context of preaching to Jews, with the second two resulting in 'Jewish' opposition. Further, they display the same syntactical form as the denial in 1 John 2:22.[37] So the denial of this message would fit a Jewish background.

Ἰησοῦς ἐστιν ὁ ποιήσας αὐτὸν ὑγιῆ) which context requires ὁ ποιήσας αὐτὸν ὑγιῆ to be the subject and Ἰησοῦς the complement since the question that the healed paralytic is answering is not 'who is Jesus' but who 'made you well' (ὁ ποιήσας με ὑγιῆ – 5:11). This example directly contradicts Wallace's word order suggestion.

[35] Curtis (1992: 30–3) proposes that the first-person plural is exclusive like 1:1–4 so the false teachers have left the apostolic community.

[36] The verb εἰμί is understood in this clause.

[37] Griffith (2002: 170–9) uses this material to identify the antichrists as Jewish Christians who have rejected that 'Jesus is the Christ' and thus defected back to Judaism. However, Griffith does not consider the option that the first-person plural in 2:19 is based on Judaism and not Christianity and so unwittingly sees the apostles' preaching in Acts as a new religion (Christianity) and not the fulfilment of Judaism.

Table 8. *Parallels between 1 John 2:19 and Deuteronomy 13:12–13*

1 John 2:19	Deuteronomy 13:12–13
They went out from us (ἐξ ἡμῶν ἐξῆλθαν), but they did not really belong to us. For if they had belonged to us, they would have remained with us; but their going showed that none of them belonged to us.	If you hear it said about one of the towns the LORD your God is giving you to live in that wicked men have arisen (ἐξήλθοσαν) among you (ἐξ ὑμῶν) and have led the people of their town astray, saying, 'Let us go and worship other gods'… (LXX 13:13–14)

Second, the description of the schism in 2:19 sounds similar to Deuteronomy 13:12–13 (see Table 8).[38]

The context of these verses is Moses warning Israel about false prophets who arise within the people of Israel (Deuteronomy 13:1). The false prophets urge Israel to turn to other gods (Deuteronomy 13:2). Two examples of false prophets are then given – those who are personally known to the hearer (brother, son, daughter, wife, close friend – Deuteronomy 13:6) and those who are not personally known (Deuteronomy 13:12). The message of both of these groups is the same – to worship other gods (Deuteronomy 13:6, 13). The similarity in description between these false prophets (Deuteronomy 13:13) and anti-christs (1 John 2:19) is the vocabulary used to describe their separation (ἐξέρχομαι) from the audience (ἐξ ὑμῶν/ἐξ ἡμῶν). Thus those who went out are described in terms used in the Old Testament to describe false prophets. Given the immediate context in 1 John of the 'two ways' topic paragraph (2:15–17), describing the schism in terms of apostasy drawn from Deuteronomy makes good sense.[39]

Third, the vocabulary used to describe the schism also occurs in Acts 15:24 (ἐξ ἡμῶν ἐξελθόντες).[40] The people described in this phrase went

---

[38] Klauck 1988: 55; Klauck 1991: 153–4.

[39] It should be noted that the apostasy in Deuteronomy 30:17 discussed in the context of 1 John 2:15–17 was worshipping other gods, the same as Deuteronomy 13:2, 6, 13. This seems to lay the ground for interpreting the command of 1 John 5:21 to be about following an idolatrous version of 'Judaism' that does not identify Jesus as the Christ.

[40] ἐξελθόντες has a C rating since it may have been inserted under the influence of Galatians 2:12, even though it is well attested in the external evidence (𝔓33,[74] א2 A C and D). Metzger (1994: 385) notes that the equivocal nature of this evidence resulted in ἐξελθόντες being enclosed within square brackets [] in the text. Whether the word was in the original manuscript or was the insertion of a copyist does not matter to the argument here. It either reflects that the phrase was used in the original or that it became a very early way of speaking of schism within Judaism.

out from Judea (15:1), from the Jewish Jerusalem church, and were teaching that Gentile believers had to obey the law, i.e. live as 'Jews'. The phrase describes a split within first century Judaism over what it meant to be a true Jew – whether the Gentiles had to become Jews once they acknowledged the Jewish Messiah, Jesus.

These three lines of evidence support the suggestion that the antichrists could be identified as faithless Jews who were denying that Jesus is the Christ and so leaving the True Israel. The first-person pronouns could refer generally to Judaism and not just a specific community.

An intertextual reading of 2:18–27

A reading of 2:18–27 is required in order to test the suggestion that identifies the antichrists with faithless Jews. The reading will pay particular attention to the limiting device, the use of γράφω in 2:21 and 26.

This part has four sections – 2:18–19, setting the historical context, and then three paragraphs (20–23, 24–26, 27), each of which starts with (καὶ) ὑμεῖς, interrupting the flow of the sentences.

The historical context is described in apocalyptic terms as the last hour (ἐσχάτη ὥρα) in which antichrists have come (2:18).[41] There is a broad consensus that in the word ἀντίχριστος, the preposition ἀντί indicates 'opposition to' rather than 'substitution for', resulting in the meaning being opponents to the Christ.[42] The origin of the term appears to be the Old Testament apocalyptic teaching of an end-time opponent to God and his people.[43] This understanding seems best, given the apocalyptic motifs in this passage and the definition of the antichrists in 2:22 as denying that Jesus is the Christ (see below for fuller exegesis of this point). These antichrists were once part of Israel, along with the author and audience, but have left the authentic Israel, revealing that they were never really part of it (2:19). Given this historical context, the author moves in the next three paragraphs to assure the audience of their difference to the antichrists.

So verse 20 assures the audience that they have the anointing (χρῖσμα) from the Holy One (ἀπὸ τοῦ ἁγίου) and that they know all things (οἴδατε πάντες).[44] Before expanding on what the anointing is, the author uses

---

[41] Neufeld 1994: 103; Strecker 1996: 62.

[42] Grundmann, Hesse, de Jonge, and van der Woude 1974: 571–2; Kauder 1986; Strecker 1988; Peerbolte 1996: 110; Watson 1997. For the contrary view see Callahan 2005: 28.

[43] Jenks 1991: 341–2; Peerbolte 1996: 110–11; Strecker 1996: 236–41.

[44] Black (1992) argues that πάντα should be preferred to πάντες, however πάντες seems to be the harder reading.

the limiting device of a reason for writing statement (ἔγραψα ὑμῖν ὅτι) to discuss the assurance that they know all things (2:21). The audience knows all things – especially 'the truth' and that 'no lie is from the truth'. This last idea gives occasion for the author to return briefly to the antichrists, since they are liars (2:22) . Their denial that 'Jesus is the Christ' is a denial of the Father and the Son (2:22). The Father and Son imagery finds its source in Psalm 2:7, where God adopts the Messiah, calling the Messiah his Son just as God is his Father. The denial of the Son results in the antichrists not having the Father, in contrast to the person who confesses the Son and so has the Father (2:23).[45] The Father and Son in these verses are God the Father and his Son Jesus Christ (1:3; 2:1). That is, in the antichrists' denial that Jesus is the Christ, they are denying both the Father and the Son. They do not have the Father because they deny the Son. In contrast, those who have the Son are the people who have the Father.

These verses make good sense if the antichrists are understood to be faithless Jews and the audience think of themselves as true Jews. The faithless Jews deny 'Jesus is the Christ' with the result that they do not have either the Father or the Son.[46] They can no longer claim to be Jews who have the Father, because in denying the Son they do not have the Father. In contrast, those who confess the Son – that Jesus is the Christ – have both the Son and the Father. They are the True Israelites who have fellowship with the Father and his Son based on the confession of the resurrection of the incarnate Christ. This confession – that 'Jesus is the Christ' – is a thoroughly Jewish confession. Χριστός is a title in this context and not a personal name, because it is articular, in parallel with υἱός, and part of the 'anointed' wordplay (ἀντίχριστος, χρῖσμα and Χριστός) of this section.[47] When this confession is understood within the parameters of the christology of the introduction (1:1–2:11) – the affirmation of the resurrection of the incarnate Christ – a Jewish understanding of the title makes sense. This is because the event that demonstrates that Jesus, as opposed to any other Jewish man, is the Christ, is his physical resurrection (cf: John 20:31; Acts 2:25–36; 13:32–7; Romans 1:4). Further, understanding Χριστός within the Jewish framework is consistent with

[45] 'Have' (ἔχω) in these verses means 'to possess' and describes the believer's relationship with God, see Malatesta 1978: 204–9; Smalley 2007: 110–11.

[46] Goulder (1999: 344) says something close to this although he views the opponents as Jewish Christians with an Ebionite Christology.

[47] Anderson 1990: 43; Griffith 2002: 173–4; Streett 2011: 158–9; contra Smalley 2007: 107–8.

its usage in John's Gospel, where it is specified as the equivalent of the only two occurrences of Μεσσίας in the New Testament (1:41; 4:25).[48] This understanding of 2:22–3 is supported in the exhortation and reasoning contained in the second paragraph.

In the second paragraph, the audience is urged to remain in what they have heard from the beginning (ἀπ' ἀρχῆς) because when they do this they will remain with the Son and the Father (2:24). The message they heard from the beginning, that resulted in their fellowship with the Father and the Son, is the resurrection of the incarnate Christ (1:1–3).[49] Further, this is the promise that they heard – eternal life (τὴν ζωὴν τὴν αἰώνιον in 1:2 and 2:25). The last verse in this paragraph provides an opportunity to check this reading because it contains a γράφω content clause (2:26). It indicates that the last few verses are about those who are trying to deceive (τῶν πλανώντων ὑμᾶς) the audience. Denying that Jesus is the Christ is a lie that the audience, who know the truth, should avoid. They do this by remaining in the message they have heard from the beginning, the message of the resurrection of the incarnate Christ that results in eternal life.

The third paragraph (2:27) returns to discuss the anointing (χρῖσμα) that the audience were told they had received from the Holy One back in 2:20. The anointing will teach them all things so that they have no need of a teacher. Carson has demonstrated the intertextual links between this verse and Jeremiah 31:29–33, where the prophet affirms that under the New Covenant all the people will know God directly and not need a teacher as they did under the Old Covenant.[50] These verses in Jeremiah were alluded to in the claims in 1 John 1:6–2:11, in particular 1:6, 2:4, and 2:6. The gift of the Spirit to each believer is the χρῖσμα referred to in these verses.[51] The reason for using χρῖσμα and not the regular πνεῦμα is to maintain the contrast between the antichrists who deny 'Jesus is the Christ' and the readers who have the Spirit of the Christ. The χρῖσμα was given in the Old Testament to prophets, priests, and kings. The antichrists may claim to be real Jews, but they lack the fulfilment of the Old Testament promise of God giving his Spirit to his people in the last days (Joel 2:28–30), a result of the resurrection of the incarnate Christ (Acts 2).

---

[48] Griffith 2002: 171.
[49] Note the repetition of vocabulary: ἀπ' ἀρχῆς in 1:1 and 2:24; ὃ ἠκούσατε in 1:1, 3 and 2:24.
[50] Carson 2004: 277–80; Carson 2007: 1065–6.
[51] Coetzee 1979: 53–4.

Plausiblity tangents

This section provides a secondary line of evidence that demonstrates the plausibility of the proposed reading. It shows that the earliest Christians thought of themselves as the True Israel from which some Jews had departed when they denied that Jesus was the Christ. This section on tangents is more substantial than elsewhere in the thesis because understanding the historical background in this way is a major contribution of this study.

After answering the objections to identifying the opponents as Jewish and briefly discussing how Christianity and Judaism split, this section provides evidence that first-century Judaism was composed of many groups who claimed to be the authentic version of Judaism, one of which was Christianity. Evidence is provided from Josephus, Qumran, and the Samaritans. Further evidence is provided from the earliest Christian writings (primarily Acts) to indicate that Christians thought that they were the true version of Judaism.[52] Finally, evidence is provided from John's Gospel to support the historical reconstruction.[53]

Objections to identifying the opponents as Jewish

The review of the secondary material in chapter 1 outlined three weaknesses with the identifications of the opponents as Jewish.

---

[52] There is also material from the Roman historians suggesting that Rome understood Christianity to be a group within Judaism. Claudius could not differentiate between Jews and Christians. He expelled the Jews from Rome in AD 49 because they were fighting about someone called Chrestus, i.e. Christ, (Suetonius, *Claudius* 25.4). He expelled them whether or not they were holding Jesus to be the Christ, for example Aquilla and Priscilla (Acts 18:2). It could be argued that by AD 64 Nero was able to differentiate between Jews and Christians because he blamed the fire in Rome on Christians (Tacitus, *Annals* 15.44.2–5). However, Tacitus' account of Christ as executed in Judea from which the movement spread to Rome, implies that even *c*. AD 120 when he wrote, Tacitus understood Christianity to be some species of Judaism. Nero did not differentiate between Christianity and Judaism as religions but rather saw the Christians as a target group among the wider Jewish community. It is not until Pliny and Trajan's discussion in AD 111–12 that evidence exists of some understanding of Christianity as separate to Judaism, being called a 'political society' and a 'cult', and not recognised as part of the accepted religion of Judaism (Pliny, *Letters* 10.96–7). For a contrary interpretation of this material see Judge 1994 and Jossa 2006.

[53] This thesis holds no firm decision on the date and location of 1 John, rather it assumes a mid to late first century date resulting in many different materials from different locations being cited. Thus the tangents indicate a general response to Christianity across the known world, though there would have been some localised differences.

First, the opponents 'went out from' the community (2:19), thus indicating that they were once with John and not just non-Christian Jews.[54] This objection contains the assumption that the author thought of himself primarily as a Christian as distinct from being Jewish. The first-person plural of 2:19 is understood to be the Christian church and thus the opponents could not be non-Christian Jews because they were once part of the Christian church. The assumption reads in differences between the religions of Judaism and Christianity, as evident in later history, ignoring the first-century context where the division was not the same. As will be argued, the earliest Christians understood Jesus to be the fulfiller of Judaism and so they considered themselves to be true Jews. Those of their countrymen who rejected Jesus as the Christ were no longer Jews, but had left true Judaism to follow some false version of Judaism. They were like the northern kingdom of Israel who rejected God's king Rehoboam and, even though descended from Abraham, were apostate and no longer part of God's kingdom.

Second, the absence of Old Testament quotes in 1 John was seen as contravening the expected style of argumentation if addressing Jews.[55] This objection is an argument from silence and in light of the recent intertextual discussion outlined in chapter 2, this objection no longer holds.

Finally Lieu's objection, that Christ is spoken of in the context of Jesus being the Son of the Father,[56] is not a weakness if the Father and Son language is understood in the context of Psalm 2:7, where the Father God adopts the Messiah as his Son. This understanding builds on the observation of Hengel and Kruse that in 1 John, the titles 'Christ' and 'Son of God' are both messianic and almost interchangeable.[57] That the discussion of 'the Christ' occurs in the context of Jesus being the Son of the Father seems to support the understanding proposed here rather than weaken it.

The Parting of the Ways

This reconstruction locates 1 John against the historical backdrop of the 'Parting of the Ways'. There are four ways in which the schism between

[54] Marshall 1978: 17; Brown 1982: 52; Schnackenburg 1992: 18; Lieu 2008a: 105.
[55] Brown 1982: 52.
[56] Lieu 2008a: 106. See also Morgen (2005a: 106–7) who argues that the concept of 'Son' is the larger christological concept in 1 John and determines the meaning of 'Christ'.
[57] Hengel 1989: 59; Schnackenburg 1992: 146; Kruse 2000: 174.

Christianity and Judaism is understood. First, some scholars argue that Christianity and Judaism were clearly differentiated from the time of Paul, if not earlier.[58] However, exponents of this view often do not explore how the early Christians understood their relationship to Judaism.[59] Second, older scholarship holds Judaism as a constant from which Christianity emerged. This model fails to recognise the different voices in Judaism in the first century, and reads later Rabbinic Judaism into the first century. A third understanding is that the Judaism of the first century had many forms (Pharisee, Sadducee, Essene …) including Christianity. These different forms grew out of the Second Temple period but eventually gave way to Rabbinic Judaism after Yavneh.[60] Some time between AD 70 and 135 Christianity parted ways with the emerging Rabbinic Judaism. This view can be misleading, because Judaism was not split into these groups but these groups existed as minorities within a common Judaism.[61] Each group adhered to the elements of a common Judaism, but claimed their version was the authentic form of Judaism. Fourth, Bauckham suggests that Christianity started as a group within common Judaism but became marginalised or separate to Judaism, just like the Qumran community or the Samaritans.[62] This did not stop Christianity thinking of itself as true Judaism, just like Qumran and the Samaritans thought of themselves as true Jews. However, over time common Judaism, that later became Rabbinic Judaism, started to define Christianity as separate from 'Judaism'. This last view seems to describe the first-century setting most naturally.

Many groups claiming 'authenticity' within Judaism

Josephus reveals that Judaism in the first century was made up of many groups who each thought that they were the authentic version of Judaism. On four occasions Josephus writes of groups (αἵρεσις) that constitute Judaism: Pharisees, Essenes, and Sadducees (*War.* 2.8; *Ant.* 13.5.9; 18:1; *Life* 2). On two of these occasions a fourth group is included on the list,

---

[58] Judge 1994; Jossa 2006.

[59] Even where Jossa 2006 does investigate Christian self-understanding, he does not seem to fully appreciate the Jewishness of the categories used in speaking of Jesus' exaltation and quickly separates the Gentiles from the Jews in Paul's mission.

[60] Dunn 1991; Dunn 1992.

[61] Bauckham 1993: 137. Deines (2001) argues that the Pharisees were the voice of common Judaism, thus defining the limits of Judaism. But this does not mean that the common people were consistently Pharisaic in belief and practice.

[62] Bauckham 1993.

the followers of Judas the Galilean (*War.* 2.8; *Ant.* 18:1).[63] These groups co-existed inside a broad understanding of Judaism defined mainly by birth.[64] Their beliefs and practices were different, yet each claimed to be the authentic version of Judaism.[65] The Essenes did not offer sacrifices in the temple because they offered themselves (*Ant.* 18.1.5) – they were their own priests. They claimed to have received their prayers from their forefathers (*War.* 2.8.5), thus making them authentic. Members of the other groups were not allowed to eat lunch or dinner with the Essenes in their houses (*War.* 2.8.5), thus revealing the Essenes' view of their own purity and the impurity of the other groups. The Pharisees claimed authenticity with regard to interpreting the law. Their practices were delivered by succession from the fathers or derived from the tradition of the forefathers (*Ant.* 13.10.6; 13.16.2), revealing that their belief and practice can be linked to the (fore)fathers. They interpreted the laws more accurately than the other groups (*Ant.* 17.2.4; *War.* 1.5.2; *Life* 38). The Sadducees' disputes with the other groups (*Ant.* 18.1.4) displayed their view that the other groups were not authentic. The Sadducees (contra the Pharisees) thought that there was no obligatory place for observances that were not written in the Law of Moses (*Ant.* 13.10.6; 18.1.4). This suggests a claim to authenticity, as their practice was based on the Law of Moses only and not on other things. However, the Sadducees did not deny the Jewishness of the Pharisees because when the Sadducees had to act as magistrates they followed the ideas of the Pharisees for the sake of the multitude (*Ant.* 18.1.4). So even though they claimed authenticity, they refrained from considering the other groups as non-Jewish.

The Qumran documents reveal that this community made the negative claim that the other groups were not authentic.[66] Like the understanding of the groups obtained from Josephus, the Qumran community understood itself to be the authentic version of Judaism (1QS 2:22; CD 12:22), the

[63] However Josephus describes Judas as a Gaulonite in *Ant.* 18.1.1, which is different from his other references to Judas as Galilean, cf: *Ant.* 18.6; 20.5.2; *War* 2.8.1; 2.17.8.

[64] Vermes (1997: 73) states: 'The ordinary Jew envisaged entry into the congregation of the chosen primarily through birth, and secondly through the symbolic initiation of an eight-day-old male infant submitted to circumcision.'

[65] Since Josephus lists the fourth group as agreeing with the Pharisees in everything, except the extent to which they are willing to carry it out (*Ant.* 18.1.6), only the beliefs and practices of the three main groups are described.

[66] Primary documents from the other groups are not as plentiful. Yet, even without being able to identify which text belongs to which group, Deines (2001: 477–91) demonstrates that Jewish texts with a Palestinian provenance written after the immediate context of the Maccabean revolt but before AD 70 are 'characterised by vehement internal Jewish conflicts' (2001: 490).

True Israel (1QS 5:5, 22), with the only true interpretation of the Law (4Q266 fr. 11; 4Q270 fr, 7 ii). Although some early texts indicate salvation was for ethnic Israel (CD 1:1–4; 1QM 10:9–10; 12:13–14; 17:8), other texts restrict salvation to the Qumran community (1QH 12:7–20; 13:17–39; 15:34), acknowledging that some members of ethnic Israel would not be saved due to their failure to repent from wickedness and sin (1QS 3:13 – 4:1; CD 20:17–34).[67] In order to be part of the True Israel and be saved, Jews had to join the Qumran community (CD 4:2; 4Q266 fr. 5 i). This restriction reveals that the Qumran community viewed the other groups as false.[68] Vermes argues that this is evident in the *Commentary on Nahum* where 'Ephraim' and 'seekers of smooth things' symbolise the Pharisees, and 'Manasseh' refers to the Sadducees: '[T]he sect saw its defectors as "Ephraim" and "Manasseh", these being the names of the sons of Joseph, associated in biblical history with the apostate Northern kingdom, and referred to itself as the "House of Judah", the faithful South.'[69] Bockmuehl summarises the Qumran community's understanding of themselves and their relationship to the rest of Judaism in this way:

> Qumran's restrictive definition of the covenant is in many ways typical of a sectarian mindset: despite their sometimes idiosyncratic and innovative beliefs and practises, embattled religious minorities not infrequently take the view that they themselves are the only surviving group that is faithful to the letter and the spirit of the original religious reality, and that they are the loyal standard bearers in a sea of apostates and renegades … As for every sectarian grouping (including early Christianity), the new movement's relationship with the majority is fractious and ambivalent, holding together a belief in the judgment of all apostasy with an expectation of the comprehensive eschatological realisation of the promises for the greater whole – however that may turn out to be defined.[70]

So not only did the Qumran community understand themselves to be the authentic version of Judaism, they viewed the other groups as false but still part of Israel.

[67] Vermes (1997: 74) states: 'They, the elect, were guided by the spirit of truth in the ways of light, while the unprivileged, Jew and Gentile alike, were doomed to wander the paths of darkness.'

[68] Bockmuehl (2001: 389–90) notes that the nature of the relationship between the Qumran community and Israel is not one of replacement, contra Seifrid (1992: 87–8), but representation in accord with the Old Testament remnant motif (CD 1:4; 2:12–14; 1QM 13:7–9; 14:8–9).

[69] Vermes 1997: 62.   [70] Bockmuehl 2001: 393.

Bauckham suggests that the Samaritans form a heuristic model for understanding the parting of Christianity from Judaism.[71] First, the Samaritans thought of themselves as Jewish, just like some Christians thought of themselves as Jewish. The Samaritans shared a number of points in common with Judaism. They 'claimed descent from the patriarch Joseph, worshipped the God of Israel as the one and only God, kept the law of Moses rigorously, practised circumcision as a sign of the covenant, [and] understood themselves to be the faithful part of the elect people of God'.[72] They even called themselves Israelites.[73] These parallels are so strong that some scholars even argue that Samaritanism should be regarded as a form of Judaism.[74]

Second, the Jews did not view the Samaritans as truly Jewish, just as the Jews did not view Christianity as truly Jewish. For instance, Sirach 50:25–6 states:

> Two nations my soul detests, and the third is not even a people:
> Those who live in Seir (Σαμαρείας), and the Philistines, and the
> foolish people that live in Shechem.[75]

Josephus on three occasions (*Ant.* 11.4.9; 11.8.6; 12.5.5) explains that the Samaritans are not really Jews, because even though they claim to be Jews, it is only when it is opportune and at the first sign of trouble they disassociate themselves from Israel. The narrator in John's Gospel also reveals the antagonism between the Jews and the Samaritans, indicating that the Jews do not think that the Samaritans are truly Jewish. In 4:9 he explains in an aside that Jews and Samaritans do not associate, and in 4:22, Jesus explains that the Samaritans worship in contrast to the Jews, and ultimately salvation is from the Jews.

Even though Bauckham suggests this as a model for describing the Parting of the Ways, it also demonstrates that Jews in the first century rejected the claims of other Jewish groups to be Jews. Common Judaism rejected the Samaritans as Jews even though the Samaritans claimed they were Jews. Rabbinic Judaism rejected the Christians as Jews even though they claimed they were Jews. So it is not without precedent that in the reconstruction of the situation behind 1 John, the author would view other groups who were once connected to Judaism as no longer

---

[71] Bauckham 1993.   [72] Bauckham 1993: 139.

[73] Josephus reports this in *Ant.* 9.14.3; 11.8.6; 12.5.5 and Bauckham (1993: 149) notes an inscription in Schurer, Vermes, Millar and Goodman (1986: 3.1.71) where the Samaritan community on Delos call themselves Israelites.

[74] For example Pervis 1986: 90–2.

[75] NRSV with LXX inserted.

truly Jewish. The author would only be doing what common Judaism did to the Samaritans and later Rabbinic Judaism would do to Christianity. Porton summarises the situation:

> [I]f Judaism around the turn of the era was based on interpreting God's revelation to Moses, it stands to reason that each group would have its own set of interpretations which it favored, while rejecting those of the other groups ... it is unlikely that any group in the 1st century would have claimed that they were not in fact offering the 'literal,' or correct, interpretation of the Mosaic revelation. Each group would claim that it alone was faithful to the Law and that it taught only things contained in the Law.[76]

So Josephus and the documents at Qumran reveal that Judaism in the first century was made up of many groups who each thought that they were the authentic version of Judaism. Yet the Qumran community's insistence that they were the remnant through whom the rest of Israel would be saved, and the denial of Jewishness to the Samaritans by the rest of Judaism, reveals that there was a view that some Jewish movements were false. This shows that for the author of 1 John to understand himself and his group as being the true Judaism from which people had left is consistent with knowledge of other Jewish groups within the first century.

Christianity is the 'genuine' Judaism

Earliest Christianity understood itself in the same way as the other first-century Jewish groups. It was a group within Judaism that was the authentic version because it identified Jesus as the Christ, who fulfilled Old Testament expectations. Since its defining element was the confession that Jesus was the Christ, this authentic version of Judaism was brought into conflict with the rest of Judaism over Jesus' identity. Thus Christianity understood that not all Jews were really members of Israel. In particular, when people denied that Jesus was the Christ, they had left the True Israel.

Christianity: a group within Judaism

Christianity is presented in Acts as one of the groups within Judaism. Acts uses the same Greek word as Josephus (αἵρεσις) in describing the

---

[76] Porton 1992: 893. Vermes (1997: 69) agrees with Porton: 'All the Jews of the inter-Testamental era, the Essenes as well as their rivals, agreed that true piety entails obedience to the Law.'

groups within Judaism. In 5:17 the High Priest and his associates are described as being of the group of the Sadducees (ἡ οὖσα αἵρεσις τῶν Σαδδουκαίων). At the Council of Jerusalem in 15:5 some of the believers in the earliest church are described as being from the group of the Pharisees (τινες τῶν ἀπὸ τῆς αἱρέσεως τῶν Φαρισαίων πεπιστευκότες).[77] At Paul's trial before Felix in 24:5, Tertullus, the prosecution lawyer representing the High Priest and some of the Elders, describes Paul as a ringleader of the group of the Nazarenes (πρωτοστάτην τε τῆς τῶν Ναζωραίων αἱρέσεως). Paul in his defence, 24:14, admits that he is a member of 'the way' – labelled by the prosecution as a group (κατὰ τὴν ὁδὸν ἣν λέγουσιν αἵρεσιν) – but then describes this group in Jewish terms as worshipping the Father God and believing everything written in the Law and Prophets (οὕτως λατρεύω τῷ πατρῴῳ θεῷ πιστεύων πᾶσι τοῖς κατὰ τὸν νόμον καὶ τοῖς ἐν τοῖς προφήταις γεγραμμένοις). In Paul's defence speech before King Agrippa in 26:5, Paul describes his former way of life as a member of the group of the Pharisees, a group he describes as the strictest within Judaism (κατὰ τὴν ἀκριβεστάτην αἵρεσιν τῆς ἡμετέρας θρησκείας ἔζησα Φαρισαῖος).[78] Finally, in 28:22, the Jews in Rome label Christianity a group (περὶ μὲν γὰρ τῆς αἱρέσεως ταύτης). So, the word αἵρεσις is used to describe the Sadducees and the Pharisees as groups within Judaism just as in Josephus. However, αἵρεσις is also used to describe Christianity. Paul's use in 24:14 indicates that he understood it as a group within Judaism. That the Jews in Rome also used it suggests that they understood Christianity as claiming to be a group within Judaism.[79]

Christianity: the authentic Judaism

However, earliest Christianity did not see itself as just a group within Judaism, but as the authentic version of Judaism, due to Jesus' fulfilment of Old Testament expectations.

The speeches of the apostles recorded in Acts present Christianity as the authentic version of Judaism, restoring Israel, because Jesus' resurrection was the fulfilment of Old Testament expectations. With Jesus' resurrection the apostles expect the kingdom to come again to Israel (Acts

---

[77] The preposition ἀπό indicates that these believers originated in the group of the Pharisees.

[78] The use of νῦν in 26:6 indicates a contrast between this previous lifestyle and the present.

[79] The context of Paul's defence of Christianity as Jewish directly before the Roman Jews' response (28:17–20) seems to confirm this understanding.

1:6). Peter's model sermon in Acts 2 explains the phenomenon of the gift of tongues as fulfilment of Joel 2:28–32, signalling the start of the last days in which God would give his people his Spirit and restore them as a nation. The event that started these last days was the exaltation of Jesus (2:33–5) in fulfilment of Old Testament expectation (Psalm 110:1), evident in his resurrection (2:24–31), again fulfilling Old Testament expectation (Psalm 16:8–11), as witnessed by the apostles (2:32).[80]

Paul's first recorded speech in Acts 13 also reveals these same themes. Jesus' resurrection fulfils God's promises to Israel as recorded in the Old Testament (13:32–5, quoting Isaiah 55:3 and Psalm 16:10). The result is forgiveness of sins for Israel (13:38), a justification that was not available through the Law of Moses (13:39). So Paul pleads with his audience not to reject the message and so fall under the judgement of God like the Israel of old (13:40–1 quoting Habakkuk 1:5).

At the Council of Jerusalem (Acts 15), the issue of the Gentiles joining Israel comes to the fore. This chapter seems to corroborate the understanding of Acts given so far and also the historical situation proposed for the background of 1 John. Some believing Pharisees were arguing that the Gentiles had to be circumcised and obey the Law of Moses (15:5). This reveals that they did not think of Christianity as a separate religion, but rather the fulfilment of Judaism, because they were requiring any Gentile who believed to become Jewish. The situation of the relationship between the believing Gentiles and the Jews is then understood in light of the Old Testament (15:15–18). James argued from Amos 9:11–12 that God had taken some people from the Gentiles since he had restored Israel. These Gentiles came to Israel but were not required to become Jewish. Instead, they were required to keep some laws that would maintain their ability to have fellowship with Jews (15:20).

John's Gospel also supports the idea that earliest Christianity saw itself as the authentic version of Judaism due to Jesus' fulfilment of Old Testament expectations. This is explicitly evident in the formulae used to introduce quotations of the Old Testament in John. Craig Evans identified and analysed the quotation formulae used by John in introducing Old Testament quotations.[81] He noted that the quotation formulae demonstrated the idea of fulfilment.[82] The quotations in the first half of the Gospel are designed to prove that Jesus is the Messiah – that his public

---

[80] Peterson (2009: 271) in commenting on Stephen's use of scripture states: 'Stephen spoke from the perspective of a personal commitment to Jesus as Lord and Christ and that he has a belief that the messianic community is the true Israel.'

[81] Evans 1982; Evans 1987.   [82] Evans 1987: 225–6.

ministry has certain correspondences to Old Testament passages. The quotations in the second half of the Gospel are made to demonstrate that the glorification of Jesus fulfils scripture.[83]

Judaism: in conflict over Jesus' identity

The earliest church thought of itself as authentic Judaism and faced opposition from within traditional Judaism over the identification of Jesus as the Christ.

Acts presents this conflict as occuring all over the known world. The Jewish hierarchy persecuted the earliest church.[84] From the start, the apostles were commanded by the rulers and elders of the people not to teach about Jesus (4:17–18; 5:28, 40). Stephen was tried by the Sanhedrin and stoned to death for claims about Jesus and the temple (6:12–7:60). Saul threatened to kill Jesus' followers (9:1), seeking and obtaining permission from the high priest to find and arrest these people for extradition to Jerusalem for punishment (9:2; 22:4–5; 26:9–11).[85] The Jews in Damascus plotted to kill Saul because he proclaimed '[Jesus] is the Christ' – οὗτός ἐστιν ὁ χριστός (9:22–23). The Jews of Thessalonica who did not believe Paul's message that 'this Jesus is the Christ' – οὗτός ἐστιν ὁ χριστὸς [ὁ] Ἰησοῦς (17:3) – started a riot in Thessalonica (17:5) and then also followed Paul to Berea, where they again stirred up the crowd (17:13). Some of the Jews in Corinth opposed Paul and became abusive after hearing his message that Jesus was the Christ – εἶναι τὸν χριστὸν Ἰησοῦν (18:5–6).[86] These Jews brought Paul to court under the charge of leading people to worship God in ways contrary to the law (18:12–13). Gallio, who was the proconsul hearing the proceedings, noted this to be an internal Jewish disagreement (18:15).[87] Some Jews plotted against Paul's life again in 20:3. When Paul reached Jerusalem, again some of the Jews from Asia stirred up the crowd, causing a riot, with the result that Paul was arrested (21:27–32). Some Jews hatched another plot against Paul's life in 23:12, resulting in Paul's transfer from Jerusalem to Caesarea. The centurion's letter to Governor Felix revealed

---

[83] Evans 1982: 82–3.   [84] See further Reicke 1984.

[85] 1 Corinthians 15:9; Galatians 1:13, 22–3; Philippians 3:6. See further Hultgren 1976; Hengel 1991; Legrasse 1995.

[86] It should be noted that each of these confessions that result in Jewish persecution has the same grammatical form as the confession in 1 John 2:22.

[87] Although not explicitly linked to the identification of Jesus as the Christ, the same sort of persecution of Paul by the 'Jews' is evident at Pisidian Antioch (13:45, 50–1), Iconium (14:2–5), and Lystra (14:19).

that the issue causing the disagreement between Paul and the Jews was intra-Jewish, a matter of their law (23:29). Felix's successor Festus also expressed the opinion that the point of difference was something internal to Judaism and about Jesus (25:19).[88]

John's Gospel also reveals that there was conflict within first-century Judaism over the identity of Jesus. In particular, 'the Jews' decided that the confession 'Jesus was the Christ' (τις αὐτὸν ὁμολογήσῃ χριστόν) would result in synagogue expulsion (9:22; 12:42; 16:2).

This 'Jewish' persecution of Christianity supports the proposed reconstruction of the situation behind 1 John because it records disagreement inside Judaism about whether Jesus was the Christ. This disagreement was not geographically isolated to Jerusalem, but seems to have been the response of 'Jews' across the known world. There may have been localised expressions of the disagreement, but the disagreement itself was not localised.

Not all Judaism is authentic

There are a number of scattered references in the New Testament documents to people who claim to be Jews but are not really Jews.

Jesus denounces the Pharisees and teachers of the law in Matthew 15:1–20 and Mark 7:1–22 as people who follow the traditions of the elders but not God. They nullify God's word through Moses and follow their own traditions (Matthew 15:6; Mark 7:13). This is in fulfilment of Isaiah 29:13, where the existence of faithless people within Israel is described. Matthew 15:13 then makes it stronger, as Jesus suggests that they were not planted by God and would be pulled up from his garden of Israel.

Romans argues that not all who are descended from Abraham and call themselves Jews are really Jews. In Romans 9:6, Paul states that not all

---

[88] One piece of evidence outside of Acts for this persecution of the earliest church by the Jews is found in 1 Thessalonians 2:14. Paul speaks in passing of the persecution of the Judean churches at the hand of the Jews. Bruce (1982: 45–6) rejects the idea that this persecution was either that associated with Saul or Herod, instead favouring the persecution of the Jews by the new procurator Ventidius Cumanus in AD 48 as a result of increased Zealot activity. However, this is not persecution of the church by the Jews, but persecution of Jews by Romans. Reicke (1984: 150–1) argues that a second and different period of persecution began under Nero *c.* 54–66. This persecution was at the hands of Zealous Jews who, in the desire to keep Judaism from becoming Hellenised at the hands of Nero, sought out Jews in Jerusalem and Judea and enforced Jewish customs. Reicke argues that this lies behind most of Paul's conflicts with Judaisers reflected in Galatians and Philippians, and the issues recorded in Acts 21.

Israel is Israel. Some reject the message in fulfilment of Old Testament expectation, demonstrating that they are not part of the remnant of Israel (Romans 11:2–5 quoting 1 Kings 19:18). This view also finds expression in Romans 2, especially 2:28–9, where it is not the outward (i.e. circumcision) that makes someone Jewish but the inward. These verses are not contrasting Jew and Christian, but unbelieving Jew (i.e. not really a Jew) and believing Jew.

Further, the only two occurrences of Ἰουδαῖος in Revelation both reveal people who claim the heritage but are not really Jews. In both Smyrna and Philadelphia there were people claiming to be Jews who John says were not Jews (2:9; 3:9). Both situations describe these people as belonging to the Synagogue of Satan. This is also similar to the idea in John 8:44, where 'the Jews' are called the children of the Devil. Bauckham comments: 'Such polemic suggests at least incipient schism of the Jewish/Samaritan kind, rather than mere diversity, and it suggests two groups, like Jews and Samaritans, both understanding their self-identity as Jewish, while denying Jewish identity to the other.'[89] Thus, there were people in the first century claiming to be Jews who John says were not really Jews.

Denying Jesus' identity is Jewish apostasy

For the authentic Judaism (that is, Christianity), the event that revealed if someone was an authentic Jew or was apostate, was the denial that Jesus was the Christ.

As just noted, in Romans 9–11 it is the rejection of the gospel message that Jesus is Lord as demonstrated in his resurrection (10:9–10) that leads to some of Israel not being True Israel.

The view that those Jews who reject that Jesus is the Christ are leaving true Judaism is also evident in Hebrews. The 'falling away' passages (especially 6:4–8; 10:26–31 and 12:15–17) are often understood to be speaking about (Jewish) Christians rejecting the Christian message in favour of becoming Jewish. Hence the strong language in Hebrews that the system described in the Old Testament was only a shadow (8:5; 10:1). However, this overlooks the equally strong emphasis in Hebrews that Jesus is the fulfiller of the Old Testament. If this level of continuity is appreciated, and Christianity is not seen as a separate religion from Judaism but the true Judaism, then another understanding of the falling away passages emerges. The passages are speaking about falling away

---

[89] Bauckham 1993: 141.

from true Judaism (belief in Jesus) to some false shadowy version of it.[90] To defend this reading in its entirety would move beyond the scope of this study, so it must suffice to respond to the main perceived objection that the gifts described in 6:4–5 are those of the Christian existence. It is true that the gifts of 6:4–5 can describe elements of the Christian existence. However, they also depict experiences under the Old Covenant, especially those associated with becoming Israel during the Exodus.[91] The reason they are part of the Christian experience is due to Christianity being the fulfilment of Judaism, or the true Judaism. The salvation experience of Christians is based typologically on the Exodus. Thus rejecting Jesus as the Christ, hardening the heart and not listening to God's word (Hebrews 3–4), results in someone leaving true Judaism for some false aberration.

Judaism and 'the Jews' in John

The historical reconstruction proposed in this chapter may not appear to be evident in John's Gospel. In John's Gospel, the title 'the Jews' seems to suggest a clear distinction between Jesus and the Judaism of his day, rather than a conflict within Judaism. Further, it seems inconsistent for the author of 1 John to view himself as Jewish and those who have left as leaving Judaism, when 'the Jews' are presented as opponents in John's Gospel. Yet these initial observations, rather than denying the reconstruction, prompt questions whose answers support the historical proposal being argued here. Before demonstrating this, a few observations about the historical situation of John are required.

Dunn presents a case for understanding John as revealing an intra-Jewish conflict over Jesus' messiahship. He cites the factionalism of first-century Judaism as the historical context of John:[92]

> Jesus and the earliest Christian congregations were in effect part of that ongoing debate as to what it meant to be a Jew, what was involved in being Israel. Within the spectrum which was

---

[90] Weeks 1976.

[91] See *Ibid.*: 78. Israel is described as enlightened, something achieved for them by God when he sent the pillar of fire to guide the people by night (Psalm 43:4; 44:3; 78:14; 105:39). Israel tasted the heavenly gift, the manna from heaven (Psalm 78:24; 105:40). Israel's elders shared the Holy Spirit in leading the people in judgement (Numbers 11:17ff). And Israel tasted the goodness of the word of God as he fulfilled his promises to rescue them and gave them the law (Psalm 119, especially verse 103), as well as experiencing the powers of the coming age in the parting of the Red Sea and destruction of Egypt.

[92] Dunn 2001: 49–53.

Second Temple Judaism, the Christian belief in Messiah Jesus, initially at least, was not much more than another element in the range of options which individual Jews might follow in practising (their) 'Judaism'.[93]

He further notes that the polemical tone of argumentation used in John should not be understood against the background of disagreement between Christians and Jews, but rather in the context of first-century disagreement and debate.[94] It is anachronistic to read back into John the forms of Christianity and Judaism that are current today:[95]

John's language is more the language of intra-Jewish polemic than of anti-Jewish polemic. He seeks by it to warn fellow Jews not to follow what was emerging as the dominant view of 'the Jews' ... This is indeed 'anti-Jewishness' of a sort. But it is not 'anti-Judaism' as we understand it today. It does not presuppose two monoliths, Judaism and Christianity, clearly distinct and clearly separate in identity, denouncing one another in anathemas and open hostility.[96]

Given this view, how then are 'the Jews' to be understood? Previous research contains many identifications for 'the Jews' in John. They are Judeans, the representatives of unbelief, an indefinite description, the Jewish authorities, ambivalent or divided figures, and the religious of Judea – to cite just a few alternatives.[97] However, none of these identifications appears to be able to account for every use of Ἰουδαῖος in John. So there are two possibilities – that Ἰουδαῖος is used with different senses throughout John (the reader decides in context), or that Ἰουδαῖος should be understood in its most general meaning. The second option seems disagreeable to scholarship due to a perceived resultant anti-Judaism in John.[98] It could also fall into the trap of assuming that every word has only one meaning, or of illegitimately transferring every sense of the word into every occurrence. Therefore, it seems better to opt for the first

---

[93] *Ibid.*: 51.

[94] See also von Wahlde 2001. For discussion of perceived anti-Semitism in the context of polemic language see Johnson 1989; Evans 2001.

[95] Dunn 2001: 57–60.   [96] *Ibid.*: 59.

[97] For a brief description and review of each position see Motyer 1997: 46–57. To this list can also be added the view that 'the Jews' are Christians who are not of the Johannine community; see de Jonge 2001.

[98] Bieringer, Pollefeyt, and Vandecasteele-Vanneuville (2001: 18–23) point out that limiting the meaning of Ἰουδαῖος can reflect the desire to lessen the perceived anti-Judaism of John.

option and require the reader to decide the sense in each usage. This allows for positive uses of Ἰουδαῖος, as in 4:22, where Jesus states that salvation is from the Jews, neutral uses, as in 11:45–46, where it seems to refer to the crowd – both those believing and rejecting Jesus – and negative uses, as in 9:22, where it refers to those who put out of the synagogue (ἀποσυνάγωγος) anyone who believes Jesus is the Christ. Understanding Ἰουδαῖος in this manner recognises the strengths of identifications listed above but avoids their inability to explain every occurrence. However, the existence of the negative sense could still call into question the historical reconstruction proposed above. So how are the negative uses to be understood?

De Boer asks a similar question about the negative uses of Ἰουδαῖος in John. He is motivated by the charge that John is anti-Jewish, as evident in the negative uses of Ἰουδαῖος. However, he notes that this negative evaluation does not sit comfortably with all the evidence in John. For instance, Jesus is presented as Jewish (4:9), observing the Jewish feasts by travelling to Jerusalem to participate in the official celebrations (2:13; 5:1; 7:10; 10:22; 12:12). The titles ascribed to Jesus originate in Jewish tradition ('Christ', 'Son of God', 'Son of Man'). There is dependence on the Old Testament, both explicitly, in quotes, and implicitly, in allusions/language in John. Jesus is even presented twice as the King of Israel (1:49; 12:13–15).[99] So de Boer narrows the issue of the negative uses of Ἰουδαῖος down to the question: '[W]hy does John refer to those who are hostile to Jesus and his disciples as "the Jews", with the potentially misleading implication that Jesus himself and his (initial) disciples as well as the Gospel's writer(s) and original, intended readers were not themselves Jews?'[100]

His answer is that John's negative use of Ἰουδαῖος is part of his irony, even sarcasm.[101] The self-description of 'the Jews' in 9:28 is that they are disciples of Moses, in contrast to the man born blind who is a disciple of Jesus. This fits with both contemporary evidence (b. Yoma 4a) and Jesus' understanding of them as searching the scriptures for knowledge of the Messiah (5:39–47) and claiming to be children of Abraham (8:31–58). Yet 'the Jews' understand discipleship to Jesus and discipleship to Moses to be mutually exclusive. However, this is not the perspective of John's Gospel. Jesus does not replace Judaism but rather fulfils it, as evident in the quotation formulae (noted above), along with the evidence cited in the last paragraph.[102] So the negative use of Ἰουδαῖος

---

[99] de Boer 2001: 263–4.   [100] *Ibid.*: 270.
[101] *Ibid.*: 271–80.
[102] See also Klappert 2001. For a contrary view see Culpepper 2001.

in referring to those who are disciples of Moses, rejecting Jesus, is '*an ironic acknowledgment of their claim to be the authoritative arbiters of Jewish identity*'.[103] The irony of rejecting Jesus is that they have 'forfeited their Jewish identity and heritage (cf, 19:15)'.[104] As a result, their accuser is Moses in whom they believe (5:45–47). When the negative occurrences of Ἰουδαῖος are understood in this way, there is no apparent difficulty with the historical reconstruction proposed above. The description is not an acknowledgment that those who rejected Jesus as the Christ were 'the Jews'. Rather, those who claimed to be Jews but were in fact disciples of Moses misunderstood their Scriptures and were not really Jews at all. They had the basis of Judaism, descent from Abraham (8:33), and Moses' writings (5:46), but did not believe, thus fulfilling Isaiah's prophecy as quoted in John 12:37–41.

A particular example of someone who 'left' true Judaism to follow the deviant understanding of Moses is Judas.[105] In John 13:30 Judas is described as 'going out' (ἐξέρχομαι), the same verb used in 1 John 2:19, from the apostles, who are presented as the restored Israel (John 20:22).[106] Judas goes out to betray Jesus to 'the Jews'.[107]

So the evidence in John supports the proposed historical reconstruction of an intra-Jewish disagreement over Jesus' identity. John presents Jesus as the Christ, the fulfiller of Old Testament expectation. There was conflict in the first century over this identification; however, those who believed in him were made into a new Israel, while those who rejected Jesus were ironically called 'the Jews' because they rejected the fulfilling of the expectations of Judaism in Jesus. In this way, salvation is understood as coming from the Jews (4:22), while those who deny Jesus have departed true Judaism to follow some deviant understanding of Moses.

Summary

This section has provided a secondary line of evidence to demonstrate the plausibility of the proposed reading. It showed that first-century Judaism was composed of many groups who claimed to be authentic, one of which was Christianity. Earliest Christianity claimed authenticity

---

[103] de Boer 2001: 278 (italics his).   [104] *Ibid.*: 278.

[105] For parallels between 1 John's 'opponents' and Judas see Witetschek 2004.

[106] In John 20:22, the resurrected Jesus gives his disciples the Spirit in fulfilment of Ezekiel 37. Jesus breathes the Spirit into the bones of Israel and so they are resurrected and restored; see Dumbrell 1991: 92.

[107] For a description of how Judas is presented as apostate in John see Kim 2004; Witetschek 2004.

because it identified Jesus as the Christ who fulfilled Old Testament expectations. With Christianity's defining element as the confession that Jesus was the Christ, it was brought into conflict with the rest of Judaism over Jesus' identity. The result was that Christianity understood that not all Jews were really members of Israel. When Jewish people denied that Jesus was the Christ, they left true Judaism. As Evans states in response to the charge that earliest Christianity is anti-Semitic:

> Early Christians did not view themselves as belonging to a religion that was distinct from Judaism. New Testament Christianity *was* Judaism, that is, what was believed to be the true expression of Judaism. Just as Pharisees, Essenes, Sadducees, and who knows what other teachers and groups believed that their respective visions of religious faith were the true expressions of what God promised Abraham and commanded Moses, so also early Christians believed that in Jesus God had fulfilled all that the prophets had predicted and all that Moses required. Early Christianity was one Jewish sect among several.[108]

So the proposed reading of 1 John 2:18–27 gains support from the tangent of history and thus appears plausible.

Conclusion

This chapter provided a reading of 1 John 2:15–27. Following the proposed identification made in the introduction of the 'claimants' as Jews, it argued that this section warns a Jewish audience against apostatising. In 2:15–17, they are commanded not to love the world but to be obedient to God, in terms and language that is reminicent of the 'two ways' rhetoric of the Old Testament. In 2:18–27 the particular issue facing the audience is addressed, the schism within the community that has led to some leaving (2:19). Those who have left have denied that Jesus is the Christ (2:22) and so have lost the relationship they claim with God the Father (2:23). It was argued that this situation describes an intra-Jewish disagreement about the identity of Jesus, where the author presents those who deny Jesus' messiahship as leaving the True Israel. Given the original nature of this proposal of the historical situation behind 1 John, a lengthy section outlined the material from the first century that supports this reading of the text. It was argued that first-century Judaism consisted of many groups all claiming authenticity, some of whom thought

---

[108] Evans 2001: 91.

the other groups had left authentic Judaism. Material from the earliest Christian sources demonstrated that Christianity also understood itself in these same terms.

The next chapter continues presenting a reading of 1 John, particularly 2:28–3:24. The reading stops at 3:24 because the following unit (4:1–6) presents what is considered to be the most explicit support for the view that the opponents deny the incarnation in 1 John, and this therefore merits a whole chapter devoted to the exposition of these crucial verses.

6

THE AUDIENCE: 1 JOHN 2:28–3:24

This chapter outlines the results of applying the reading method of chapter 2 to 1 John 2:28–3:24 within the framework established in the introduction (1:1–2:11). The two particular aspects of the framework that inform this reading are the affirmation of the resurrected incarnate Christ (1:1–3), and the audience's view of themselves as the True Israel.

Since there are two units in this section of 1 John (2:28–3:12 and 3:13–24), the chapter has two parts. The next chapter is devoted to a detailed study of 4:1–6 because this is the section of 1 John that is perceived to most clearly affirm the incarnation in light of the opponents' denial.

1 John 2:28–3:12

1 John 2:28 starts with the same three elements observed in 2:18 – a vocative (τεκνία) combined with an eschatological statement (ἐν τῇ παρουσίᾳ αὐτοῦ) and the use of the adverb νῦν. So the unit discusses a second aspect of living in the world described in 2:15–17 – the identity of the audience as children of God. A closing boundary seems to occur at 3:13 where there is a change in theme from 'sin' to 'love', hence the unit is 2:28–3:12.

Gaps and limiting devices

This unit presents two gaps to the reading of 1 John proposed in this research so far. First, φανερόω in 3:5 and 8 can be understood to refer to the incarnation. For instance Marshall comments on φανερόω in 3:8: 'Here John assumes the reality of the incarnation, which was accepted by his adherents but doubted by his opponents.'[1] However, under the influence of the immediate context (the abolition of sin), many scholars suggest φανερόω is a shorthand way of referring to the whole of Jesus'

---

[1] Marshall 1978: 185. See also Johnson 1993: 40; Beutler 2000: 38, 85.

incarnate activities and not just the incarnation *per se*.[2] Yet evidence for widening the meaning of φανερόω in this way is lacking. This reading's proposed christology, that understands 1 John as affirming not just the incarnation but the resurrection of the incarnate Christ, may provide a clearer explanation of 3:5 and 8.

Second, the statements regarding the sinlessness of the audience cause a gap since they appear to be in contradiction to the statements about sin contained in 1:8 and 10. Scholars generally experience this second gap irrespective of which historical reconstruction they adopt or literary methods they use, as evident in the lengthy discussions in the secondary literature.[3] As such, a review of the fills is unnecessary because the issue at hand is how this research fills the gap in light of the proposed understanding of 1 John's argument up to this point.

In terms of the limiting devices, the verb γράφω does not occur in the unit. There are three uses of the vocative (2:28 – τεκνία, 3:2 – ἀγαπητοί, 3:7 – τεκνία) that may afford some opportunity to review the proposed reading. The final boundary does not appear to be marked with a summary statement, but the negative imperative seems to signal a movement in the argument, as the vocabulary of 'sin' ceases, replaced with a discussion of 'love'.

An intertextual reading of 1 John 2:28–3:12

These verses are made up of two main sub-units: 2:28–3:3 and 3:4–12. The first sub-unit describes the status of the audience as children of God (τέκνα θεοῦ in 3:1 and 2). This status is made prominent through a repetition of vocative forms in 2:28 (τεκνία) and 3:2 (ἀγαπητοί) and the repeated use of νῦν in 2:28 and 3:2. This sets the basis for the discussion of sin that dominates the second sub-unit (3:4–12).

The sub-units are linked both formally and logically. Formally, the sevenfold repetition of the phrase πᾶς ὁ that starts in the first sub-unit (2:29; 3:3) continues into the second (3:4, 6 (x2), 9, 10).[4] Logically, the link between Christ and those born of him described in 2:29–3:3 is assumed in, and underlies, 3:4–12. So in 2:29, knowing that Jesus is righteous results in knowing that those who do righteousness are born of

---

[2] Westcott 1966: 103; Houlden 1973: 96; Schnackenburg 1992: 174; Kruse 2000: 119, 123; Smalley 2007: 148–9.

[3] It takes Griffith (2002: 128–36) nine pages just to present and critically evaluate the six most common positions before he adds a seventh alternative. See also Kotzé 1979; Kruse 2003.

[4] Brown 1982: 118.

God. In 3:1, the world does not know those born of God because it did not know Jesus. In 3:2, the children of God will be made like Jesus when he returns because they will see him as he is. In 3:3, the child of God, holding on to the hope of being made like Jesus, makes himself holy just as Jesus is holy. This logic is evident in the second sub-unit in 3:7, where the one who does what is right is righteous just as Jesus is righteous.[5]

1 John 2:28–3:3

This sub-unit starts with the command to remain in Jesus so that on his appearance (φανερόω) the audience may not be ashamed (2:28). It continues, describing this appearance as his coming (ἐν τῇ παρουσίᾳ αὐτοῦ), a reference to Jesus' second coming to judge, hence the fear of shame (αἰσχύνομαι). This eschatological reference gives way to a couple of statements positing links between those who remain in Christ and Christ himself – righteousness (2:29), and non-recognition by the world (3:1). It is not until Jesus appears (φανερόω) that the audience will be made like him (3:2). It is this hope of being made like him that purifies the audience since Jesus is pure (3:3) and they remain in him (2:28).

This sub-unit picks up the christology of the introduction (especially 1:1–2:2). The appearing (φανερόω) of Jesus is from heaven (1:2), where he lives as the advocate (παράκλητος) for his people (2:1). Further, Jesus is described as righteous (2:29), the same description used of Jesus in 2:1, a description that has not occurred between 2:1 and 2:29.[6] With this christology established, the author turns to discuss the theme of sin, the same theme evident in 1:6–2:2. Sin has not been discussed since 2:2 and is reintroduced in 3:4, dominating 3:4–9.[7]

1 John 3:4–12

Just as the first sub-unit twice states that the audience are the children of God, the second sub-unit contains a repetition of ideas. There is a parallelism between 3:4–6 and 3:7–9.[8] Both start with discussions of sin (3:4, 7–8a), move to reasons for Jesus appearing (3:5, 8b), and then return to discuss sin, apparently affirming the ability to stop sinning (3:6, 9). That

---

[5] For a contrary view that δίκαιός ἐστιν (2:29; 3:7) refers to God rather than Jesus see von Wahlde 2002.

[6] The δίκ– word group does not occur between 2:1 and 2:29.

[7] There is one reference to sin in 2:12; however since this reference is in the poem, it seems to summarise one element of the introduction, namely the theme in 1:6–2:2.

[8] Klauck 1991: 190; Smalley 2007: 167.

the second part of the parallel starts with the vocative τεκνία (3:7) draws the readers' attention to the repetition and suggests that 3:4–6 and 3:7–9 should be read together and interpreted in light of each other. Further, it reminds the reader of the christology of 2:28–3:3 (and thus 1:1–2:2) since it again describes Jesus as righteous (καθὼς ἐκεῖνος δίκαιός ἐστιν). The section is rounded off with a test and an example of recognising the children of God by their actions (3:10–12).

The two gaps that require filling are the second and third lines of the parallel – that Jesus appeared in order to bear sin (3:5) and destroy the Devil (3:8b), and that everyone who remains in Christ does not sin (3:6, 9a) and is not able to sin (3:9b).

Given the christological context, where Jesus is understood to be in heaven, where he is the παράκλητος for his people and from where he will return, the appearing of Jesus in these verses could be his appearing in heaven to present his sacrifice (ἱλασμός). In this way, he is the one that bears the sin of the world and destroys the Devil's works. There are two lines of evidence that support this reading.

First, to interpret 'appearing' (φανερόω) as always referring to Jesus' incarnation is suspect. In 2:29 and 3:2, the verb is used to describe Jesus' return to earth to judge. The location of appearing may be the same, earth, but the incarnation is not on view in the second set of uses. However, it should also be noted that the verb does not specify where the appearing takes place. The location is determined by the context of the discussion. Since the default location of Jesus in this section is in heaven, it seems that φανερόω in 3:5 and 8 is referring to Jesus' appearing in heaven.

Second, the links in christology between this unit and 2:1 indicate a High Priestly activity for Jesus in heaven. The solution to the problem of sin in 1:6–2:2 takes place in Old Testament cultic terms. So for instance it is the blood (τὸ αἷμα) of Jesus that cleanses (καθαρίζει) from sin in 1:7. Further, confession (ὁμολογῶμεν) of sin is required for forgiveness (ἀφῇ) and cleansing (καθαρίσῃ) in 1:9. Finally, Jesus is described as a sacrifice of atonement (ἱλασμός) in 2:2. So when Jesus' present role in heaven is described as the advocate (παράκλητος), it is describing Jesus' priestly action. Just as the priest entered the temple and God's presence to present the sacrifice of atonement for his people, so Jesus entered God's presence with his sacrificial blood to bring forgiveness for sins. This understanding matches the order of the verses in 2:1–2 where the description of Jesus' present activity occurs before reference to his death. Since 2:28–3:12 starts with Jesus in heaven and contains the cultic language of holiness (3:3) that then gives way to the discussion of sin (3:4–9), it seems that 3:5 and 8 should be understood in the same

vein. The order of the descriptions of Jesus appearing and dealing with
sin in 3:5 and 8b are the same as in 2:1–2 – mention of Jesus' appearing
precedes the action that deals with sin and the Devil.

Hence Jesus' 'appearing' in 3:5 and 8 is his appearing in heaven as the
High Priest to bring the sacrifice that deals with sin. This understanding
is corroborated by two elements in 3:5. The description of Jesus as bearing (αἴρω) sins is reminiscent of the High Priest carrying the sacrifice of
atonement for sins into the Holy of Holies (Leviticus 4:5; 16:15) – Jesus
bears sins. Further, the description of Jesus as sinless could be taken
to refer to Jesus' sinless sacrifice of himself. However, it could also be
referring to the qualification he required in order to appear as the High
Priest in heaven to bear the sin offering (Hebrews 4:15; 7:26–28).

This understanding of 1 John 3:5 and 8 helps to fill the gap experienced
in reading 3:6 and 9, where the audience's sinlessness is affirmed. The
larger unit (2:28–3:12) desires that the readers remain in Christ (2:28).
Since Christ is righteous, holy and sinless, the believer is also seen to
be these things by God because Christ is in heaven representing them as
their High Priest. So 3:6 can say that no one who remains in Christ sins,
because the perspective of this section is of Christ in heaven bearing his
blood for his people. This fulfils the Old Testament promises of God for
his faithful people alluded to in the introduction (1:7, 9; 2:2). Similarly
in 3:9, everyone born of God from the heavenly perspective does not sin,
because the seed (σπέρμα) of God remains in them. Given the context,
σπέρμα seems to refer to the χρῖσμα of 2:27 as it was given to them and
remains in them.[9] This then is a reference to the Spirit that unites the
believer to Christ and so means that, from the heavenly perspective, the
believer does not and cannot sin, because in God's eyes they are seen
as Christ. The believer has the identity of being a child of God who is
represented in heaven by the resurrected incarnate Christ who is their
παράκλητος with the Father, holding his sacrificial blood that pays the
penalty for sin.

Yet, as believers live in this world waiting to be made completely like
Jesus at his return (3:2), there is still the issue of how the children of
God and the children of the Devil can be recognised. 1 John 3:10–12
concludes the unit with a test and an example. Everyone who does not
do what is right or love his brother is not from God (3:10). The reason
for this (ὅτι) is found in the message that they should love one another
(3:11) – not following the example of Cain, who under the influence

---

[9] For a review of the different ways σπέρμα has been understood see du Preez 1975;
Dryden 1999: 85–8.

of the Evil One killed his brother (3:12), but under the influence of the resurrected incarnate Christ – the message which they have heard from the beginning and which has the imperatival element of love for one another (1:5; 2:7–11).

Tangents

Some of the other earliest Christian documents provide three sources of tangents to this reading that demonstrate its plausibility.

First, Streett suggests that Jesus is presented in John's Gospel as a High Priest. Jesus intercedes for his disciples as the divine-name bearer (John 17:6, 11–12, 26), and sanctifies himself in order to sanctify his disciples (John 17:19).[10]

Second, Hebrews 9:24–28 describes Jesus entering heaven to 'appear' for his people in God's presence. 'Appear' in 9:24 is not φανερόω as in 1 John 3:5 and 8, but ἐμφανίζω. However, Ellingworth comments that '[t]here is no sharp distinction or contrast in Hebrews between ἐμφανίζω and φανερόω'.[11] Jesus appears in heaven where he presents the sacrifice of himself for sin once for all. Further, his appearing and interceding for his people is based on his resurrection. So in Hebrews 7:23–25, because Jesus lives for ever, he is able to always intercede for his people. He represents his people as the exalted High Priest who is sinless (7:26–28). The same thought is evident in Romans 8:34, where Jesus, the one who died and was resurrected, is now at God's right hand interceding for his people, and 1 Timothy 2:5–6, where Jesus, who is described in sacrificial terms as giving himself as a ransom for all (ὁ δοὺς ἑαυτὸν ἀντίλυτρον ὑπὲρ πάντων), is the mediator between man and God.[12]

Third, the New Testament contains other passages that view the believer as in heaven. In Ephesians 2:6, Paul describes the believer as being raised up with Christ and seated in heaven. The same idea is evident in Colossians 3:1–4, a passage that Wright notes corresponds quite closely with 1 John 2:28–3:3 in its sequence of thought.[13]

---

[10] Streett 2011: 319–20. Streett also includes Jesus' seamless garment (John 19:33) as an allusion to the high priest's garment, and his washing of the disciples' feet (John 13:5f) in order to sanctify them as priests as an allusion to Moses' washing of Aaron so he could become the high priest (Exodus 29:4). However, these allusions are not as convincing.

[11] Ellingworth 1993: 480.

[12] Further, 1 Timothy 2:5–6 even conforms to the order of the verses here in 1 John, where the present work of Jesus as the mediator precedes the description of his death.

[13] Wright 2003: 464.

1 John 3:13–24

The second unit starts with a negated imperative (μὴ θαυμάζετε) and has 'love' as its theme.[14] The lack of vocabulary associated with the 'love' in 4:1–6 confirms a closing boundary at 4:1.[15]

Gaps and limiting devices

There are four cataphoric occurrences of the demonstrative pronoun οὗτος in this part (3:16, 19, 23, and 24). However, the referent of three of these occurrences is supplied within a clause of the demonstrative and therefore they do not constitute a gap. So the postcedent of τούτῳ in 3:16 is ἐκεῖνος ὑπὲρ ἡμῶν τὴν ψυχὴν αὐτοῦ ἔθηκεν, the postcedent of αὕτη in 3:23 is πιστεύσωμεν τῷ ὀνόματι τοῦ υἱοῦ αὐτοῦ Ἰησοῦ Χριστοῦ καὶ ἀγαπῶμεν ἀλλήλους, and the postcedent of τούτῳ in 3:24 is ἐκ τοῦ πνεύματος οὗ ἡμῖν ἔδωκεν. The fourth cataphoric occurrence of οὗτος constitutes a gap because of the large distance between τούτῳ (3:19) and its postcedent μείζων ἐστὶν ὁ θεὸς τῆς καρδίας ἡμῶν καὶ γινώσκει πάντα (3:20). The discussion of this gap is limited as it does not affect either the historical reconstruction or the christology proposed in this thesis. There are no reader-experienced gaps in this unit as both the themes and christology of this part are consistent with, and support, the reading of 1 John developed so far in this research.

Of the three limiting devices used in 1 John, only vocatives occur in this part – ἀδελφοί in 3:13, τεκνία in 3:18, and ἀγαπητοί in 3:21. The first two of these occur with an exhortation – μὴ θαυμάζετε in 3:13 and μὴ ἀγαπῶμεν in 3:18. As such, they draw the reader's attention to the implication of the argument resulting in them marking a summary sentence. The first, μὴ θαυμάζετε, ἀδελφοί in 3:13, draws together a summary of the two aspects of living in the world – there are antichrists in the world and the readers are the children of God, so do not be surprised that the world hates the readers (εἰ μισεῖ ὑμᾶς ὁ κόσμος). The second, τεκνία, μὴ ἀγαπῶμεν in 3:18, summarises the argument of 3:13–17 – even though the world hates them (3:13–15), the readers should be people who love their brothers (3:16–18). The third vocative, ἀγαπητοί in 3:21, seems to stress that the readers can have confidence before God even when their hearts condemn them.

---

[14] ἀγαπάω, its cognates ἀγάπη and ἀγαπητός, along with its antonym μισέω, occur nine times in these 10 verses.

[15] The vocative that starts 4:1 (ἀγαπητοί) links the two units but this is the last of the ἀγάπη word group until 4:7.

An intertextual reading of 1 John 3:13–24

Three of the occurrences of οὗτος in this part are in sentences phrased so similarly that they appear to mark paragraphs or stages in the argument:

3:16 ἐν τούτῳ ἐγνώκαμεν τὴν ἀγάπην

3:19 ἐν τούτῳ γνωσόμεθα ὅτι ἐκ τῆς ἀληθείας ἐσμέν

3:24 ἐν τούτῳ γινώσκομεν ὅτι μένει ἐν ἡμῖν

Each clause starts with the same prepositional phrase (ἐν τούτῳ) and the verb γινώσκω, although each has a different tense-form of γινώσκω. In this way the phrase alerts the reader to the theme of each paragraph – so 3:16–18 is about love (ἀγάπη), 3:19–22 is about the heart (καρδία) and confidence in prayer,[16] and 3:23–4 is about a command (ἐντολή).[17] The formula (ἐν τούτῳ + γινώσκω) and the themes of love (ἀγάπη) and commandment (ἐντολή) link this section to the third unit of the introduction (2:3–11). The formula occurred four times in 2:3–5, and the vocabulary of love and commandment were both introduced in 2:3–11. Thus this unit's contribution to the themes is its discussion of the heart and confidence in prayer in 3:19–22.

When the formula and themes are used to map the argument it appears that the part starts with a discussion of the world's hatred of the believer (3:13–15) that is contrasted with the believer's love (3:16–18). The loving actions of the believer give them confidence in their hearts when they pray (3:19–22) because they obey the commandment to believe in the name of Jesus Christ and love one another (3:23–24).

The gap in this part, the distance between οὗτος in 3:19 and its antecedent in 3:20, slows the reader down to appreciate the development of the themes of love and the commandment already discussed in 2:3–11. This development is the confidence in prayer that the readers should have, based on their knowledge that God is greater than their hearts, and their obedience to his commandment (3:24).

Overall, this unit supports the reading developed in this research in six areas.

First, the description of the readers in 3:14 as passing from death to life (μεταβεβήκαμεν ἐκ τοῦ θανάτου εἰς τὴν ζωήν) reveals the same metaphorical understanding of life and death, light and darkness discussed in the introduction (1:3–5). It pictures the world as existing in the realm of death, seen in its actions of hate and murder (ὁ μὴ ἀγαπῶν

---

[16] καρδία does not occur in 1 John outside these verses.
[17] ἐντολή occurs in five clumps in 1 John (2:3–4; 7–8; 3:22–24; 4:21; 5:2–3).

μένει ἐν τῷ θανάτῳ. πᾶς ὁ μισῶν τὸν ἀδελφὸν αὐτοῦ ἀνθρωποκτόνος ἐστίν – 3:14–15). This is similar to the ideas expressed in 2:9–11 where hating one's brother was the action of existing in the darkness.

Second, the christology of this unit is consistent with the introduction (1:1–2:11). Jesus' death (ἐκεῖνος ὑπὲρ ἡμῶν τὴν ψυχὴν αὐτοῦ ἔθηκεν – 3:16), is the model of love.[18] It is not the incarnation that reveals and demonstrates love, but the death of the incarnate Christ.

Third, the ethic of love described in this section (3:16–18) has inter-textual links with Deuteronomy 15:7–8, where Moses commands the people of Israel:

> If there is a poor man among your brothers in any of the towns of the land that the LORD your God is giving you, do not be hardhearted (τὴν καρδίαν σου) or tightfisted toward your poor brother. Rather be openhanded and freely lend him whatever he needs. (NIV)

There are two links between Deuteronomy 15:7–8 and 1 John 3:16–21 – both are about seeing a brother in need, and both speak of the heart response to seeing this need. The readers of 1 John are to follow the love ethic of the Old Testament, not just in word but in action (3:18). This extends the proposed historical reconstruction, providing evidence that the audience should act as faithful Israel in their dealings with each other. Further support for the reading is observed if, following the Old Testament links, ἀδελφός is taken as referring to a fellow Israelite, a descendant of Abraham (rather than the historically anachronistic 'Christian').

Fourth, when the first two points are read together, the christology of the message involves in it the ethical imperative of love. This is consist-ent with the introduction, especially the movement noted in 1:3–5, where 1:5 was a summary of the message that involved the ethic of living in the light. The movement was also evident in 2:7ff, where the commandment to love was linked to living in the light.

Fifth, the logic of love gives confidence of knowledge of God. This is evident in 3:19–24, where obedience to the commandment to love results in assurance for the heart. This is consistent with 2:3–11, where knowledge of fellowship with God was assured in the action of keep-ing the commandment to love. There is a development of this theme in 3:19–24 with regards to confidence in prayer that was not evident in the introduction.

---

[18] Kruse 2000: 137.

Sixth, one difference between the themes of love and commandment in this part and the introduction is that the commandment also calls for belief in the name of God's Son Jesus Christ (3:23). This difference supports the research so far, because linking faith and love together again demonstrates an ethical imperative to the message of the resurrected incarnate Christ. It also supports the understanding of the historical situation outlined in this research, that the antichrists deny that Jesus is the Christ, while the True Israel confess him and should love one another.

Tangents

There are two tangents to this reading that demonstrate its plausibility. First, Jesus' death is presented as the model of love elsewhere in the New Testament. In John 10:11, 15, Jesus uses the same vocabulary as 1 John 3:16 in calling himself the Good Shepherd who lays down his life for his sheep.[19] Further, in John 15:13 Jesus states that this 'laying down of life' demonstrates his love.[20] In Romans 5:8, Paul argues that God's love is seen in Jesus' death.[21] In 1 Peter 2:21, Jesus' suffering (and death) are presented as the model for slaves to follow when their masters mistreat them.

Second, James 2:15–17 speaks about seeing a brother or sister in need and the requirement on those with faith to act. The Jewish audience of James (1:1) suggests these brothers and sisters are Jewish. Given this and the parallel ethic with 1 John 3:16–18, the reading gains further support for its proposed historical reconstruction.

Conclusion

This chapter has provided a reading of 1 John 2:28–3:24 that is consistent with the research's understanding of 1 John 1:1–2:11. In particular, the resurrection of the incarnate Christ was seen to lie behind both the identity of the readers as the children of God and the ethical system the author endorsed. Further, the proposed historical situation made sense of the appeal to ethical behaviour that stemmed from the Old Testament and treated other believers as True Israelites.

---

[19] John 10:11: τὴν ψυχὴν αὐτοῦ τίθησιν; John 10:15: τὴν ψυχήν μου τίθημι; 1 John 3:16: τὴν ψυχὴν αὐτοῦ ἔθηκεν

[20] Again, the same vocabulary is used in describing Jesus' death: τὴν ψυχὴν αὐτοῦ θῇ (John 15:13).

[21] See also Galatians 2:20.

7

THE CONFESSION: 1 JOHN 4:1–6

This chapter provides a reading of 1 John 4:1–6, especially the confession of 4:2–3, that demonstrates its consistency with the christology and historical situation proposed above.

Following the reading method, this chapter has four main parts. The first part outlines the gap and structure of 1 John 4:1–6. The second part critically reviews how previous research has filled this gap. The third part then proposes that the phrase Ἰησοῦν Χριστὸν ἐν σαρκὶ ἐληλυθότα (4:2) refers to Jesus' resurrection appearances that demonstrated he was the Christ. This reading is made under the influence of intertextual appeal to the resurrection narratives of John's Gospel. A reading of 4:1–6 is then undertaken to test this understanding. The fourth part provides some tangents to further demonstrate its plausibility.

The reasons these verses receive such a detailed treatment are because the confession is the basis for many of the historical reconstructions of 1 John, and previous research understands it to affirm a christology different from that proposed above. So for example:

> 1 John 4:2, which speaks of 'Jesus Christ having come in the flesh,' has played a prominent role in the interpretation of 1 John since it seems to provide a basic clue to the issue that divides the author from his adversaries[1]

> The whole weight of the docetic-cum-gnostic case in 1 John rests on the modifying phrase 'has come in the flesh'.[2]

> It seems clear then that the secessionists are Christians with a different christology. The key verses here are 1 John 4:3 and 2 John 7.[3]

---

[1] de Boer 1991: 326.
[2] Griffith 1998: 269. Griffith (2002: 179) states: 'This passage [4:2–3] is the sole foundation for all docetic interpretations of the controversy in the letter.'
[3] Trebilco 2004: 285. See also Uebele 2001: 119.

The gaps, limiting devices and structure of 4:1–6

In order to set the context for the discussion of filling the 'gap' in 4:1–6, this section identifies the 'gap' and the limiting devices in 4:1–6, before briefly reviewing the structure of 4:1–6.

Gaps

Most of the sentences in this part are asyndetic (4:1, 2, 4, 5, 6), causing the syntactical appearance of interruptions to the flow of the sentences. However, the phrase ἐκ τοῦ θεοῦ is used six times in these verses, giving them a unity. So, 4:1 commands the audience to test if the spirits are 'from God'. Verses 2 and 3 outline the test that indicates whether a spirit is 'from God' or not. Verses 4, 5, and 6 are all asyndetic but start with a personal pronoun (ὑμεῖς, αὐτοί, ἡμεῖς) discussing the results of the test – that the audience is 'from God' but the antichrists are 'from the world'. Thus there are no gaps caused by an interruption to the flow of the sentences.

There is only one cataphoric use of a pronoun – τούτῳ in 4:2. However, this does not cause a gap since the postcedent of τούτῳ is the test of 4:2b–3a that follows almost immediately. The cataphoric phrase ἐν τούτῳ γινώσκετε has been used five times in 1 John so far and has a prominence-marking function.[4] So in this context it highlights the confessional test of verses 2–3.

There is one reader-experienced gap in these verses – the meaning of the confession in 4:2. As Perkins states: 'The real exegetical problem in this section is the confession mentioned in v.2 and the associated testing of spirits.'[5] In addition to the uncertainty as to how the phrase Ἰησοῦν Χριστὸν ἐν σαρκὶ ἐληλυθότα should be understood, the understanding expressed here, that the christology of 1 John affirms the resurrection of the incarnate Christ, runs counter to the understandings of the confession found in previous research. As a result, the meaning of the confession and its contribution to the christology of 1 John is a gap that requires investigation.

Limiting devices

In terms of limiting devices, there are no uses of γράφω in these verses. Of the two vocatives, both appear to be prominence-marking. The first

---

[4] 2:3, 5; 3:16, 19, and 24. It also occurs in 4:13 and 5:2. The variant phrase ἐκ τούτου γινώσκομεν is found in 4:6.

[5] Perkins 1979: 51.

(ἀγαπητοί in 4:1) draws the reader's attention to the imperative that starts the unit. The second (τεκνία in 4:4), alerts the reader to the movement in the argument from the test to the conclusions that can be drawn from the results of the test. This second vocative limits how the gaps are filled because it gives prominence to the results of the test, thereby indicating the nature of the test – namely, that it reveals whether a spirit has its origins in God. The last limiting device is the boundary evident at the end of 4:6 that is marked by a change in theme. The phrase ἐκ τοῦ θεοῦ ceases to be used after 4:6, while the vocabulary of love (ἀγαπάω, ἀγάπη, ἀγαπητός), which stopped with the vocative in 4:1, is reintroduced in 4:7. This boundary is further observable due to the anaphoric demonstrative phrase ἐκ τούτου γινώσκομεν that starts the last sentence in 4:6, acting as a summary statement of the paragraph. Thus the boundary limits the way gaps can be filled, as it indicates that the unit is about discriminating between spirits based on their origin – either being ἐκ τοῦ θεοῦ or not.

Structure

This unit contains three parts. First, the imperatives and the reason (ὅτι) for the commands are given in verse 1. The use of a negative imperative to start a unit suggests a pattern, since it was also used in 2:15 and 3:13. The imperatives flow from the assurance the readers received in 3:24 that God has given every believer his Spirit, yet the spirits require testing. The second part contains the test – the confession that indicates if the spirit is from God or not (4:2–3). The cataphoric phrase ἐν τούτῳ γινώσκετε draws the reader's attention to the test, marking it as a progression in the argument. The third part (4:4–6) outlines the results of the test for the readers – that they are from God and the antichrists are from the world. The asyndetic start to 4:4, along with the personal pronoun (ὑμεῖς) and vocative (τεκνία), indicates a new part. That the other verses in this part are also asyndetic and begin with personal pronouns (αὐτοί, ἡμεῖς) reveals similarity to verse 4; however, the lack of a vocative indicates that they are not new parts but other conclusions within the same part. The anaphoric demonstrative phrase ἐκ τούτου γινώσκομεν concludes the paragraph.[6]

---

[6] This progression in thought from imperatives to test to results to conclusion indicates that the chiastic pattern proposed by some scholars is unlikely; see for example Malatesta 1978: 284–6. It also explains the repetition of vocabulary and themes that these chiastic patterns are based on, since the results and conclusions of 4:4–6 are drawn from 4:1–3. Consequently it warns against understanding some phrases in light of parallels, since the chiasm does not exist.

Table 9. *A syntactical diagram of 1 John 4:2–3*

ἐν τούτῳ γινώσκετε τὸ πνεῦμα τοῦ θεοῦ·
πᾶν πνεῦμα ὃ ὁμολογεῖ
  Ἰησοῦν Χριστὸν ἐν σαρκὶ ἐληλυθότα
ἐκ τοῦ θεοῦ ἐστιν,
καὶ
πᾶν πνεῦμα ὃ μὴ ὁμολογεῖ
  τὸν Ἰησοῦν
ἐκ τοῦ θεοῦ οὐκ ἔστιν (1 John 4:2–3)

The 'confession' in previous research

Understanding the confession in 4:2–3 is a gap that requires filling to produce a reading of these verses. There are two related sub-issues in understanding these verses. First, there is disagreement about the syntactical relationship between its three parts – Ἰησοῦν, Χριστόν, and ἐν σαρκὶ ἐληλυθότα. Second, there are a variety of ways the semantics of the confession are understood, especially the phrase ἐν σαρκὶ ἐληλυθότα. This section will critically discuss how this gap has been filled in previous research.

The syntax of the confession of 4:2–3

There are two ways the syntax of the confession is understood that result in three options for understanding the confession.[7]

First, the whole phrase (Ἰησοῦν Χριστὸν ἐν σαρκὶ ἐληλυθότα) is understood as the object of the verb ὁμολογέω. In translation this would mean the confession was 'Jesus Christ come in the flesh'.[8] Scholars who argue for this option often cite as support the similar expression in 2 John 7 and the parallel with the next verse, ὃ μὴ ὁμολογεῖ τὸν Ἰησοῦν, that contains only a single object.[9]

---

[7] For a review of the options see Brown 1982: 492–3.

[8] Brooke 1912: 109; Westcott 1966: 141; Brown 1982: 493; Burdick 1985: 295; Morgen 2005a: 152–3; Smalley 2007: 212; Lieu 2008a: 166–7.

[9] See for instance Brown 1982: 492, though he does not agree that μὴ ὁμολογεῖ is part of the text, favouring λύει. A number of scholars prefer reading λύει instead of μὴ ὁμολογεῖ, arguing that it is the harder reading – see for instance Gore 1920: 170–1; Piper 1947: 440–4; Bultmann 1973: 62–3; Brown 1982: 494–6; Hengel 1989: 57; Schnackenburg 1992: 201–2. However, the lack of external witness to λύει (only one tenth-century Greek manuscript contains it, and even then it is in the margin (1739), and some Church Fathers (Socrates, Irenaeus, Origen)), the difficulty in the present reading (μὴ ὁμολογεῖ where οὐχ ὁμολογεῖ would be more 'grammatically correct'), and the ability to explain how λύει

Second, the verb ὁμολογέω is understood to take a double accusative, or more accurately a double accusative of object-complement. Wallace defines this as: 'a construction in which one accusative substantive is the direct object of the verb and the other accusative (either noun, adjective, participle, or infinitive) complements the object in that it predicates something about it.'[10] Wallace notes that ὁμολογέω is one of the verbs in the New Testament that can take this double accusative of object-complement.[11] This results in two other options for understanding the confession.[12] The direct object of the verb is Ἰησοῦν Χριστόν, with its predicate being ἐν σαρκὶ ἐληλυθότα. That is, Ἰησοῦν Χριστόν is understood as a personal name and so the confession is that he ἐν σαρκὶ ἐληλυθότα. In translation this would mean the confession was 'Jesus Christ has come in the flesh'.[13] Or the third option is that the object of ὁμολογέω is Ἰησοῦν, with its predicate being Χριστὸν ἐν σαρκὶ ἐληλυθότα. In translation this would mean the confession was 'Jesus is the Christ having come in the flesh'.[14]

The first option, that takes the whole phrase as the object of the confession, does not seem best. The evidence cited for this view is open to debate. The parallel expression in 2 John 7 can be understood to be another example of the double accusative of object-complement.[15] The parallel in 1 John 4:3 is clearly different, as the content of the confession is different in expression and length (τὸν Ἰησοῦν). Further, the length of the original confession suggests that a statement in the form of a sentence is on view. This suggestion gains weight when it is noted that the emendations in both Vaticanus and Polycarp *Philippians* indicate that the confession was taken to be a sentence at an early date.[16] Even Brown, who prefers to understand the whole clause Ἰησοῦν Χριστὸν ἐν σαρκὶ

---

could have come about as a reading, mean that μὴ ὁμολογεῖ should be preferred. For a full defence of this position see Ehrman 1988.

[10] Wallace 1996: 182. See also Wallace 1985.

[11] Wallace 1996: 183. See also BDF §157; Klauck 1991: 228; Schnackenburg 1992: 200.

[12] Streett (2011: 173) lists a further possibility that sees ἐν σαρκὶ ἐληλυθότα as separate from Χριστόν. This would be translated 'Jesus as the Christ as having come in the flesh'. However, in effect this appears to be just a variant of the third option where the phrase ἐν σαρκὶ ἐληλυθότα becomes an appositional phrase modifying Χριστόν.

[13] Bultmann 1973: 62; Marshall 1978: 205; de Boer 1991: 334; Klauck 1991: 228; Loader 1992: 49; Schnackenburg 1992: 200–1; Rensberger 2001: 69; Brown 2003: 237.

[14] Haupt 1879: 246; Coetzee 1979: 52; Law 1979: 94; Stott 1988: 159; Neufeld 1994: 71; Griffith 2002: 187; Schmid 2002: 167; Witherington 2006: 524.

[15] Wallace 1996: 188.

[16] Both Vaticanus and Polycarp, *Philippians* 7:1, read ἐληλυθέναι in place of ἐληλυθότα.

ἐληλυθότα as the object of ὁμολογέω, acknowledges that the ὁμολογέω takes a double accusative on occasions, noting the parallel with John 9:22, Romans 10:9, and 1 John 4:15.[17] Finally, Streett points out that this option is not helpful because the confession must express some relationship between the three constituent parts.[18] Therefore this option does not seem likely.

A decision between the second and third options depends on a decision about the use of Χριστός – either as a personal name, thus going with Ἰησοῦς, or as a title, and so going with ἐν σαρκὶ ἐληλυθότα. The evidence cited for understanding Χριστός with Ἰησοῦς includes the other occurrences in 1 John, where the expression occurs as a seemingly fixed formula (1:3; 2:1; 5:6, 20; and especially 3:23, given its proximity to the confession).[19] Further, it is noted that where Χριστός is not read as the personal name type expression, it is articular and accompanied by the copula (2:22; 5:1).[20] However, this evidence does not rule out the third option. The places where the expression Ἰησοῦς Χριστός is used do not preclude its meaning as a title – the promised Messiah of the Old Testament. As Streett comments: 'When the Epistles speak of ὁ υἱός αὐτοῦ (i.e., θεοῦ) Ἰησοῦς Χριστός (1 John 1:3; 3:23; 5:20; 2 John 3), they are ascribing to Jesus his dual (related) titles, Son of God and Messiah.'[21] Further, there are occurrences where Χριστός lacks the article and copula, and maintains its titular force. So for instance, in the confession of John 9:22, where the same verb ὁμολογέω is used, Χριστός lacks both the article and a copula.[22] The same is also evident in Romans 10:9 and 1 Corinthians 12:3, both of which are reporting statements of belief.[23] Thus these are not good grounds for ruling

---

[17] Brown (1982: 493) argues against 4:2 being a double accusative of object-complement because John 9:22 has a different word order where the verb ὁμολογέω is placed between the accusatives, and in 1 John 4:15 the copula is used to indicate in particular that the confession is a statement. However, he has no explanation of Romans 10:9. Lieu (2008a: 166–7) also notes the use of the article and copula in 2:22; 4:15; and 5:5 as evidence against the statement being a sentence. However, she notes that the participial phrase results in an understanding of the statement much like the second option.

[18] Streett 2011: 173.

[19] Bultmann 1973: 62; Marshall 1978: 205; Schnackenburg 1992: 200; Lieu 2008a: 166–7.

[20] Lieu 2008a: 166.   [21] Streett 2011: 241–2.

[22] Streett (2011: 243) notes that Brown's objection that the verb occurs between the object and the complement does not disqualify John 9:22 as a parallel, since both 𝔓⁶⁶ and 𝔓⁷⁵ place the verb before both the object and the complement.

[23] These examples are taken from Streett (2011: 244–6), who also gives examples from Acts 3:20, John 1:41, Luke 23:2, the Second Century and Ancient Titulature. He concludes that the examples 'undercut the facile claim of so many scholars that without an article, Χριστός must be construed as a personal name'.

out the third option. In favour of the third option are the links between 4:2 and 2:22, where the issue of Jesus' identity as the Messiah is on view. Both passages occur in apocalyptic contexts of opposition from people known as 'antichrists' and affirm who Jesus is in contrast to these opponents. The way that 4:1–3 is structured, with the antichrists being mentioned after the confession, further suggests that what is on view is Jesus' identity as the Christ.

So, this research will follow the third option and read 4:2–3 as 'Jesus is the Christ having come in the flesh'.[24]

The meaning of the confession

There are six main ways that the meaning of the phrase ἐν σαρκὶ ἐληλυθότα is understood in previous research.[25]

The incarnation

First, ἐν σαρκὶ ἐληλυθότα is understood to be an affirmation of the incarnation.[26] This understanding often perceives the false prophets as Docetists who deny that Jesus Christ was fully human. The view places stress on the words ἐν σαρκὶ and usually appeals to the existence of Docetic opponents addressed by Ignatius, Marcion, and Polycarp. Polycarp even quotes 1 John 4:2 in *Philippians* 7:1–2 when speaking against his opponents.

There are two main problems with this view. First, if the confession was affirming the incarnation, it would have been more natural to use εἰς σάρκα rather than ἐν σαρκί. Brown comments: 'It must be noted that the author says "come in the flesh" not "come into the flesh," and so the act of

---

[24] The issue over identifying the subject and complement of this statement is difficult. Since Χριστός is being used in a titular sense, little hangs on the outcome of the decision.

[25] A seventh alternative understands ἐν σαρκὶ ἐληλυθότα as referring to the sacrament. Vouga (1988: 376) bases his argument on the use of σάρξ in John 6:51–58 which he understands to be about the sacrament, see also Vouga 1990: 64. However, as Streett (2011: 176) comments, this view 'has not been very well received by scholarship'. One of the reasons for this is that 'there are no explicit indications in the Epistles that the sacraments are an issue'.

[26] Haupt 1879: 244–9; Brooke 1912: 108–9: Gore 1920: 166–71; Windisch 1930: 126; Dodd 1946: 99; Bultmann 1973: 62; Wengst 1976: 17–8; Richter 1977: 128; Bruce 1979: 105; Barker 1981: 340; Wengst 1988: 3759; Larsen 1990b: 35; Klauck 1991: 233; Loader 1992: 67; Johnson 1993: 95; Toribio Cuadrado 1993: 274–5; Sloyan 1995: 42–3; Womack 1998: 100–1; Goulder 1999: 342; Beutler 2000: 103–4; Uebele 2001: 120–2; Beeke 2006: 152–3; Yarbrough 2008: 223; Jones 2009: 166–7.

the incarnation is not the point.'[27] Second, using the participle ἐληλυθότα results in emphasis on the identity of the person rather than the coming. Schnackenburg comments on the perfect participle ἐληλυθότα that it: 'lays no particular stress on the historical event or moment of time when the incarnation occurred.'[28] Both of these problems were felt in the early church, since they were both 'corrected' when this confession was used in disagreements with Docetists and Gnostics. So the docetic teaching of Simon and Cleobius is reported in 3 Corinthians as εἰς σάρκα ἦλθεν ὁ κύριος.[29] The participle was changed to an infinitive in both Polycarp, *Philippians* 7:1 and Tertullian, *Against Marcion* 3:8 when facing Doectic or Gnostic opposition.

Jesus' permanent humanity

Second, ἐν σαρκὶ ἐληλυθότα is understood to stress the permanent existence of Jesus in the flesh.[30] This understanding places a great deal of weight on the perfect tense-form of the participle. It follows a traditional understanding of the perfect tense-form (a past action with ongoing consequences).

This view has two main weaknesses. First, it suffers the same weakness as the incarnation view outlined above with respect to the phrase ἐν σαρκί. If the incarnation, or in this case the permanent incarnation, was on view, εἰς σάρκα would have expressed the thought more clearly. Second, understanding the perfect tense-form of the participle as implying permanency seems an over-reading of the Greek grammar.[31] The recent advances of aspect theory in understanding Biblical Greek warn against understanding the perfect as 'a past action with an ongoing consequence'.[32] The perfect tense-form used in 1 John 4:9 reveals the extent to which the perfect can be understood as a past action with ongoing consequences since Jesus is not still being sent into the world.[33] Further,

---

[27] Brown 1982: 493. See also Plummer 1911: 142; Griffith 2002: 183; Streett 2011: 192.
[28] Schnackenburg 1992: 201.   [29] Griffith 2002: 183.
[30] Plummer 1911: 142; Brooke 1912: 109; Marshall 1978: 205; Coetzee 1979: 52; Law 1979: 99; Burdick 1985: 295–6; Stott 1988: 157–8; Hengel 1989: 63; Hiebert 1991: 182–3; Burge 1996: 174–5; Strecker 1996: 134–5; Akin 2001: 172–3; Thomas 2003: 203; Kinlaw 2005: 101; Smalley 2007: 212.
[31] Brown 1982: 493.
[32] Porter 1994: 40; Campbell 2008a: 24–6.
[33] Streett 2011: 182.

Table 10. *Comparison of 1 John 4:2 and 2 John 7*

1 John 4:2	Ἰησοῦν Χριστὸν ἐν σαρκὶ ἐληλυθότα
2 John 7	Ἰησοῦν Χριστὸν ἐρχόμενον ἐν σαρκί

the parallel expression in 2 John 7 uses a present participle in apparently speaking of the same situation.

The difference in tense-forms cautions against placing too much stress on the perfect tense-form as determinative of meaning. The difference in tense-forms is consistent with Campbell's argument that both tense-forms semantically encode the imperfective aspect. If anything is to be established on the basis of the tense-form, it is that the choice of the perfect results in prominence or intensification of the action of 'coming' in 1 John 4:2.[34]

Christ's present presence

Third, ἐν σαρκὶ ἐληλυθότα is understood to refer to Christ's present presence in the believing community. Minear argues that the phrase ἐν σαρκί 'should be understood as a parallel and synonymous expression for "in you" in 4:4'.[35] Further, Minear argues that the references to Christ in 1 John are most often and decisively about his indwelling.[36] The result is that ἐν σαρκὶ ἐληλυθότα refers to the indwelling of Christ within the believer and the church.[37]

There are a couple of weaknesses with this view. It is unclear why ἐν ὑμῖν is an analogous phrase for ἐν σαρκί. There are no syntactical or semantic reasons for linking the two phrases. Minear bases the decision on his reconfiguration of 1 John's themes. However, of the other times ἐν ὑμῖν is used in 1 John, it refers to the indwelling of the word of God (2:14), the message the audience have heard (2:24), the anointing (2:27), and the truth that is not only in them but also in Jesus (2:8). Even in 4:4, where the masculine article could suggest that Jesus is on view, it seems more natural to understand the antecedent as God via his Spirit, since the section is about testing if spirits are from God or not.[38] Second,

---

[34] Campbell 2008a: 27–9.
[35] Minear 1970: 292; Callahan 2005: 41.
[36] Minear 1970: 299.   [37] *Ibid.*: 302.
[38] Brown (1982: 505) comments on Minear's view that 'in Johannine thought the divine indweller is scarcely Christ *in the flesh*' (italics his).

Streett notes that this view 'subsume[s] Christology into ecclesiology in a way that the Epistles do not … in the conceptual world of 1 John, Jesus is presently a heavenly resident – the παράκλητον πρὸς τὸν πατέρα – whose second appearance is still awaited (2:28; 3:2)'.[39] He indwells the believer by his Spirit, the very thing that is being tested through this confession.

Jesus' earthly life

Fourth, ἐν σαρκὶ ἐληλυθότα refers to the earthly life of Jesus.[40] This view understands σάρξ as referring to human existence in general and so σάρξ is speaking about the whole human existence of Jesus – from incarnation through to death. The verb ἔρχομαι is understood against the background of Old Testament expectation voiced in John 11:27, where the Messiah is described as the coming one (σὺ εἶ ὁ χριστὸς ὁ υἱὸς τοῦ θεοῦ ὁ εἰς τὸν κόσμον ἐρχόμενος). So the phrase describes Jesus as the Christ who came into human existence in fulfilment of Old Testament expectation. This is not limited to his incarnation but describes his whole life (including death) as salvific. So Brown comments: '[T]he point of difference between the secessionists and the epistolary author [is] … the salvific value of Jesus' career in the flesh and the degree to which that career was part of his identity as the Christ, inevitably the attitude towards his death will be crucial.'[41]

This view has much to commend it. Understanding σάρξ as referring to human existence in general finds support in 1 John 2:16. Further, understanding ἔρχομαι in light of another affirmation of Jesus' identity (John 11:27) and thus referring to the expectations of first-century Jews, makes good sense. However, there are also some weaknesses with this view. First, it is not just the word σάρξ that is used but the phrase ἐν σαρκί. Brown was quick to criticise understanding σάρξ as a reference to the incarnation on the basis of the preposition, but his explanation does not explain the contribution of the preposition. The grammar of the confession has ἐν σαρκί as a phrase which should therefore be treated as a unit when it comes to meaning. Second, it is unclear as to how the verb ἔρχομαι leads to Brown concluding that the issue at stake is the 'salvific

---

[39] Streett 2011: 175. See also Strecker (1996: 134) who argues that Minear 'improperly confuses the christological and ecclesiological aspects by choosing to understand the expression ἐν σαρκὶ as parallel to ἐν ὑμῖν'. Kruse (2000: 147) finds Minear's argument 'unconvincing'.

[40] Brown 1982: 505; Schnackenburg 1992: 201; Neufeld 1994: 119; Kruse 2000: 146–7; Michaels 2002: 160.

[41] Brown 1982: 77.

value of Jesus' career in the flesh'. The verb is used to express Jewish expectation, but how this results in the phrase being about the salvific value of Jesus being in the flesh is not explained.[42]

Jesus' death

Fifth, ἐν σαρκὶ ἐληλυθότα denotes the death of Jesus.[43] Building on the observations of the view that interprets ἐν σαρκὶ ἐληλυθότα as referring to the whole of Jesus' earthly life including his death, de Boer argues that: '[T]he confession found in 1 John 4:2 is a statement not about the concrete reality of the humanity of Jesus Christ as such, nor even about the "salvific importance" of his earthly career in general (Brown). The confession of 4:2 makes a claim about the death of Jesus Christ.'[44] De Boer argues this by linking 4:2 to 5:6, since both verses contain the verb ἔρχομαι with a prepositional phrase beginning with ἐν. Since de Boer understands 5:6 to be about the death of Jesus,[45] he concludes that the phrase ἐν … ἐληλυθότα is also about the death of Jesus.[46] This he sees confirmed when the contribution of σάρξ is taken into account since it refers to Jesus' self-giving death in John 6:51ff.[47] Within the context of 1 John 4:2, this reference to Christ's self-giving flesh in death is not a reference to the atonement but to the example that it sets for believers to follow.

This interpretation has a few weaknesses. First, de Boer's exegesis divides the phrase into ἔρχομαι + ἐν, and then σάρξ. This division runs contrary to the written order of the text that, by placing the phrase ἐν σαρκί before the participle ἐληλυθότα, indicates that the two parts of the phrase are ἐν σαρκί and ἐληλυθότα. This does not deny the links between 4:2 and 5:6, but rather suggests that the semantic units are ἐν σαρκί and the verb ἔρχομαι, which when studied may result in a different interpretation of the phrase. Second, to read 4:2 in light of 5:6 seems problematic since it both runs contrary to the reading order of the text and interprets a difficult text in light of another difficult text. Third, Griffith points out that the verses cited as support for interpreting σάρξ as referring to Jesus' self-giving death (John 6:51–8) do not use ἔρχομαι.[48] This leads Streett to conclude that it 'is difficult to see how dying on the cross could be described as "coming"'.[49]

---

[42] Streett 2011: 225.   [43] de Boer 1991: 345–6.
[44] *Ibid.*: 332.   [45] *Ibid.*: 337. See also de Boer 1988.
[46] *Ibid.*: 340.   [47] *Ibid.*: 340–1, 44–5.
[48] Griffith 2002: 184.   [49] Streett 2011: 226.

A Messianic affirmation

Sixth, ἐν σαρκὶ ἐληλυθότα is an affirmation that Jesus is the Christ.[50] This view is very similar to understanding ἐν σαρκὶ ἐληλυθότα as referring to the earthly life of Jesus. It avoids one weakness of the 'earthly life of Jesus' understanding (focussing just on the meaning of σάρξ) by reviewing how the phrase ἐν σαρκί is used in other early Christian documents. It reaches roughly the same conclusion as the 'earthly life of Jesus' view, that as a phrase it describes the sphere of humanity in general, but this is as the result of more nuanced investigation. Griffith's examination of the phrase's occurrence elsewhere in the first- and second-century Christian documents (Galatians 2:20; Philippians 1:22, 24; 1 Timothy 3:16; 1 Peter 4:2; Ignatius, *Ephesians* 1:3; 2 Clement 8:2; Barnabas 5:6–7, 10–11; The Long Recession of Ignatius, *Smyrnaeans* 6:1; Epistle of Diognetus 5:8–9; 6:3),[51] allows him to conclude: '[T]he phrase ἐν σαρκὶ ἐληλυθότα in 1 Jn 4.2 is to be taken in the neutral sense of existence in the realm of space and time. There is no need to import any special theological significance into the word sarx, whether in promoting a particular view of the incarnation or of soteriology.'[52] Further, it builds on the 'earthly life of Jesus' observation that ἔρχομαι is used in John's Gospel to refer to Jewish expectation.[53] However, this view does not attribute any particular meaning to this verb, such as that proposed in the 'earthly life of Jesus' understanding (that it indicates that the opponents rejected the salvific nature of Jesus' flesh). Instead, it reads the confession of 4:2 in the light of the denial in 2:22. Thus it argues that 4:2 is restating 2:22 in the positive – that Jesus is the Christ, the expected one in the sphere of humanity.

Even though this proposal avoids the pitfalls of 'the earthly life of Jesus' understanding and provides a consistent reading with 2:22, it suffers one major weakness. The proposal is unable to account for why the phrase was added. If 4:2 simply affirms the same confession as 2:22, why add ἐν σαρκὶ ἐληλυθότα? There should be a reason for the addition of the phrase and an explanation for its contribution to the argument of the text of 1 John.[54]

---

[50] Wurm 1903: 53–62; Lampe 1973: 261–2; Thyen 1988: 193; Griffith 2002: 184–8; Witherington 2006: 524; Streett 2011: 238–51.

[51] Griffith 2002: 181–3.

[52] *Ibid.*: 184.

[53] Griffith (*Ibid.*: 187) notes the use of ἔρχομαι in John 4:25; 6:14; 7:27, 31, 42; and 11:27. See also Streett 2011: 191.

[54] Since the phrase appears in a credal test where so much is at stake, it is difficult to put the addition down to stylistic reasons.

Summary

From this survey it becomes apparent that there are weaknesses in each of the proposed understandings of the phrase ἐν σαρκὶ ἐληλυθότα. The evidence indicates that the phrase ἐν σαρκί should be understood as referring to the world of humanity in general. However, the meaning of the verb ἔρχομαι has not been explained in a satisfying way, so it requires further examination and elucidation. Further, the question of the significance of the phrase's inclusion in such a prominently marked test also requires an answer.

Conclusion

Although previous scholarship fills the gap of the confession in many and various ways, it seems best to understand the syntax as affirming that 'Jesus is the Christ having come in the flesh'. Further, the phrase ἐν σαρκί appears to refer to the world of humanity in general. The point of investigation that remains is the meaning of ἔρχομαι and the ability of any proposed reading to explain the addition of the phrase ἐν σαρκὶ ἐληλυθότα to the confession.

An intertextual reading of 4:1–6

Given the weaknesses of each of the above proposals for understanding ἐν σαρκὶ ἐληλυθότα, it is proposed that the gap may be filled by understanding the phrase as referring to Jesus' resurrection appearances. These appearances demonstrated that he was the Christ. This reading is made under the influence of intertextual appeal to the resurrection narratives of John's Gospel.

In accord with the reading method outlined in chapter 2, this section has two parts. The first outlines the intertextual evidence for understanding the phrase ἐν σαρκὶ ἐληλυθότα, in particular the verb ἔρχομαι, as referring to Jesus' resurrection appearances. The second section tests this proposal by presenting a reading of 4:1–6, paying special attention to the limiting devices that occur in the verses.

The demonstration of the resurrection

As seen in the review above, the confession itself is similar to 2:22 in that it identifies Jesus as the Christ. Given the context of opposition and antichrists, this parallel is not unexpected. However, this verse lengthens the statement by adding the words ἐν σαρκὶ ἐληλυθότα. The review of how this phrase is understood in the secondary literature revealed that ἐν σαρκί seems to mean the realm of human existence.[55] The questions that remained related to the meaning of the verb ἔρχομαι, and the reason for the addition of the phrase ἐν σαρκὶ ἐληλυθότα to the confession.

ἔρχομαι

The verb ἔρχομαι is such a commonly occurring verb that BDAG comments it 'is not readily susceptible to precise classification' and so instead BDAG is satisfied to outline a number of uses of the verb in the New Testament and other early Christian literature.[56] It most commonly conveys the sense of motion and so is translated with the English words 'come' or 'go'.

The review above revealed two of the uses of ἔρχομαι preferred in understanding ἐν σαρκὶ ἐληλυθότα. Those views that understood the phrase to refer to the incarnation (be it the event or the ongoing continual state), understood ἔρχομαι as describing motion, primarily the motion of the second person of the Trinity's descent from heaven to earth into human flesh. The evidence cited to support this understanding is John 1:9, 11; 3:19. On the other hand, the views that saw the phrase ἐν σαρκὶ ἐληλυθότα as referring to the whole of Jesus' life (including death) or his Messianic status, understood ἔρχομαι not so much in terms of motion but in terms of appearance. Jesus was the one who appeared, thereby fulfilling the Old Testament expectation. The evidence cited as support for this view is John 4:25; 6:14; 7:27, 31, 42; and 11:27. However, neither of these options, even though they are supported with references to John's Gospel, seems to make sense of the phrase. So maybe one of the other uses of ἔρχομαι better suits 1 John 4:2.[57]

In order to suggest a use that better suits the meaning of ἔρχομαι in 4:2, this thesis will again return to the resurrection narratives of John's Gospel for an intertextual link. These narratives were a significant factor in understanding 1:1 and thus important in comprehending the christology of 1 John so far presented in this reading.

[55] See Griffith (2002: 181–3) who cites Galatians 2:20; Philippians 1:22, 24; 1 Timothy 3:16; 1 Peter 4:2; Ignatius, *Ephesians* 1:3; 2 Clement 8:2; Barnabas 5:6–7, 10–11; The Long Recession of Ignatius, *Smyraneans* 6:1; Epistle of Diognetus 5:8–9; 6:3. See also Brown 1982: 493.

[56] BDAG: 393.

[57] Knox (2000) argues that the verb ἔρχομαι is used with reference to five comings of Jesus in the New Testament.

The verb ἔρχομαι is used four times in the resurrection narratives of John 20:19–21:14 to describe the bodily appearances of the resurrected Jesus.[58] First, it is used to describe Jesus' 'coming' or appearance to the disciples (20:19). Usually this would not be significant, given the frequent use of the verb. So for instance, BDAG lists this as an occurrence of the verb 'used w[ith] other verbs to denote that a person, in order to do someth[ing], must first come to a certain place'.[59] However, the second occurrence of the verb cautions against such a view. The verb occurs a second time in 20:24 and is used to summarise the whole first resurrection appearance – 'Thomas ... was not with them when Jesus *came*' (Θωμᾶς ... οὐκ ἦν μετ' αὐτῶν ὅτε ἦλθεν Ἰησοῦς). The aorist tense-form of ἔρχομαι (ἦλθεν) being perfective in aspect indicates this is a summary.[60] That ἔρχομαι is used to summarise the first resurrection appearance reveals that the resurrection was thought of as a 'coming' of Jesus. The verb ἔρχομαι seems to have started to take on some specialised meaning.[61] The third instance of the verb is in 20:26, where it again refers to the appearance of the resurrected Jesus to his disciples, in particular Thomas, so that he could see and feel Jesus' resurrected body. The final occurrence of ἔρχομαι is in 21:13, where again it describes the appearance of the resurrected Jesus. Here again it seems to be used to summarise the resurrection appearance. The conclusion of 21:14 states that this was the third time that the resurrected incarnate Jesus had appeared to his disciples (τοῦτο ἤδη τρίτον ἐφανερώθη Ἰησοῦς τοῖς μαθηταῖς ἐγερθεὶς ἐκ νεκρῶν).[62] Here, ἔρχομαι and φανερόω are similar in meaning, a point Minear observed with reference to 1 John. He comments that ἔρχομαι: 'probably has the force of "to appear, to make an appearance, to come within public view," and is closely aligned to phaneroo, which on the whole seems more characteristic of Johannine thought (1:2; 2:19, 28; 3:2, 5, 8, 10; 4:9).'[63] Minear observes the similarity but understands each as referring to the incarnation. However, in John 20–1 ἔρχομαι and φανερόω are explicitly linked to the resurrection. Each of the three appearances uses the verb ἔρχομαι to describe the action of

---

[58] It is also used with the common meaning of motion in 21:3 and 8, both of which have the disciples as the subject. For a detailed examination of the verb ἔρχομαι in the Johannine literature see Toribio Cuadrado 1993 although, as Silva (1995) points out, Toribio Cuadrado's study suffers major linguistic flaws that limit its results.

[59] BDAG: 394.   [60] Campbell 2008b: 34–9.

[61] The BDAG article does not include the use of ἔρχομαι in John 20:24 in any of its number of meanings.

[62] The aorist tense-form of φανερόω indicates that it is summarising the previous resurrection appearances; see Campbell 2008b: 34–9.

[63] Minear 1970: 294.

appearing (20:19, 24, 26; 21:13), while φανερόω is used to summarise the appearances (21:1, 14).

That ἔρχομαι is used to describe the resurrection appearances of Jesus and structure the resurrection narrative of John's Gospel has not gone unnoticed. In the article on ἔρχομαι in TDNT, Schneider recognises that ἔρχομαι is used to refer to the resurrection appearances. In his section on the verb's use in the Johannine writings, he has a separate section on the use of ἔρχομαι referring to the resurrected Jesus.[64] Further, in this section he notes that the verb structures the resurrection narrative. He states: 'The Johannine accounts of the resurrection appearances are introduced by the words ἔρχεται and ἦλθεν.'[65] ἔρχομαι also refers to the resurrection outside of the resurrection narratives in John's Gospel. It is used this way in the Upper Room Discourse in 14:3, 18, and 28.[66] Scholars have even linked the two sets of passages. Both Schnackenburg and Brown make the link, and note that ἔρχομαι is referring to the resurrection, but fail to make this connection when commenting on 1 John 4:2. So Schnackenburg comments on 20:19: '"He came" just as he had promised his "coming" to the disciples at the time of his farewell (cf. 14:18, 28).'[67] Brown states: 'John's use of "came" may be accidental, but many commentators see here a specific fulfilment of the promise to come back in xiv 18, 28 (same verb).'[68] Following this understanding of ἔρχομαι results in identifying the phrase ἐν σαρκὶ ἐληλυθότα with the resurrection appearances of Jesus in the realm of humanity. The result is that the confession of 4:2 fits with the christology of the rest of 1 John.

It could be objected at this point that this understanding promotes a specialised meaning of ἔρχομαι that is not warranted given its wide usage.[69] However, the fact that the parallel resurrection accounts in Luke do not use the word with reference to Jesus' appearing indicates

---

[64] Schneider 1964: 672–3.

[65] *Ibid.*: 672. It should be noted that Schneider does not think that this use is on view in 1 John 4:2. Under the influence of identifying the opponents as Docetic, Schneider prefers to understand it as a reference to the incarnation (1964: 674). Toribio Cuadrado (1993: 362–363) also notes that ἔρχομαι introduces the resurrection narratives.

[66] BDAG: 394, understands this as a separate usage but fails to recognise the references in John 20:19, 24, 26, and 21:13 as the same meaning. For a contrary view see Moloney 1998: 534.

[67] Schnackenburg 1982: 323.   [68] Brown 1970: 1021.

[69] The wide usage is evident even in 1 John 4:1–3. The cognate ἐξέρχομαι occurs in 4:1 describing the false prophets as those who had 'gone out from' the audience. Further, the antichrists are described as those who the readers have heard 'are coming' (ἔρχεται). However, both these instances are obviously different in that their context is that of the opponents (2:18–19) and not the resurrection christology so far encountered in 1 John.

that John is using it with a particular meaning. Brown notes the lack of ἔρχομαι in Luke 24:36, a verse that 'has almost the same expression' as John 20:19.[70]

It could further be objected that understanding ἔρχομαι as referring to the resurrection lacks precedent in the early church.[71] However, this gives the early church an inappropriately determinative role in assigning meaning and misunderstands the nature of the early church's use of 1 John 4:2. 1 John 4:2–3 is not quoted or alluded to in order to explain what it meant in its original context but rather for the sake of the arguments of the time.[72] The confession was used both in situations of conflict over the incarnation (Polycarp, *Philippians* 7:1; Tertullian, *The Flesh of Christ*, 24; *Against Marcion*, 3.8; 5:16; *Prescription against Heretics*, 33; 3 Corinthians 1:14),[73] and other situations – such as the present life of the believer (Origen's use of 1 John 4:2 in *Homilies on Genesis* 3:7; *Homilies on Exodus* 7; and *Commentary on Romans* 5.8.10),[74] a means of determining between Jewish and Christian prophets (Origen's use of 1 John 4:2 in *Commentary on 1 Corinthians* 12:3),[75] and as referring to the coming of Jesus as the incarnate Messiah fulfilling Old Testament expectation (Origen's use of 1 John 4:2 in *Homilies on Psalms* 49:3; 67:5).[76] This demonstrates that the early church did not understand these verses as only an affirmation of the incarnation, but rather used the confession for their purposes in argument. The earliest uses are not purporting to give the original intent of the confession. So, the fact that the early church does not reflect an understanding of 4:2 proposed in this research does not weaken this reading.

Therefore, this reading proposes that the phrase ἐν σαρκὶ ἐληλυθότα refers to the resurrection 'coming' of Jesus back into the realm of humanity.[77]

---

[70] Brown 1970: 1021. ἔρχομαι does not occur in the Matthean resurrection narrative to refer to the appearance of the risen Jesus; however, one of its cognates does occur – προσέρχομαι (28:18).

[71] I am not aware of it being understood this way anywhere in the history of the church.

[72] Streett 2011: 194–6.

[73] *Ibid.*: 194–5. However, Streett, following Hartog 2005, questions whether Polycarp is written against Docetism. Further, Streett (2011: 195–6) argues that the changes made by both 3 Corinthians and Tertullian of the participle to an infinitive demonstrate that 'the confession as it appears in 1 John is inadequate for rebutting docetism'. The confession is being used for a purpose for which it was not written.

[74] Streett 2011: 175.   [75] *Ibid.*: 196.

[76] *Ibid.*: 196.

[77] This understanding fits well with the parallel non-confession in 4:3 of τὸν Ἰησοῦν since what is on view is the identity of Jesus, that he is the Christ having appeared resurrected in the world; see *Ibid.*: 247.

The reason for the addition of ἐν σαρκὶ ἐληλυθότα

The addition of ἐν σαρκὶ ἐληλυθότα, understood as a reference to the resurrection, should not surprise the reader of 1 John for two reasons.

First, the addition of the phrase links together two of the streams of the christology of 1 John. The first is the affirmation of the resurrection of the incarnate Christ, witnessed and proclaimed by the author (1:1–3). The second is the identification of this risen Christ as Jesus (2:22). Thus the addition to the confession is in keeping with the christology of 1 John.

Second, these two themes are related to each other in the logic of the earliest church, since it is the physical resurrection of Jesus that is seen as the proof that he is the Christ. So, in John's Gospel, the purpose statement of 20:30–1 – revealing that the aim of the author is to move the reader to faith that Jesus is the Christ, the Son of God – follows the resurrection narratives (20:19–29).[78] Thomas confesses that Jesus is God because he meets the physically resurrected Jesus (20:28). In Matthew's Gospel, it is at the resurrection that Jesus states that all authority has been given to him (28:18). Further, the logic is also present in the preaching of the earliest church. Peter cites the physical resurrection as the proof that Jesus is the Christ (Acts 2:25–36), as does Paul (Acts 13:32–7).

So the addition is in keeping with the logic of both the christology of 1 John and the earliest church. It is an addition that states the reason for the identification of Jesus as the Christ, since it is the resurrection that demonstrates that Jesus is the Christ.

The demonstration of the resurrection and 4:1–6

In order to test the viability of understanding ἐν σαρκὶ ἐληλυθότα as referring to the resurrection of Jesus in the sphere of humanity, this section provides a reading of 4:1–6. Since this unit is comprised of three parts – the imperatives and reasoning of 4:1, the test of 4:2–3, and the results of the test in 4:4–6, the reading to test the proposed understanding has three parts. It pays particular attention to the limiting devices (the vocative in 4:4, the closing boundary, and the concluding statement in 4:6) as they are encountered in the reading.

---

[78] It is Jesus' self-designation as 'the resurrection and the life' that causes Martha to confess that 'Jesus is the Christ, the Son of God' (John 11:25–7).

The imperatives and reasoning (4:1)

1 John 3 ends by stating that God has given his Spirit to his people from which they can be confident that they know him (3:24). This prompts the author to warn his readers that not every spirit is to be believed but rather the spirits should be tested. The first verse of 1 John 4 opens with the vocative ἀγαπητοί that directs the readers' attention to two imperatives concerning the spirits (μὴ παντὶ πνεύματι πιστεύετε ἀλλὰ δοκιμάζετε τὰ πνεύματα). This prominence-marking function of the vocative reinforces the seriousness of the commands. The spirit should not be automatically believed but tested to see if its origin is God (εἰ ἐκ τοῦ θεοῦ ἐστιν). Verses 2–3 provide the test to use in ascertaining the origin of the spirits, but before the test is outlined, the author stops to give the reason for the imperatives. The reason (ὅτι) is the existence of many false prophets (πολλοὶ ψευδοπροφῆται) who have gone out (ἐξεληλύθασιν) into the world (εἰς τὸν κόσμον).

In this verse, πνεῦμα refers to the supernatural powers that motivate people. These powers have two sources. They may be evil, as is evident in those that control the false prophets. Or they may be from God, his Spirit who he has given to his people (3:24).[79] This meaning of πνεῦμα continues throughout the rest of 4:1–6.[80] Given the existence of false prophets, the spirits must be tested.

The command to test false prophets, or in this case the spirit that motivated them, was not something new but is evident in the Old Testament (Deuteronomy 13:1–5; 18:15–22). There the test seems to have two parts – that words foretelling the future come to pass (13:1; 18:21–2), and in Deuteronomy 13:2, that the words of the prophet do not encourage apostasy from God and the worship of false gods.[81] The second part of the test is not just applied to false prophets but also to fellow Israelites who have arisen from within the nation (ἐξήλθοσαν ἄνδρες ... ἐξ ὑμῶν) and are encouraging apostasy from God and the worship of false gods (13:12–13).[82] The repetition of the verb ἐξέρχομαι in 2:19 and 4:1 suggests a link between the passages.[83] What is on view in this verse is the spirit that motivated the schism, a spirit that causes people to go after

---

[79] Brown 1982: 486.

[80] Understanding humanity as being motivated by spirits is also evident at Qumran; see 1QS 3:17–21.

[81] Kruse (2000: 147) also notes that Deuteronomy 13:2–6 uses a test of speech to identify false prophets, along with a parallel in *Didache* 11:7–8.

[82] Deuteronomy 13:13–14 (LXX).

[83] 1 John 2:19 and 4:1 are the only two places the verb occurs in 1 John.

other gods and serve them. These false prophets have gone out from the real Israel into the world – that is, they have committed apostasy and are teaching others to do the same, just like the fellow Israelites in Deuteronomy 13:12–13.

The test (4:2–3)

These two verses outline the test that enables the readers to discern between spirits. The opening cataphoric statement causes the reader to search for the postcedent of ἐν τούτῳ and thus gives prominence to the test. It is given as the means by which the readers can know or recognise the Spirit of God (γινώσκετε τὸ πνεῦμα τοῦ θεοῦ). If the spirit is able to make the confession, then it is from God (ἐκ τοῦ θεοῦ ἐστιν), if not, then it is not from God (ἐκ τοῦ θεοῦ οὐκ ἔστιν). The second part of the confession is abbreviated so that the text only contains the words τὸν Ἰησοῦν instead of the full phrase of the confession in 4:2 Ἰησοῦν Χριστὸν ἐν σαρκὶ ἐληλυθότα.[84] The abbreviation results in a shorter second line but the article before Jesus in 4:3 (τὸν Ἰησοῦν) is anaphoric, referring to the Jesus described in the confession.[85] This further supports the contention that the confession is about the identity of Jesus – that he is the Christ having appeared in the sphere of humanity.

The spirit that does not confess this is identified as not from God but as the antichrist (ἐκ τοῦ θεοῦ οὐκ ἔστιν· καὶ τοῦτό ἐστιν τὸ τοῦ ἀντιχρίστου). This reference again links this unit and the confession with 2:18–27, since this is the last place that the antichrists were mentioned in 1 John. Further, the existence of this opponent to the Christ (i.e. to identifying Jesus as the Christ), was foretold to the readers (ὃ ἀκηκόατε ὅτι ἔρχεται) and is present in the world (καὶ νῦν ἐν τῷ κόσμῳ ἐστὶν ἤδη). This repeats 2:18, forming another link between the two units.

Thus the test reveals those who speak by the Spirit of God, because they can confess that Jesus is the Christ having come in the flesh, and those who speak under the influence of the spirit of the antichrist, the false prophets, who deny that understanding of Jesus.

The results (4:4–6)

There are three results that the writer draws from the test. The vocative τεκνία towards the start of verse 4 indicates that the writer has progressed

[84] Loader 1992: 50.
[85] de Boer 1991: 333; Griffith 1998: 270.

from the test to the results, each of which start with a plural personal pronoun (ὑμεῖς, αὐτοί, ἡμεῖς). The paragraph concludes with an anaphoric pronominal phrase (ἐκ τούτου) that summarises the paragraph as the means by which the audience distinguish the spirits (γινώσκομεν τὸ πνεῦμα τῆς ἀληθείας καὶ τὸ πνεῦμα τῆς πλάνης).

The first result is that the readers can be confident that they are from God (ἐκ τοῦ θεοῦ) and have conquered the false prophets motivated by the spirit of the antichrist (καὶ νενικήκατε αὐτούς).[86] This is because (ὅτι) God, who is in them by his Spirit, is greater than the antichrist who is in the world.[87]

The second result is in contrast to the first because it describes the false prophets as from the world (ἐκ τοῦ κόσμου).[88] Because the false prophets are from the world, they speak in terms drawn from the world (ἐκ τοῦ κόσμου) and the world listens to them. The phrase ἐκ τοῦ κόσμου occurs twice in this verse but it occurred before in the description of the world in 2:15–17. There, the apostate desires of 2:16 were said to stem from the world (ἐκ τοῦ κόσμου). That is, the false prophets speak a message of apostasy that draws people out of the True Israel into the world at large, a world against God. This message does not affect all the True Israel but it does seduce those who were not part of the True Israel, those who were masquerading under the guise of Israel.[89] This reading of the verse continues the theme of true and faithless Israel as the self-understanding of the audience as presented in the exegesis of 1:6–2:11 and especially 2:19f.

The third result sees a return to the use of the first-person plural (ἡμεῖς), aligning the author with the audience. The author assures the readers that they, together with the readers, are from God and then adds that those who know God listen to them, while those who do not know God do not listen to them. This assurance that they are heard further supports the proposal that the readership thinks about themselves as the True Israel. Israel's task was to declare the praises of God to the nations (Exodus 19:5–6) and to be a light to the nations (Isaiah 2:2–5 echoed in 1 John 1:7).

---

[86] Understanding ψευδοπροφῆται to be the antecedent of the masculine plural pronoun αὐτούς. Strecker 1996: 137.

[87] θεός is the subject of the masculine article in this clause and ἀντίχριστος is the subject of the masculine article in the next clause. *Ibid.*: 137.

[88] This again understands ψευδοπροφῆται as the antecedent of αὐτοί.

[89] Perkins (1979: 53) notes that 'Verse 5 is just another of the author's appeals to the rhetoric of the fourth gospel to identify the opponents with the "unbelieving Jews" (who are "from the world," Jn 8:23).'

The paragraph concludes with a summary that the test provides results that display the spirit of truth and the spirit of deception (τὸ πνεῦμα τῆς ἀληθείας καὶ τὸ πνεῦμα τῆς πλάνης).

Summary

This reading of 4:1–6 has demonstrated the viability of the proposal that ἐν σαρκὶ ἐληλυθότα refers to the resurrection appearances of Jesus in the realm of humanity. It supports the understanding of the christology of the introduction and explicitly refers to the resurrection of the incarnate Christ. Further, it harmonises with the understanding of the denial of the antichrists as understood in 2:22, that they denied that Jesus was the Christ. In these verses, the confession that the antichrists are not able to make is the resurrection of the incarnate Christ, the very proof that Jesus was the Christ.

Plausibility tangents

This final section aims to present tangents to this reading to demonstrate its plausibility. There are three sets of tangents that provide support for this reading of 4:1–6.

First, understanding ἐν σαρκὶ ἐληλυθότα to be a reference to the resurrection appearances of Jesus in the human sphere finds parallel in the confession of faith in 1 Timothy 3:16.

This confession opens with the clause ἐφανερώθη ἐν σαρκί that refers to the resurrection appearances of Jesus.[90] There is general agreement among scholars that ἐν σαρκί is being used in the same way in 1 Timothy 3:16 and 1 John 4:2 as a reference to the realm of humanity. However, some scholars understand 1 Timothy 3:16 to affirm the incarnation and not the resurrection appearances.[91] This understanding is often under the influence of thinking the use of φανερόω in 1 John 1:2; 3:5 and 8 refers to the incarnation.[92] However, this research has noted Minear's observation that ἔρχομαι and φανερόω are similar in 1 John,[93] and that 1 John 1:2; 3:5 and 8 do not refer to the incarnation but rather the appearances of the incarnate Christ, both resurrection appearances and appearances as the high priest in heaven. Further, Collins finds ἐφανερώθη ἐν σαρκί

[90] Collins 2002: 108–9.
[91] Bockmuehl 1988: 98; MacLeod 2002: 339–40.
[92] For example Mounce 2000: 227; Towner 2006: 278–80.
[93] Minear 1970: 294.

Table 11. *Comparison of 1 John 4:2 and 1 Timothy 3:16*

1 John 4:2	ἐν σαρκὶ ἐληλυθότα
1 Timothy 3:16	ἐφανερώθη ἐν σαρκί

in 1 Timothy 3:16 as a reference to the resurrection, citing the resurrec-tion narratives of Luke 24:36–43 and John 20:24–9, the use of φανερόω in Mark 16:12, 14; John 21:2, 14; and Barnabas 15:9 as support for his conclusions. Additionally, Marshall, in a review of Griffith (2002), notes that Barnabas 5:6 uses the same vocabulary (ἐν σαρκὶ ἔδει αὐτὸν φανερωθῆναι) in a context where the resurrection is clearly the referent. The result is that Marshall links 1 John 4:2 with the resurrection of Jesus: 'I doubt whether the reference in Barnabas 5:6f. can be emptied of mean-ing: there the fact that Jesus was manifested "in the flesh" is significant in relation to the concept of the resurrection.'[94] Marshall does not take this line of observation any further than a point of weakness in Griffith's argument. However, his observation furthers the reading proposed above because it demonstrated that the vocabulary was used of the resurrection in the early church.

Second, this understanding of ἐν σαρκὶ ἐληλυθότα is similar to two of Paul's confessions. In 1 Corinthians 12:3, Paul states that only people speaking under the influence of the Holy Spirit can say 'Jesus is Lord' (Κύριος Ἰησοῦς). The similar context of spirit inspired speech along with the confession being about Jesus reveals parallels between 1 John 4:2 and 1 Corinthians 12:3.[95] The confessions are equivalent if ἐν σαρκὶ ἐληλυθότα is understood to be a reference to the resurrection appearances of Jesus, since it is these that confirm he is both the Lord and Christ.[96] These parallel passages support the plausibility of under-standing ἐν σαρκὶ ἐληλυθότα to be about the resurrection appearances of Jesus. The same confession occurs again in Romans 10:9, where the

[94] Marshall 2003: 94.
[95] Dodd (1946: 98–9) is one of many scholars who acknowledge the parallel between 1 Corinthians 12:3 and 1 John 4:2. However, he does not pursue the parallel as a means for understanding what is meant by ἐν σαρκὶ ἐληλυθότα but rather assumes it is a reference to the incarnation, under the influence of his historical reconstruction that identifies the opponents as forerunners of the Gnostics.
[96] Peter draws this conclusion from the resurrection at the end of his first sermon at Pentecost (Acts 2:36 – καὶ κύριον αὐτὸν καὶ χριστὸν ἐποίησεν ὁ θεός, τοῦτον τὸν Ἰησοῦν ὃν ὑμεῖς ἐσταυρώσατε). In personal conversation David Jackson pointed out to me the option that the phrase καὶ χριστὸν could be epexegetical here and so 'Lord' and 'Christ' are two ways of referring to the same concept. This would fit the paralleling of the confessions.

Lordship of Jesus is explicitly linked to the resurrection. Dunn comments on Romans 10:9 that: '[B]elief in the resurrection of Jesus is here a corollary of the confession that Jesus is Lord.'[97] This again reveals the logic of linking the resurrection with Jesus' Lordship or his identification as the Christ. This further supports the suggestion that ἐν σαρκὶ ἐληλυθότα be understood to be a reference to the resurrection appearances of Jesus in the realm of humanity.

Third, the denial of the resurrection is evident in the earliest church. To start with, the resurrection was denied in the philosophical and religious context of the earliest church.[98] Epicurean philosophers (Acts 17:18) and the Sadducees (Matthew 22:23, 28, 30ff.; Mark 12:18, 23; Luke 20:27, 33, 35ff.; Acts 23:8) both denied the physical resurrection. Further, the Jewish leaders in particular denied Jesus' resurrection from the very start. So, in Matthew 28:12–13, the Jewish leaders bribe the soldiers who were guarding the tomb when Jesus was raised, not to tell others about the resurrection, but rather to report that his disciples stole the body. The idea of the resurrection continued to be problematic in the earliest church, with some denying it (1 Corinthians 15:22ff.) and others stating that it had already come (2 Timothy 2:16–18). So it makes sense for a confession to include a reference to the resurrection as a means of testing the spirits.

Thus this reading, that understands the confession as 'Jesus is the Christ having appeared in the realm of humanity', is consistent with the teaching of the early church's confessions. Further, given the philosophical and religious climate of the earliest church, where the resurrection of Jesus was in dispute, it would have served well as a test of the spirits.

Conclusion

This chapter explicated 1 John 4:1–6, arguing that the confession of 4:2 is a reference to the resurrection appearances of Jesus in the sphere of humanity. Intertextual links with the resurrection narratives of John's Gospel were cited as the reason for this understanding, before an intertextual reading of 4:1–6 was carried out in order to demonstrate the validity of the proposal. Finally, three tangents to the understanding were suggested that demonstrate its plausibility.

This chapter has demonstrated that the resurrection is mentioned in at least one other place than the introductory verses. Therefore it refutes the view that the resurrection is not referred to in 1 John. The consistency

[97] Dunn 1988: 609.   [98] See further Bolt 1998.

of the christology across the text so far has reinforced the decision to understand 1:1–3 as affirming the resurrection of the incarnate Christ. This chapter has further supported this argument.

The next chapter of this thesis presents the results of the application of the reading method to the remaining verses of 1 John.

8

THE RESURRECTION OF THE CRUCIFIED JESUS: 1 JOHN 4:7–5:21

This chapter outlines a reading of 1 John 4:7–5:21 that is consistent with the christology of the resurrection of the incarnate Christ and the audience's view of themselves as the True Israel as presented in 1 John 1:1–4:6. It continues to utilise the method described in chapter 2, giving the results of the method rather than reviewing each step in detail. Particular attention is paid to 4:9–10; 5:6–8, and 20 since these passages are often understood to affirm a christology that is different from that suggested here, and 5:21 since it is usually understood as supporting a historical reconstruction different from the proposal suggested in chapters 4 and 5. There are three main parts to this chapter: 4:7–5:4a, 5:4b–15, and 5:16–21.

1 John 4:7–5:4a

The body of 1 John started with the topic paragraph about the world (2:15–17) and then described two aspects of the world – the existence of antichrists (2:18–27) and the identity of the readers as being born of God (2:28–3:12). The next two units started with negative imperatives (3:13; 4:1), seemingly providing some implications of living in this world. These implications continue, with the opening boundary of this unit (4:7) containing a cohortative (ἀγαπῶμεν). The change from a negative imperative to a positive command may flow from the double imperative of 4:1, where the first is negative and the second is positive. The language of 'love' reappears and continues as a theme until 5:4a, where the vocabulary ceases to occur, indicating a closing boundary.

Gaps and limiting devices

At first glance this unit seems to be a series of unrelated sentences due to the high frequency of asyndesis, so there should be a significant amount of interruption to the flow of sentences. However, no real interruption to the flow of sentences is experienced due to the high repetition of vocabulary that holds the unit together. The verb ἀγαπάω and its cognates ἀγάπη and ἀγαπητός occur 34 times in this unit of 16 verses. As a result there are no real gaps in this section due to an interruption to the flow of the sentences.

Cataphoric pronouns occur in four places in this unit. Three of these four involve the phrase ἐν τούτῳ.[1] In each case the postcedent of the phrase closely follows the pronoun (τὸν υἱὸν αὐτοῦ τὸν μονογενῆ ἀπέσταλκεν ὁ θεὸς εἰς τὸν κόσμον ἵνα ζήσωμεν δι' αὐτοῦ in 4:9, ἡμεῖς ἠγαπήκαμεν τὸν θεὸν ἀλλ' ὅτι αὐτὸς ἠγάπησεν ἡμᾶς καὶ ἀπέστειλεν τὸν υἱὸν αὐτοῦ ἱλασμὸν περὶ τῶν ἁμαρτιῶν ἡμῶν in 4:10, and ὅταν τὸν θεὸν ἀγαπῶμεν καὶ τὰς ἐντολὰς αὐτοῦ ποιῶμεν in 5:2), resulting in the reader experiencing no gap. The other cataphoric use of a pronoun occurs in 5:3 (αὕτη γάρ ἐστιν ἡ ἀγάπη τοῦ θεοῦ). Its postcedent (ἵνα τὰς ἐντολὰς αὐτοῦ τηρῶμεν) is the next clause, so there is no gap.

There is only one reader-experienced gap in this unit – the christological affirmations that the Father sent (ἀποστέλλω) his Son into the world (4:9, 10, 14). When stress is placed on the verb ἀποστέλλω, the verses appear to be about the incarnation.[2] This impression is further strengthened due to the perceived parallels with 1 John 1:1–3, a passage also understood in the secondary literature as affirming the incarnation.[3] This impression could be understood to be contrary to the christology proposed in this reading's understanding of 1 John, thus causing a gap.

Therefore there is only one gap in this unit that requires attention – the Christological affirmations of 4:9, 10, and 14. Are they consistent with the understanding of the christology of 1 John as presented in this research or do they question this proposal?

Of the three limiting devices, there are no uses of γράφω in these verses. There are two vocatives in this unit that limit the possible way gaps are filled. The first (ἀγαπητοί) in 4:7 draws the readers' attention to the cohortative that starts the unit and seems to signal a progression in the argument with the reintroduction of the theme of love. The second

---

[1] The phrase ἐν τούτῳ also occurs in 4:17, where it is anaphoric rather than cataphoric.

[2] See for example Westcott (1966: 125), who lists them in his additional note on 3:5 – Aspects of the Incarnation. Further, both Dunn (1980: 56–9) and Brown (1982: 517) call them 'incarnational formulas'. Westcott (1966: 148) even states: 'The manifestation and the essence of love … are distinguished, though both are seen in the Incarnation.'

[3] Bultmann (1973: 67) and Painter (2002: 266, 269) both see parallels with 1:1–3 on the basis of ἐφανερώθη and ἐν ἡμῖν. This leads Bultmann to say 'ἐφανερώθη ("made manifest") means the revelation in the historical event of Jesus' appearance'. Smalley (2007: 229) acknowledges that in general φανερόω as a verb can refer to the resurrection but understands it in 1:1–3 as alluding to the incarnation.

vocative in 4:11 (ἀγαπητοί again) draws the readers' attention to the way of living that the audience should follow (ἡμεῖς ὀφείλομεν ἀλλήλους ἀγαπᾶν). This vocative marks the conclusion of the paragraph, since the cohortative of 4:7 (ἀγαπῶμεν ἀλλήλους) is followed with reasoning in 4:8–10 before it is restated in 4:11. These vocatives limit the way the gaps in 4:9 and 10 can be filled because they indicate that 4:8–10 are giving reasons for the command to love one another.

The closing boundary of the unit (5:4a) also limits how gaps are filled. The boundary was identified on the basis of repeated vocabulary – the theme of love. Since the vocabulary of love (ἀγαπητός, ἀγαπάω and ἀγάπη) is absent from 5:4b onwards, it appears that the gaps in 4:9, 10, and 14 should all be filled with reference to the theme of love.

Within this theme, three other vocabulary clusters are also evident. In 4:9–10 and 14, there is a cluster of the verb ἀποστέλλω. In 4:17–18 there is a cluster of vocabulary associated with fear (φόβος). Again, in 4:19–21 there is a cluster of vocabulary associated with loving the brothers (ἀδελφός). These clusters seem to indicate paragraphs within the progression of the argument of this unit. These clusters again limit the way these verses can be understood.

An intertextual fill

These verses require a decision about the meaning of ἀποστέλλω and the significance placed on the meaning. The verb need not be a reference to the incarnation but rather it could be a reference to a mission. Elsewhere, the verb is used of people, angels, and even spirits being sent on a mission.[4]

This meaning of mission is evident in John's Gospel. So for example, in 1:6 God sends John the Baptist, in 1:19 the Jews of Jerusalem send Priests and Levites, in 1:24 some Pharisees had been sent, in 3:28 John the Baptist was sent. None of these occurrences implies a divine pre-existence. Rather, the people mentioned are all sent on a mission. Even the first occurrence of ἀποστέλλω with Jesus as the object (3:17) does not imply incarnation but rather mission.[5] Thus if the gap is filled by understanding ἀποστέλλω as referring to Jesus' mission rather than his incarnation, then there is no need to question this reading of 1 John's christology.

---

[4] Yarbrough 2008: 238.

[5] Westcott (1966: 125) notes that mission is the key element to this verb's meaning but still places the verb in the group of words used to describe the incarnation.

Table 12. *Statements using ἀποστέλλω in Parallel*

4:9	τὸν υἱὸν αὐτοῦ τὸν μονογενῆ *ἀπέσταλκεν* ὁ θεὸς εἰς τὸν κόσμον ἵνα ζήσωμεν δι' αὐτοῦ.
4:10	*ἀπέστειλεν* τὸν υἱὸν αὐτοῦ ἱλασμὸν περὶ τῶν ἁμαρτιῶν ἡμῶν.
4:14	ὁ πατὴρ *ἀπέσταλκεν* τὸν υἱὸν σωτῆρα τοῦ κόσμου.

Further, when the three verses that use ἀποστέλλω are placed in parallel to each other, it is evident that the verb is used to introduce an aspect of Jesus' mission. The aspect is given in the rest of the sentence.[6]

So Jesus was sent in order that the readers might have life (4:9), to be a propitiation for sin (4:10), and to be the saviour of the world (4:14). Each of these descriptions of Jesus' mission are elements or results of his death and resurrection. So, when emphasis is not placed on the incarnational meaning of ἀποστέλλω, there is no challenge posed to this research's understanding of the christology of 1 John. On the contrary, when the verb is understood in terms of mission and the focus is shifted to understanding the mission in terms of the rest of the sentence, the christology of the glorification of the incarnate Christ is affirmed in these verses. A number of scholars understand these references in this manner.[7] Even Painter, who prefers the incarnation meaning of ἀποστέλλω, concedes that: 'The sending is understood to have a saving purpose, to save the world (4:14), that we might live through him (4:9). Involved in this is the death of the Son as an expiation for sins (4:10; ... 2:2; cf. 1:7).'[8] Thus when the gap in meaning of ἀποστέλλω is filled with a reference to 'mission' and stress is placed evenly across the sentence and not just on the verb, rather than questioning this research, these verses are seen to support this reading's proposed christology.

---

[6] Strecker (1996: 150) quotes Kramer (1966: 113) that there is 'a definite pattern, for the first clause speaks of the sending, the next unfolds its saving significance, sometimes by means of a ἵνα-clause, sometimes by phrase of apposition'.

[7] See for instance Brown 1982: 551–2; Strecker 1996: 150; Smalley 2007: 230; Streett 2011: 191. Kruse (2000: 160) warns against denying any reference to the incarnation in these verses. This research aims to avoid this denial by understanding the verses as affirming the death and resurrection of the incarnate Christ. The point of dispute in this gap is with the stress being placed on ἀποστέλλω at the expense of the following clause so that it is interpreted as a reference to the incarnation alone.

[8] Painter 2002: 207.

An intertextual reading of 4:7–5:4a

These verses can be grouped into three sub-units. The first (4:7–11) gives the command to love one another and provides theological reasoning for the command. The second sub-unit (4:12–16) addresses the issue of remaining in an unseen God. The third sub-unit (4:17–5:4a) outlines three implications of loving God – confidence before God (4:17–18), the need to love one's brothers (4:19–21), and the means of recognising one's brothers (5:1–4a).

The first sub-unit (4:7–11) starts with the command to love one another (ἀγαπῶμεν ἀλλήλους). Three reasons (ὅτι) are given for this command in 4:7b–8: love is from God, the one loving has been born of and knows God, and the one not loving does not know God because God is love. The unit then provides two examples (4:9–10) of how God's love is revealed, demonstrating both that the love is from God and that God is love. Both examples cite God's action of sending (ἀποστέλλω) his Son, first to achieve life for his people (4:9) and second as a propitiation for their sins (4:10).[9] Jesus' mission, as God assigned it, resulted in the readers living since Jesus acted as a sacrifice for the readers' sins. The final verse in this unit (4:11) restates the command of 4:7 to love (ἀλλήλους ἀγαπᾶν) but ties it explicitly to God's love, as is evident in the conditional statement (εἰ οὕτως ὁ θεὸς ἠγάπησεν ἡμᾶς, καὶ ἡμεῖς ὀφείλομεν). Thus the mission meaning of ἀποστέλλω fits within the logic of the first sub-unit.

The second sub-unit (4:12–16) opens with a statement that no one has ever seen God (θεὸν οὐδεὶς πώποτε τεθέαται). Even though God's love is evident in the mission of his Son, the objection could be raised that God has not been seen. The actions of God may reveal love, but what about his person? If God is love, then how can the readers share in this love? In answering this objection the writer contends that if the readers love one another, then God remains in them and his love is made complete in them (4:12). That is, loving one another results in more than just seeing God. The result of loving one another is that God remains in the readers and perfects his love in the readers. This connection, that is greater than sight, is confirmed through God's gift of his Spirit (4:13). Yet this love is predicated on seeing the outworking of God's love. The author saw and testifies that God sent his Son to save the world (4:14).[10]

---

[9] Morris 1965: 205–8.

[10] The return to the first-person plural is in the same vein as 1:1–5. The events of Jesus' life, death, and resurrection were seen by a number of people, not just the author.

It is the confession that Jesus is the Son of God, the Messiah, that results in God remaining in the audience and the audience in God (4:15). That confession requires the audience to love (4:11) and results in the author and audience knowing and believing God's love is in them (4:16). Thus the writer can affirm that God is love, because it is seen in his actions and in the actions of his people, and so those remaining in love remain in God and He in them (4:16).

The third sub-unit (4:17–5:4a) outlines three implications of loving God and remaining in him. First, remaining in God's love means that the readers can have confidence before God on the Judgement Day (4:17–18). The phrase ἐν τούτῳ is anaphoric, indicating that the way love is made complete in the readers is by them remaining in God. The result of remaining in God is confidence on the Day of Judgement (παρρησίαν ἔχωμεν ἐν τῇ ἡμέρᾳ τῆς κρίσεως). This is because (ὅτι) the readers in this world are just as Jesus is in heaven. Since the readers remain in God and he in them, they are united to him. Even though they are in this world, they are united to Christ. This unity with Christ theme was evident in 2:28–3:12, where it allowed the author to state that the readers do not sin (3:6, 9). Thus there is no need to fear judgement because the perfect love, by which God remains in the audience and they remain in God, drives out fear (4:18). There is no punishment to be feared because they are not seen as sinners but as Jesus, due to their unity with him by perfect love.

The second implication of loving God and remaining in him is that the audience must love their brothers. The command is to love because God loved the readers first (4:19). They cannot claim to love God and not love their brothers (4:20) because God commanded that those who love him must also love their brothers (4:21).

The third implication is that this love indicates the identity of the brothers. Everyone who believes that Jesus is the Christ, is born from God and loves others who are born of God (5:1). That the readers love God's children is evident when they love God and obey his commandments (5:2). Love of God is obedience to his commands, commands that are not difficult because those who are born of him have conquered the world (5:3–4).[11]

---

[11] Smalley (2007: 258) acknowledges that believers have victory 'through the risen Christ (cf: 2:13–14, 18; 5:18–19)' but fails to expand what is meant by 'risen' and does not cite the resurrection as on view in his exegesis of either set of verses. This thesis finds an explicit reference to the resurrection in 5:20.

Tangents

There are a couple of other places in the New Testament that provide tangents to the understanding of ἀποστέλλω proposed in this reading. These tangents demonstrate the plausibility of understanding the verb to be a reference to 'a mission'.

First, ἀποστέλλω is used when referring to some people's missions. Moses was sent to be the ruler and deliver of Israel (Acts 7:35). Peter and John were sent to Samaria to confirm that the Samaritans had received the gospel (Acts 8:14). Cornelius sent messengers for Peter (Acts 10:17, 20; 11:11, 13). Preachers of the gospel in general are sent (Romans 10:15). Paul was sent to preach (Acts 26:17; 1 Corinthians 1:17). Angels are sent to minister to people (Hebrews 1:14). So to understand ἀποστέλλω as referring to 'a mission' is within the semantic domain of the verb.

Second, ἀποστέλλω is used of Jesus' mission in Acts. So, rather than referring to his incarnation, the verb occurs in 3:26 referring to his post-resurrection mission. Further, the verb is used of Jesus' second coming in 3:20. Again the 'mission' meaning, rather than incarnation, is prevalent. So the understanding of ἀποστέλλω as referring to the pre- and post-resurrection mission of Jesus, rather than his incarnation alone, is attested to elsewhere in the earliest Christian documents.

Third, a very similar formula to 1 John 4:9, 10, and 14 occurs in Romans 8:3 and Galatians 4:4.[12] In each, Jesus is presented as sent for the purpose of salvation. The mission meaning, rather than the incarnation, makes better sense of each verse. So, although Romans 8:3 uses πέμπω rather than ἀποστέλλω, Jesus was sent to be a sin-offering and so condemn sin. In Galatians 4:4–5, Jesus was sent in order to redeem his people. In each verse, there is material that could result in the 'sent' verb being understood as a reference to the incarnation (i.e. ἐν ὁμοιώματι σαρκὸς ἁμαρτίας in Romans 8:3, and γενόμενον ἐκ γυναικός, γενόμενον ὑπὸ νόμον in Galatians 4:4). However, these 'incarnation' references are used to better explain the mission of Jesus as outlined in the second part of each verse. So in Romans 8:3, Jesus is described in terms of sinful flesh because he is the one who as a sin-offering condemned sin in the flesh (καὶ περὶ ἁμαρτίας κατέκρινεν τὴν ἁμαρτίαν ἐν τῇ σαρκί). Again, in Galatians 4:4, Jesus is described as being born of a woman and born under law so that he can redeem those under the law (ἵνα τοὺς ὑπὸ νόμον

---

[12] See Kramer 1966 contra Schweizer 1966.

ἐξαγοράσῃ).[13] Thus the logic of understanding ἀποστέλλω in 1 John 4:9, 10 and 14 as referring to the mission of Jesus that is then further explicated in the following clauses is viable since it occurs elsewhere in the earliest Christian documents.

Therefore it seems plausible to understand the verb ἀποστέλλω with its 'mission' meaning.

Summary

These verses pose no difficulties to the understanding of the christology developed in this reading of 1 John. On the contrary, when ἀποστέλλω is understood with a 'mission' meaning, 1 John 4:9, 10, and 14 support the notion that the letter affirms the death of the incarnate Christ.

1 John 5:4b–15

A new unit starts at 5:4b, as the vocabulary of love ceases to be used, and extends down to 5:16, where the theme of sin reoccurs.[14] The last few verses of 1 John 4:7–5:4a reintroduce the identity of the readers as being born of God (5:1–4a). This reintroduction is coupled with a statement about the identity of Jesus as the Christ (5:1), the point of dispute with the antichrists (2:22–23). The combination of these twin aspects of this world brings 1 John to a climax outlined in 5:4b–15. This unit is held together by a threefold repetition of the cataphoric statement καὶ αὕτη ἐστὶν (5:4b, 11, 14). The readers, by believing that Jesus is the Christ/ Son of God, are born of God and so have overcome the world (5:4b), have the true testimony of God about his Son (5:11), and have confidence before God in prayer (5:14). The γράφω statement in 5:13 confirms the climactic nature of this unit and its tone of assurance.[15]

Gaps and limiting devices

There are no real interruptions to the flow of sentences in this unit. Even when the sentences are asyndetic, there is continuity as a result of

---

[13] That this verse also speaks of birth indicates that ἐξαποστέλλω alone is not enough to indicate a reference to the incarnation.

[14] Scholars who see a division of the text at 5:4 or 5:5 include Windisch 1930; Gaugler 1964; Bultmann 1973; Marshall 1978; Perkins 1979; de Boor 1982; Stott 1988; Schnackenburg 1992; Johnson 1993; Strecker 1996; Kruse 2000; Rensberger 2001; Schmid 2002; Thomas 2003; Smalley 2007; Lieu 2008a.

[15] Coetzee 1979: 45.

repeated vocabulary. So for example, the theme of witness (μαρτυρέω, μαρτυρία) links 5:9 to 5:7–8 even though 5:9 is asyndetic. The theme of life (ζωή) links 5:11–13 together even though both 5:12 and 13 are asyndetic. And the continuity between 5:13 to 5:14–15 is effected by an assuring tone evident in the repetition of the verb οἶδα (5:13, 15). This means there are no gaps as a result of interruptions to the flow of sentences in 5:4–15.

Pronouns are used cataphorically three times in this unit, all with the phrase καὶ αὕτη ἐστὶν (5:4b, 11, and 14). Since the postcedent of the pronoun closely follows each time (ἡ πίστις ἡμῶν in 5:4b, ζωὴν αἰώνιον ἔδωκεν ἡμῖν ὁ θεός in 5:11, and ἐάν τι αἰτώμεθα κατὰ τὸ θέλημα αὐτοῦ ἀκούει ἡμῶν in 5:14), the phrase does not form a gap, while its repetition gives it prominence. It seems to mark three points in the unit where conclusions are drawn. There are also two occurrences of pronouns being used in ways that could be either cataphoric or anaphoric and thus require the reader to make a choice, resulting in a momentary gap. 1 John 5:6 starts with the phrase οὗτός ἐστιν ὁ ἐλθὼν δι' ὕδατος καὶ αἵματος. This could refer to 5:5 and so be anaphoric, or to Ἰησοῦς Χριστός (the very next phrase) and so be cataphoric. Either way, the gap is quickly filled because of the proximity of the referent. In 5:9 the phrase αὕτη ἐστὶν ἡ μαρτυρία τοῦ θεοῦ occurs. Given that the phrase is followed by ὅτι, which could indicate a content clause, and the last use of the phrase in 5:6 was cataphoric, the reader would expect the same in 5:9. However, the phrase is anaphoric, referring to the three witnesses of the blood, the water, and the spirit, and the ὅτι is not recitative but causal.[16] Thus the cataphoric uses of pronouns do not seem to cause gaps in this unit.

There is one reader-experienced gap in these verses – the referents of 'water' and 'blood' in 5:6–8. The gap is felt throughout the secondary literature. For example Culpepper states: 'Verse 6 … is notorious for its ambiguity. The problem is not broken grammar or lack of clarity but our inability to determine the precise nuances water and blood would have had for the Johannine Christians.'[17] Burge also comments: 'First John 5:6 is perhaps the most perplexing verse in all of the Johannine letters.'[18] Accordingly, the secondary literature understands the christological material of 5:6–8 in a variety of ways.[19] The phrase ὁ ἐλθὼν δι' ὕδατος

[16] Yarbrough 2008: 286; Smalley 2007: 270.
[17] Culpepper 1985: 101.   [18] Burge 1996: 201.
[19] The following list is representative of the main options and groups them together for descriptive purposes. The summary nature of each group results in a loss of the particular nuances of each. For an exhaustive survey and critique of how the secondary literature

καὶ αἵματος is understood as referring to the sacraments of baptism and the Eucharist,[20] the incarnation,[21] the birth and death of Jesus,[22] the baptism and death of Jesus,[23] Jesus' baptismal ministry and sacrificial death,[24] the death of Jesus,[25] and the messianic identity of Jesus.[26] Most of these proposals are inconsistent with the understanding of the previous christological affirmations in 1 John expressed above. Thus there is a gap involving the understanding of the referent of 'water and blood' in 5:6–8.[27]

Although there are no uses of the vocative in this unit, γράφω occurs in 5:13. The anaphoric use of the pronoun (ταῦτα ἔγραψα ὑμῖν) could refer to the directly preceding verses and thus just this unit.[28] The result is that it limits how gaps in the immediate context can be interpreted. However, the pronoun could also be understood to refer to the whole of 1 John,[29] thus limiting the way that gaps can be understood, not just

has understood these verses see Streett 2011: 258–99. Briefer reviews are found in Brown 1982: 575–8; Lieu 2008a: 209–12.

[20] Westcott 1966: 182; Vouga 1990: 72–3; Burge 1996: 201; Strecker 1996: 183. Dodd (1946: 128–31) also understands the phrase as referring to the sacraments because he perceives the sacraments as continually witnessing the baptism and death of Jesus.

[21] Richter 1977: 122–34; Goulder 1999: 343–4.

[22] Witherington 1989: 160; Larsen 1990b; Culy 2004: 125–6; Witherington 2006: 545.

[23] Wurm 1903: 68; Plummer 1911: 158–9; Brooke 1912: 133; Gore 1920: 192–3; Windisch 1930: 132; Ross 1954: 213–14; Houlden 1973: 127; Bultmann 1973: 79; Wengst 1976: 18–24; Marshall 1978: 231–2; Bruce 1979: 118–19; Coetzee 1979: 47–50; Perkins 1979: 61; Barker 1981: 350; de Boor 1982: 149–51; Palmer 1982: 75; Burdick 1985: 364–8; Stott 1988: 180; Wengst 1988: 3759; Hengel 1989: 62; Hiebert 1991: 234–7; Loader 1992: 67; Johnson 1993: 126; Carson 1994: 226–30; Burge 1996: 202; Womack 1998: 122–3; Akin 2001: 196–7; Painter 2002: 306; Griffith 2002: 157–60; Brown 2003: 250–1; Heckel 2004: 440; Kinlaw 2005: 103–4; Beeke 2006: 194–6; Smalley 2007: 265–7; Yarbrough 2008: 282–3; Jones 2009: 213–14. Beutler (2000: 120–3) understands 'water' and 'blood' as referring to the baptism and death of Jesus, which is also presently testified to in the church through the sacraments of baptism and Eucharist.

[24] Kruse 2000: 178.

[25] Perkins 1979: 61; Brown 1982: 578; Culpepper 1985: 101–3; de Boer 1988; Schnackenburg 1992: 236–7; Thompson 1992: 132–5; Neufeld 1994: 131; Sloyan 1995: 51–2; Rensberger 2001: 89–92; Michaels 2002: 159–60; Schmid 2002: 202; Thomas 2003: 252; Morgen 2005a: 195.

[26] Haupt 1879: 298–313; Streett 2011: 310–37. Lieu (2008a: 212–13) presents a variant of this, arguing that the images, even though they escape identification, were common to the author and the audience, and are used to indicate that Jesus is the Son of God.

[27] The textual variant in 5:7–8 is fairly widely understood as an addition due to its lack of early external witness, and its ability to be explained as an addition as a Trinitarian formula. See for instance Brown 1982: 775–87; Klauck 1991: 303–11; Metzger 1994: 647–9; Strecker 1996: 188–91; Yarbrough 2008: 293.

[28] Schnackenburg 1992: 247; Derickson 1993: 101–2; Lieu 2008a: 220–1; Yarbrough 2008: 295–6.

[29] Westcott 1966: 188; du Toit 1979: 97–8; Brown 1982: 608, 634; Strecker 1996: 197–8; Kruse 2000: 188; Painter 2002: 313; Smalley 2007: 277.

in these verses but in the text as a whole. The statement of 5:13 reveals that the purpose of the whole of 1 John is to assure the readers that they possess eternal life when they believe in the name of the Son of God. As a result, the limit placed on any proposal is the idea of assurance. Since the immediate verses are part of the whole of 1 John, a decision about the referent of ταῦτα is not required. Any understanding of 5:6–8 should be shaped by the awareness that the purpose of the text is the readers' assurance of their eternal life when they believe in the name of the Son of God.

The closing boundary of this unit in 5:15 was identified under the influence of the reappearance of the vocabulary of sin in 5:16ff. There are sub-units within 5:4b–15 observable on the basis of repeated vocabulary. The language of witness (μαρτυρέω, μαρτυρία) occurs in 5:6–11, life (ζωή) in 5:11–13, and asking (αἰτέω, αἴτημα) in 5:14–15. These vocabulary clusters correspond to the use of the cataphoric phrase καὶ αὕτη ἐστίν in 5:4b, 11, and 14 with the result that the phrase progresses the argument and marks paragraphs. These boundaries establish limits as to how the paragraphs should be understood because they indicate the themes of each paragraph.

An intertextual fill

The difficulty in these verses is ascertaining what is meant by the clause οὗτός ἐστιν ὁ ἐλθὼν δι' ὕδατος καὶ αἵματος, Ἰησοῦς Χριστός in 5:6. In keeping with the christology of 1 John proposed above, the clause appears to refer to the resurrection of the crucified Jesus.

The last chapter of this thesis noted that ἔρχομαι is used to structure the resurrection narratives of John 20:19–21:14. This resulted in the confession of 1 John 4:2 being understood as a reference to Jesus' resurrection that demonstrated that he was the Christ. If ἔρχομαι is understood in the same way in 5:6, then ὕδατος καὶ αἵματος again refers to some aspect of the resurrection of Jesus Christ.[30] However, the link between ὕδατος καὶ αἵματος and John's resurrection appearance narratives is not obvious at first glance since neither ὕδωρ nor αἷμα occurs in John 20:19–21:14. Yet the absence of the vocabulary does not mean the link is not there, merely that it is less apparent.

The only other use of the nouns ὕδωρ and αἷμα in combination in the New Testament occur in John 19:34, where the soldier's spear pierces

---

[30] Many scholars link 5:6 to 4:2 on the basis of the repetition of the verb ἔρχομαι. See for example de Boer 1991.

the dead Jesus resulting in a flow of blood and water.[31] This observation forms the basis of some scholars' understanding ὕδατος καὶ αἵματος as referring to Jesus' death.[32] This linguistic link is compelling but is not found in the resurrection narratives. However, the marks of the crucifixion, in particular the spear wound, are evident in the resurrection narratives.

Of the five occurrences of the noun πλευρά in the New Testament, four occur in John and describe the place from which the blood and water flowed (19:34; 20:20, 25, 27).[33] In the first resurrection appearance narrative (20:19–23), the proof that Jesus offers to demonstrate that he is physically risen are the scars in his hands and side (20:20). In the second resurrection appearance narrative (20:24–9), Thomas claims that unless he sees these scars and puts his hand into Jesus' side (καὶ βάλω μου τὴν χεῖρα εἰς τὴν πλευρὰν αὐτοῦ), he will not believe (20:25).[34] When Jesus appears to Thomas, he offers the evidence of his scars, in particular his wounded side (20:27). It is these distinguishing scars that move Thomas to believe that Jesus was raised and so confess him to be his Lord and God (20:28). So even though the vocabulary of ὕδατος καὶ αἵματος does not occur in the resurrection appearance narrative, the idea is evident in the references to Jesus' side.

Further, this line of reasoning is strengthened when the two prepositions used with 'water and blood' in 1 John 5:6 are considered. Most scholars see no significant difference in John's variation between διά followed by the genitive and ἐν.[35] So the meaning lies in the overlap of the two prepositions' semantic domains – their shared meaning. One of the shared meanings is 'with'.[36] If this meaning is understood, then in 1 John 5:6 Jesus comes 'with' water and blood, that is, he is resurrected 'with' the scars of crucifixion. This proposal matches the christology of the introduction, where the resurrection was the focus of 1:1–5 while the death of Jesus was referred to in 1:6–2:2. The resurrected Christ of 1:1–5 is the crucified Christ of 1:6–2:2.

---

[31] The two also occur in the longer reading of Matthew 27:49. Although this longer reading is attested in א B C etc, it seems to be an addition made under the influence of John 19:34. See Hill 1981: 355.

[32] For example Schnackenburg 1992: 236–7.

[33] The fifth occurrence is in Acts 12:7. It also occurs in the longer reading of Matthew 27:49.

[34] The noun χείρ occues in John 20:25, 27 and 1 John 1:1.

[35] Brown 1982: 574.

[36] *Ibid.* Brown notes that this meaning is evident in the descriptions of the priest entering the holy place in Hebrews. In Hebrews 9:12 the preposition διά is used, while in the parallel description in Hebrews 9:25 ἐν occurs. Brown also notes that the meaning 'in' is evident in the parallel passages of Romans 6:4 and Colossians 2:12.

The reference to the Spirit in 5:6–8 supports this understanding since the Spirit is Jesus' gift to his disciples once they have recognised him as the resurrected crucified Christ. So in John 20:22, Jesus gives the Spirit to the disciples once they are moved to faith after witnessing the scars. This gift of the Spirit is in fulfilment of Jesus' promises that he would come and give them the Spirit (14:16–18, 26; 15:26).[37] Jesus, as a resurrected crucified man, gives the Spirit, an action that demonstrates that he is the Christ. In this way are provided three witnesses to Jesus' resurrection, meeting the requirement of Deuteronomy 19:15. The water and blood demonstrate in a twofold manner that Jesus was crucified and dead. Further, the scar, from which the blood and water flowed, is the proof that it was the crucified Jesus who was raised. The gift of the Spirit is the third witness that Jesus was resurrected from the dead because only the one who God raised is able to give the Spirit.

An intertextual reading of 5:4b–15

The threefold repetition of the cataphoric statement καὶ αὕτη ἐστίν (5:4b, 11, 14) breaks this unit into three paragraphs and reveals the theme of each paragraph.

The first paragraph (5:4b–10) is about the readers' faith (ἡ πίστις ἡμῶν) that overcomes the world (ἡ νίκη ἡ νικήσασα τὸν κόσμον). It is faith that Jesus is the Son of God (Ἰησοῦς ἐστιν ὁ υἱὸς τοῦ θεοῦ). Jesus is described as the one coming with water and blood (ὁ ἐλθὼν δι' ὕδατος καὶ αἵματος), not only with water, but water and blood (οὐκ ἐν τῷ ὕδατι μόνον ἀλλ' ἐν τῷ ὕδατι καὶ ἐν τῷ αἵματι). The readers' faith is that Jesus is the Son of God, the King of Israel, expected by the Jewish people under the influence of Old Testament prophecy.[38] That ὁ υἱὸς τοῦ θεοῦ was understood as messianic is evident in Nathanael's confession (John 1:49) where it is in apposition to βασιλεὺς ... τοῦ Ἰσραήλ. The event that demonstrates that Jesus is the eternal King of Israel is his physical resurrection from the dead as a result of crucifixion, his coming in water and blood.

The construction in 5:6 'οὐ(κ) ... μόνον ἀλλ'...' does not report the sentiments of the opponents. It is a common rhetorical device used to emphasise unity (John 11:52; 12:9; 17:20; 1 John 2:2; 2 John 1) and

---

[37] Michaels (1989: 344–5) lists the correspondences between Jesus' promises in the upper room discourse and John's resurrection accounts.
[38] 'Son of God' and 'Christ' are equivalent messianic titles in 1 John. See Hengel 1989: 59; Schnackenburg 1992: 146; Kruse 2000: 174.

there is no need to read it in a polemical context.[39] The water and blood together testify to the crucified body of Jesus. The unity of this witness also includes the testimony of the Spirit in 5:8 (τὸ πνεῦμα καὶ τὸ ὕδωρ καὶ τὸ αἷμα, καὶ οἱ τρεῖς εἰς τὸ ἕν εἰσιν).[40] The audience should not doubt that Jesus is the Son of God but have confidence based on his resurrection because God has testified to it, and his witness is greater than human witness (5:9). So the one believing in the Son of God has the witness in himself, but those who do not believe God's witness make him out to be a liar (5:10). It should be noted that this understanding of 5:4b–10 is consistent with the other occurrences of the μαρτυ-word group in 1 John, where it was used in the context of testifying to the physical resurrection of Jesus (1:2) being sent as the saviour of the world (4:14).

The second paragraph (5:11–13) is about the eternal life (ζωὴν αἰώνιον) that God has given in his Son (ἐν τῷ υἱῷ αὐτοῦ). The author has already testified to the eternal life (τὴν ζωὴν τὴν αἰώνιον) that he heard, saw, looked at, and touched – the resurrection of the incarnate Jesus in 1:1–2. Given the testimony that Jesus is the Son of God raised from the dead (5:5–10), the author can now affirm that God has given eternal life to the readers. Those who have the Son have life (ὁ ἔχων τὸν υἱὸν ἔχει τὴν ζωήν), while those who do not have the Son do not have life (ὁ μὴ ἔχων τὸν υἱὸν τοῦ θεοῦ τὴν ζωὴν οὐκ ἔχει). The γράφω statement of 5:13 supports this understanding of these paragraphs because it gives the reason for writing to be so that the audience may know that they possess eternal life (εἰδῆτε ὅτι ζωὴν ἔχετε αἰώνιον) as those trusting in the name of the Son of God (τοῖς πιστεύουσιν εἰς τὸ ὄνομα τοῦ υἱοῦ τοῦ θεοῦ). God gave them eternal life (5:10) when he testified to the resurrection of the crucified Jesus (5:5–10) and so indicated that Jesus is the Son of God (5:5).

The third paragraph (5:14–15) is about the confidence (ἡ παρρησία) the readers can have before God in prayer. The audience can know that when they ask something in accordance with God's will, their prayers are heard.

Tangents

There are three intertextual tangents that demonstrate the plausibility of understanding the clause οὗτός ἐστιν ὁ ἐλθὼν δι᾽ ὕδατος καὶ αἵματος, Ἰησοῦς Χριστός to refer to the resurrection of the crucified Jesus.

---

[39] Streett 2011: 300–2.

[40] The reference to three witnesses could appear to weaken this proposed reading because it could be argued that the proposal results in two witnesses (water and blood, the Spirit). However, this same weakness is also evident in the view that the blood and water are a reference to Jesus' death.

First, Jesus is described as the resurrected crucified incarnate Christ elsewhere in the Johannine corpus. In Revelation 5:5–6, Jesus is presented as the Lion of Judah but then appears as a slain lamb. This description corresponds to the reading presented above, that the resurrected Jesus is the crucified Jesus. The description is not confined to the Johannine corpus but also occurs in Mark 16:6, where the angels describe Jesus as the risen crucified man,[41] and 1 Corinthians 1:23, where Paul preaches a crucified Christ.[42] Thus the fill that understands the idea of coming through water and blood to be the resurrection of his crucified body, is viable.

Second, the logic that the existence of the Spirit acts as a witness to the resurrection of the crucified Jesus is evident elsewhere in the earliest Christian documents. So the first sermon in the earliest church is provoked by the gift of the Spirit (Acts 2). In Peter's sermon, the Spirit is given due to the exaltation of the resurrected crucified Christ (2:32–33). The existence of the Spirit bears witness to the fact that Jesus was raised after being crucified. In commenting on Acts 2:33 Marshall states: '[T]he bestowal of the Spirit offers further testimony that Jesus is the Messiah.'[43] The same idea is evident in Romans 1:3–4, where the Spirit and the resurrection appoint Jesus as the Son of God.[44] Thus, the witness of the Spirit, as encountered in Acts 2 and Romans 1:4, contributes to the plausibility of this reading.

The third tangent is historical in nature. The historical reconstruction proposed in this thesis is that the audience thought of themselves as the True Israel and those who had left as apostate Jews. One of the issues that caused Jews to stumble was the preaching of the crucified Christ (1 Corinthians 1:23).[45] As Fee comments: 'To the Jew the message of a crucified Messiah was the ultimate scandal.'[46] So an affirmation of the resurrection of the crucified Jesus would cause the sort of split that is described in 2:19. When Jews heard the preaching of the resurrected crucified man, Jesus, it is not surprising that some took offence and left true Judaism. Thus this reading appears plausible because its understanding of οὗτός ἐστιν ὁ ἐλθὼν δι᾽ ὕδατος καὶ αἵματος, Ἰησοῦς Χριστός fits the

---

[41] This reference was drawn to my attention in personal conversation with Peter Bolt.

[42] Fee 1987: 75, following Ellis 1978: 73–4, lists this as an option, although he is cautious in adopting it. Recent verbal aspect research may also weaken this piece of evidence.

[43] Marshall 1980: 79.

[44] It should also be noted that the Spirit in Romans 1:4 is found in parallel with the flesh in 1:3. This is reminiscent of the relationship argued for in this reading between 1 John 4:2 (flesh) and 1 John 5:6–8 (Spirit). Both describe a realm in which Jesus is understood to be the Christ.

[45] See also Galatians 3:13 and 5:11 for similar ideas.

[46] Fee 1987: 75.

historical reconstruction of this research and finds extra support in 1 Corinthians.

Therefore it seems reasonable to understand οὗτός ἐστιν ὁ ἐλθὼν δι' ὕδατος καὶ αἵματος, Ἰησοῦς Χριστός as referring to the resurrection of the crucified Jesus.

Summary

It is plausible that the clause οὗτός ἐστιν ὁ ἐλθὼν δι' ὕδατος καὶ αἵματος, Ἰησοῦς Χριστός is a reference to the resurrection of the crucified Jesus. It results in a consistent reading of 5:4b–15 within the logic of the unit as a whole, and has support from both theological and historical tangents.

1 John 5:16–21

The final unit of 1 John returns to the theme of sin and so restates the previous arguments of 1 John concerning sin. These statements are assuring in tone and are based on the identity of the readers as those born of God (5:18–19). In this way it acts as a conclusion to 1 John, reviewing the arguments of 1 John after the climax of 5:4–15.

Gaps and limiting devices

Like most of 1 John, these verses appear to contain a number of interruptions to the flow of sentences. Asyndesis is evident at the start of verses 16, 17, 18, 19, and 21, resulting in an impression of sentence interruptions. However, the asyndesis does not constitute a series of gaps, for two reasons. First, the verses have a unity of theme as revealed by the repetition of the vocabulary of sin (ἁμαρτάνω, ἁμαρτία).[47] Second, two of these asyndetic verses (18 and 19) start with the same phrase (οἴδαμεν ὅτι), indicating a structural device. A third occurrence of this phrase starting verse 20, where it is not asyndetic because of the inclusion of δέ, confirms that οἴδαμεν ὅτι is being used as a literary device.[48] It appears that the threefold repetition of οἴδαμεν ὅτι reports, in the form of a list,

---

[47] This repetition of vocabulary is the reason for dividing the text between 5:15 and 5:16, and placing 5:16–17 with 5:18–21. 5:16–17 could be understood to be an example of prayer and linked with 5:14–15 under the influence of the repetition of αἰτέω. However, since 'sin' was understood as a key theme in 1 John, under the influence of its prominence in 1:5–2:2, this reading perceives the re-emergence of the theme of sin in 5:16–17 resulting in its unity with 5:18f.

[48] Brown 1982: 118.

a series of conclusions drawn from the argument of the text. The final verse of 1 John is often understood to pose a gap because it is asyndetic, starts with a vocative and imperative, and contains material that is understood as not being discussed elsewhere in 1 John. Thus 5:21 presents a gap that requires filling.[49]

There are three reader-experienced gaps in these verses. First, the secondary literature abounds with discussion about the nature of the sin that leads to death in 5:16–17 (ἁμαρτάνοντα ἁμαρτίαν μὴ πρὸς θάνατον). Second, scholars often view the statement that the Son of God came (ὁ υἱὸς τοῦ θεοῦ ἥκει) in 5:20 as affirming the incarnation.[50] This could question the understanding of 1 John's christology presented here. As a result it forms a gap that requires filling. Third, the historical situation proposed in this thesis runs contrary to some views of 5:21. The command to keep oneself from idolatry is sometimes taken to imply that the audience is Gentile.[51] This could question the reconstruction that the audience understands itself as the True Israel, and so form a gap.

Thus there are three gaps that require filling in this unit – the nature of the sin that leads to death (5:16–17), an understanding of the clause ὁ υἱὸς τοῦ θεοῦ ἥκει (5:20), and the asyndetic final verse that commands the readers to avoid idolatry and is taken to indicate a Gentile audience (5:21).

Of the three limiting devices, there are no uses of γράφω in these verses. There is one vocative (τεκνία) in 5:21 that seems to draw attention to the final words of the book. So it seems to indicate that 5:21 is a summary statement of some kind. Further, the final verse is also a boundary for the unit (and the book as a whole), supporting the idea that the vocative indicates a summary. Thus, the final verse should limit the ways gaps are filled in this unit (and the book as a whole) because it provides a summary of the desired actions of the audience after reading the text. Since there appears to be a gap in 5:21, the way it limits interpretation requires a re-reading of the text as a whole in light of any proposed fill and thus the reading circle described in chapter 2 continues.

---

[49] There are no uses of pronouns with cataphoric referents thus there are no other gaps that arise from textual devices.

[50] Plummer 1911: 171; Bultmann 1973: 89; Marshall 1978: 253; Barker 1981: 358; Culpepper 1985: 113–4; Johnson 1993: 139; Thomas 2003: 278; Smalley 2007: 292; Yarbrough 2008: 318. Strecker (1996: 209) argues that it refers to Jesus' earthly existence.

[51] du Rand 1994: 169; Wallace 1996: 46; Painter 2002: 328–30.

An intertextual fill

The first gap in this section involves identifying what is meant by the phrase ἁμαρτία πρὸς θάνατον. This thesis understands 'the sin to death' as referring to the sin of apostasy.[52] This is because the last place the results of sin were pictured negatively in 1 John was in the 'claims' of 1:6–2:11. There the sins were those of faithless/apostate Israel. It was those 'claims' that resulted in someone being in the darkness, out of fellowship with God, and having blinded eyes. Further, this proposal explains the verses in their historical context. Some have left the True Israel (2:19) when they denied that Jesus was the Christ (2:22), thereby committing apostasy.

The second gap in this section involves the 'coming' (ἥκει) that is referred to in 5:20. In keeping with this research's understanding of 1 John's christology, this reading will identify the Son of God's coming with Jesus' resurrection appearances. The verb ἥκω is used in a variety of ways in John's Gospel. On one occasion it occurs in parallel with ἔρχομαι, revealing their shared semantic domain (6:37). Thus, it is not surprising that scholars understand it in light of 4:2 and 5:6 as referring to the incarnation. However, if 4:2 and 5:6 do not refer to the incarnation but rather to the resurrection of the incarnate Christ, then ἥκω in 5:20 could also refer to the resurrection of the incarnate Christ. This sits well with the first use of ἥκω in John, where it refers to the hour of Jesus' glorification, that is, his death and resurrection (2:4).

The third gap involves a number of decisions about 5:21 – the impression of its disconnectedness from 5:20, its apparent summary form that does not conclude the book but looks as though it introduces new material, and its content that some have taken to reveal a Gentile audience. This gap is filled by means of the following decisions. First, there is no gap on account of disconnectedness since the verse contains a semantic link with 5:20e – ὁ ἀληθινὸς θεός and τῶν εἰδώλων.[53] Further, 5:20e stands off from the rest of 5:20, and when combined with 5:21, forms the expected antithesis to 5:20a–d.[54] Again, the appeal to the vocative as an indicator of a new section is not valid, since its primary function is to draw the readers' attention to a particular point, in this case the

52 This is similar to Griffith (2002: 143–8), however the reasoning is different because he understands the theme of sin in 3:4–10 as being apostasy, an opinion that this study does not share.
53 *Ibid.*: 59–60.   54 *Ibid.*: 60–1.

summary of 5:21 and its imperative.[55] So second, the verse does contain
a summary of 1 John's message, but it is not in the form of new material.
If the referent of οὗτός in 5:20e is Jesus, then this verse contains another
christological affirmation in keeping with 2:22; 4:2–3; 5:1, 5, and 6–8.[56]
The idolatry of 5:21 is in contrast to the correct understanding of Jesus,
it is the rejection that Jesus is the Christ, the denial of those who have
departed the True Israel (2:22).[57] Following from this, the third aspect
of the gap is filled when the audience is understood to be perceiving
themselves as the True Israel. Thus the injunction to guard against idolatry is in keeping with the commands to Israel to avoid idolatry found in
such places as the second of the Ten Commandments (Exodus 20:4–6;
Deuteronomy 5:8–10).[58]

An intertextual reading of 5:16–21

These verses have 'sin' (ἁμαρτάνω, ἁμαρτία) as their theme and can be
split into two paragraphs. The first paragraph (5:16–17) continues the
discussion of prayer (5:14–15), giving a case study involving praying
about sin. The second paragraph (5:18–21) summarises the teaching of
the whole of 1 John with regards to the theme of sin and so concludes
1 John.

When the audience sees a brother (member of Israel) sin, they should
ask God and he will restore that person to life (5:16), the life that they
have when they have the Son (5:12). This is applicable to sin that does
not lead to death (ἁμαρτίαν μὴ πρὸς θάνατον). There is a sin that leads
to death – the sin of apostasy from God. 'Death' is the position of those
who do not have the Son of God (5:12).[59] The author does not want them
to pray about that sin.[60] Even though all sin is unrighteousness, there is
sin that does not lead to death about which the readers should pray if they
see their brothers committing such sin (5:17).[61]

---

[55] See the discussion of the function of a vocative in chapter 2.

[56] Griffith 2002: 76–7.

[57] This understands εἴδωλον in a metaphorical way. For the list of options as to how 5:21
can be understood see Griffith *Ibid.*: 12–27.

[58] Understanding the historical situation in this way alleviates the tension in the proposal
that there is a reversal of strategy when the idolatry polemic of the Old Testament is used
against Judaism; see *Ibid.* The Old Testament's idolatry polemic is against faithless Israel,
the very people in 1 John who are acting under the influence of the antichrist and denying
the resurrection of the crucified incarnate Christ.

[59] *Ibid.*: 144.   [60] *Ibid.*: 113–15.

[61] Tan 2002.

In bringing the book to an end, the author summarises the teaching of three themes in statements that all start with the phrase οἴδαμεν (δὲ) ὅτι. First, everyone being born from God does not sin, but the one born from God keeps him, and the Evil One cannot touch him (5:18). The references to being born from God remind the reader of 5:4, where it is affirmed that they are born by faith in the message of the resurrected incarnate Christ. As such, they can pray for their brother when they see him commit a sin that does not lead to death (5:15–16) and God will restore him to life so that the Evil One cannot touch him. The statement that those born of God do not sin links back to the heavenly perspective of Christ's work discussed in 3:4–9. Thus, this first summary statement stands in contrast to the sin that leads to death in 5:15–16, and fits within the assuring purpose of the book as a whole (5:13). Second, the readers know that they are from God, in contrast to the world that is under the control of the Evil One (5:19). This summarises the teaching of 1 John 2:15–17 and 4:1–6. The audience is of God because they are able to confess that Jesus is the Christ having come in the flesh (4:2). In contrast, the world denies Jesus (4:3) under the influence of the antichrist. The spirit of the antichrist is accepted by the world (4:4–6), a world marked by the desires of the flesh and eyes (2:16). Third, the readers know that Jesus as Israel's King, the Son of God, came in his resurrection body and gave knowledge to his people. He did this so that they would know the truth, the truth they live in when they are in Jesus Christ, who is truly and eternally alive (5:20). This statement summarises the material on the resurrection in 1 John (i.e. 1:1–3; 4:2; 5:6–8) because it is the resurrection that brings fellowship and life (1:1–3), that brings confidence of the readers' standing with God (4:2), and that brings assurance of their salvation (5:6–13).

The final command of the book summarises the issue facing the audience – they are to guard themselves from idols, or false versions of God (5:21). This is in contrast to the true God, Jesus Christ (5:20). The false versions are those promulgated by the antichrists who deny Jesus is the Christ, the very confession that gives the true and assuring knowledge the readers desire. This final command thus picks up the issue of apostasy contained in the summary statements, given that the world is under the control of the Evil One. It contrasts these with the assurance that the audience does not sin, cannot be touched by the Evil One, and on account of the resurrection of Jesus, knows that they are in the truth, in the true God and eternal life of Jesus.

Tangents

The tangents that demonstrate the plausibility of this reading fall into three categories.

First, that 'sin to death' in 5:16 should be understood as apostasy is viable when it is noted that Jeremiah is commanded not to pray for apostate Israel because they committed idolatry (Jeremiah 7:16; 11:14; 14:11). Further, in John 17: 9, Jesus does not pray for the world but for those from the world who the Father has given him. Taking the world in John 13–17 as representing faithless Jews, this again supports understanding the 'sin to death' as being apostasy from Israel.

Second, that ἥκω refers to the resurrection is supported when it is noted that understanding (διάνοια) is a cognate noun of a verb used in the other earliest Christian documents when referring to a result of the resurrection. The verb διανοίγω occurs in Luke's resurrection narratives on two occasions to describe one of Jesus' post-resurrection actions. Jesus is said to have opened (διανοίγω) the Scriptures to the men on the road to Emmaus (24:32) and the disciples (24:45). Further, the term διάνοια occurs in the New Covenant promises of Jeremiah 31:33 (=LXX 38:33) as the place where God will put his law (cf. Hebrews 8:10; 10:16). In the resurrection of Jesus, the New Covenant promise of the law on the heart was enacted, as Jesus opened the minds of the disciples so that they could understand the Scriptures.

Third, the Old Testament consistently warned against idolatry (for example Exodus 20:4; Leviticus 19:4; Deuteronomy 5:8), and condemned the people when they committed idolatry (for example Isaiah 1:29; Ezekiel 6:4–13; 8:10; Hosea 8:4–6). The idolatry in those cases was worshipping some one or thing other than the true God. So the proposed reading is supported both in its view of the audience and its understanding of these verses relating to the sin of apostasy.[62]

Summary

When these final verses are understood in this way, they support the proposal that 1 John testifies to the resurrection of the incarnate Christ. This testimony is made in the context of the audience thinking of themselves as the True Israel, while those ethnic Jews who have left are understood as faithless or apostate.

---

[62] Griffith (2002: 193–204) provides a list of other sources that support this reading.

Conclusion

This chapter has proposed a reading of 1 John 4:7–5:21 that is not only consistent with the christology and historical situation suggested in the rest of this research, but argues that the passages in question lend more evidence to the thesis. The statements that God 'sent' his son (4:9–10, 14) were not incarnational affirmations but rather mission statements, where the results of the sending were consistent with the christology of the rest of 1 John. The difficult verses of 5:6–8 were understood to emphasise the resurrection of the crucified Jesus. The resurrection was also on view in 5:20 since it was the event that brought the fulfilment of the New Covenant promise of understanding the Scriptures and having them written on the audience's heart/mind. The historical situation of the audience understanding itself as the True Israel from whom some have left, was supported in the suggestion of the 'sin to death' being apostasy (5:16), and the command to guard oneself from idols as being an anti-idolatry polemic used in the Old Testament of faithless Judaism.

CONCLUSION

This study proposed that 1 John affirms the resurrection of the incarnate Christ in the context of an intra-Jewish disagreement over Jesus' identity.

It presented a reading of 1 John shaped by its introduction. The introduction affirmed the resurrection of the incarnate Christ (1:1–3) and proposed the 'claims' of 1:6–2:11 could have been Jewish in origin. This understanding of the christology and historical situation were then tested as the rest of 1 John was 'read' in light of these twin proposals. It was argued that the schism of 2:19–23 could be identified as being an internal Jewish disagreement over Jesus' identity – the author and his readers understood those who denied that Jesus was the Christ as leaving the True Israel. Historical material was cited to demonstate the plausibility of such an understanding. It was then argued that the resurrection was the event that demonstrated Jesus was the Christ. This was why it was used in the test confession of 4:2–3. The antichrists and false prophets could not affirm that Jesus was the Christ who came in the flesh, that is, appeared in his resurrected incarnate state to his disciples. Two other explicit references to the resurrection were also noted in 5:6–7 and 20. The reading demonstrated the plausibility of understanding 1 John in light of the affirmation of the resurrection of the incarnate Christ in the situation of an intra-Jewish disagreement over Jesus' identity.

The thesis contained two main parts. The first part reviewed previous methods of reading 1 John (Historical Critical, Literary/Rhetorical), critically discussed the identifications of the 'opponents' made in the secondary literature, and then described its adopted reading method. Since all of the identifications of the opponents had weaknesses, the ground was cleared to propose a new reading of 1 John and present a new historical sitation in support of the reading. The adopted reading method paid particular attention to three sources of 'gaps' in the reading process (discontinuity between sentences, cataphoric pronouns, and reader-experienced gaps) and three devices that limited how these gaps could be 'filled' (occurrence of vocatives, the use of γράφω, and boundary crossing). It was argued that readers use intertextual connections to fill the gaps, but these connections are limited by the devices. A re-reading of the text in light of proposed 'fills' was used to test if the intertextual connections were viable. This process resulted in a circular reading, where the understanding of the text was ultimately demonstated to be viable on the basis of the text itself. To this circle, the method added tangents, lines of evidence that did not determine the meaning of the text but confirmed the plausibility of the reading. These tangents were taken from other documents of the time and it was suggested that the process as a whole healed the division between the historical and literary methods used in previous research.

This reading method creates opportunities for further research as it could be applied to other texts. The value of the approach was seen in the reading of 1 John as a whole. It has rendered an internally self-consistent reading that explains the details of the text. The tangent lines have demonstrated the plausibility of the reading, especially in presenting a first-century historical context for 1 John. Thus, applying the method to other New Testament texts could provide a fruitful avenue for further research. In terms of the details of the method, the study of the pronouns did not result in the identification of as many gaps as expected. On the other hand, the limiting devices proved crucial in interpreting the text. Although γράφω does not appear as frequently in other New Testament texts, other authorial commentary features may perform the same function.

The second part of the thesis applied this reading method to the text of 1 John. The third chapter argued that 1 John 1:1–5 affirmed the resurrection of the incarnate Christ. It noted intertextual links with both the prologue and resurrection narratives of John, and argued that what was on view in 1 John 1:1–3 was not the incarnation but rather the resurrection of the incarnate Christ. Both sets of intertextual links were acknowledged rather than one being the basis of ignoring the other. This opened the way for a new reading of the rest of 1 John with a view to testing if the christology of the resurrected incarnate Christ occurred elsewhere in the text.

The fourth chapter again applied the reading method in detail, this time to the rest of the introduction (1:6–2:11). It proposed that the claims of the introduction were Jewish in nature and demonstrated who was a member of the True Israel and who was a faithless Jew. The resulting characterisations provided the reader with expectations to use in evaluating people and actions that would occur in the body of the text (2:15–5:21).

The fifth chapter presented the results of the reading method for 1 John 2:15–27. It proposed that the historical situation behind the letter was a rejection of the confession 'Jesus is the Christ'. This type of rejection was evident within first-century Judaism and could easily result in those making the denial being thought of as leaving the True Israel. This historical situation may elucidate the other Johannine literature (and New Testament books), in particular 2 John, given its similarities with 1 John, and thus form an avenue for further research.

The sixth chapter examined 1 John 2:28–3:24, paying particular attention to texts that questioned the understanding of the christology or historical situation arrived at from the reading of 1 John 1:1–2:27. It suggested that the reference to Jesus' appearing in 3:5 and 8 had in view Jesus' appearing in heaven and not the incarnation.

The seventh chapter was devoted to a detailed examination of 4:1–6, since the confession of 4:2–3 is used in the secondary literature to define the teaching of the opponents. After examining the use of the verb ἔρχομαι in the resurrection narratives of John's Gospel, it was argued that the phrase ἐν σαρκὶ ἐληλυθότα in 1 John 4:2 refers to Jesus' appearing in his resurrected body to his disciples. Further, the reason for adding ἐν σαρκὶ ἐληλυθότα to the confession was because the resurrection of Jesus demonstrated he was the Christ. So in the context of a denial that Jesus was the Christ (2:22), the addition of the phrase is explained.

The last chapter presented the results of the reading for 1 John 4:7–5:21, focussing especially on 4:9–10, 14; 5:6–8, 20, and 21. It found that the formulae used in 4:9–10 and 14 refer to the mission of Jesus. After examining the options for understanding 5:6–8, the thesis argued that the 'water and blood' are a reference to Jesus' crucifixion. So the 'coming' in the water and blood is referring to Jesus' resurrection appearances as the crucified Christ. This understanding was supported by the third witness, the gift of the Spirit, the result of the resurrection of the crucified Jesus. The research proposed that the final verses spoke again of the resurrection of Jesus in the context of people apostatising from the True Israel.

Thus, this research has presented a reading of 1 John that understands it as affirming the resurrection of the incarnate Christ in the context of an intra-Jewish disagreement about Jesus' identity. The internal self-consistency of the reading and its ability to explain the text of 1 John demonstrated that it was possible, while the tangents to the reading (both historical and theological) revealed that it was not just possible but plausible.

APPENDIX: THE STRUCTURE OF 1 JOHN

Through the course of this research, a structure and argument for 1 John have emerged.[1] Using 2:12–14 as a starting point, 1 John appears to have two parts – an introduction (1:1–2:11) and a body (2:15–5:21).

The introduction sets the reading context through its christology (1:1–5) and establishment of two key themes – sin (1:6–2:2) and love (2:3–11). The two sets of 'claims' are in parallel to each other, both discussing implications of the preached message of the resurrected incarnate Christ (1:1–3) – fellowship and sin (1:6–2:2), and assurance and obedience (2:3–11). It has the following structure (Table 13):

Table 13. *The structure of 1 John's introduction (1:1–2:11)*

1:1–3a The preached message – the resurrected incarnate christ	
1:3b–5 Fellowship and light	2:3 Knowledge and the commands
1:6–2:2 Three case studies	2:4–11 Three case studies
1:6–7 ἐὰν εἴπωμεν ὅτι	2:4–5 ὁ λέγων
1:8–9 ἐὰν εἴπωμεν ὅτι	2:6–8 ὁ λέγων
1:10–2:2 ἐὰν εἴπωμεν ὅτι	2:7–8 Vocative purpose statement
2:1 Vocative purpose statement	2:9–11 ὁ λέγων

The two themes of sin and love are given heightened prominence in the introduction through the use of the combination of a vocative and a γράφω statement (2:1; 7–8). The body of the book uses these themes to discuss the real-life problem facing the readers – the existence of antichrists in the world.

The body starts with an introductory paragraph that sets the world as the context (2:15–17) and then outlines two particular aspects of the

---

[1] A fuller treatment of this material can be found in Jensen 2012.

world that face the readers – the existence of antichrists (2:18–27), and the readers' identity as being born of God (2:28–3:12). On the basis of these twin aspects, the body then gives commands about behaviour (3:13–5:4a), building to a climax (5:4b–21) where the readers are assured of their victory over the world, their possession of God's true testimony, their eternal life, and their position in prayer. A conclusion restates the text's teaching with regard to the themes of sin, the world, and the resurrection (5:18–21). Thus 1 John has the following structure (Table 14):

Table 14. *The structure and Argument of 1 John.*

Introduction	1:1–2:11
Message preached	1:1–5
Claims about sin	1:6–2:2
Claims about love	2:3–11
Transition	2:12–14
Body	2:15–5:21
The world	2:15–17
Two aspects of the world	
Antichrists exist	2:18–27
Readers are God's children	2:28–3:12
Commands concerning the world	
Do not be surprised but love	3:13–24
Do not trust but test spirits	4:1–6
Love one another	4:7–5:4a
Climactic assurances	5:4b–15
Conclusion	5:16–21

BIBLIOGRAPHY

Akin, D. L. (2001). *1, 2, 3 John*. Nashville, TN: Broadman & Holman.
Anderson, J. (1990). 'Cultural Assumptions behind the First Epistle of John'. *Notes on Translation* 4:39–44.
Anderson, J. L. and Anderson, J. (1993). 'Cataphora in 1 John'. *Notes on Translation* 7:41–6.
Baker, R. O. (2004). *Little Children Keep Yourselves From Idols: A Retrospective Reading of 1 John*. PhD thesis: Baylor University, Waco, TX.
Barclay, J. M. G. (1987). 'Mirror-Reading a Polemical Letter: Galatians as a Test Case'. *Journal for the Study of the New Testament* 31:73–93.
Barker, G. W. (1981). '1 John' in *The Expositor's Bible Commentary*. Edited by F. E. Gaebelein; vol. xii; Grand Rapids, MI: Zondervan, 293–358.
Barnwell, K. (1974). 'Vocative Phrases'. *Notes on Translation* 53:9–17.
Barthes, R. (1977). 'The Death of the Author' in *Image Music Text*. Edited by S. Heath; London: Fontana Press, 142–8.
Bauckham, R. J. (1993). 'The Parting of the Ways: What Happened and Why'. *Studia Theologica* 47:135–51.
Baylis, C. P. (1992). 'The Meaning of Walking "in the Darkness" (1 John 1:6)'. *Bibliotheca Sacra* 149:214–22.
Beeke, J. R. (2006). *The Epistles of John*. Darlington: Evangelical Press.
Beekman, J. and Callow, J. (1974). *Translating the Word of God, with Scripture and Topical Indexes*. Grand Rapids, MI: Zondervan.
Beutler, J. (1988). 'Die Johannesbriefe in der neuesten Literatur (1978–1985)'. *Aufstieg und Niedergang der Römischen Welt* 25.5:3773–90.
(2000). *Die Johannesbriefe*. Regensburg: Pustet.
Bieringer, R., Pollefeyt, D. and Vandecasteele-Vanneuville, F. (2001). 'Wrestling with Johannine Anti-Judaism: A Hermeneutical Framework for the Analysis of the Current Debate' in *Anti-Judaism and the Fourth Gospel*. Edited by R. Bieringer, D. Pollefeyt and F. Vandecasteele-Vanneuville; Assen: Royal Van Gorcum, 3–44.
Black, D. A. (1992). 'An Overlooked Stylistic Argument in Favor of πάντα in 1 John 2:20'. *Filologia Neotestamentaria* 5:205–8.
Bockmuehl, M. (1988). 'Das Verb phaneroo in Neuen Testament: Veruch einer Neuauswertung'. *Biblische Zeitschrift* 32:87–99.
(2001). '1QS and Salvation at Qumran' in *Justification and Variegated Nomism: Volume 1, The Complexities of Second Temple Judaism*. Edited by D. A. Carson, P. T. O'Brien and M. A. Seifrid; vol. i; Tubingen: Mohr Siebeck, 381–414.

Bogart, J. (1977). *Orthodox and Heretical Perfectionism in the Johannine Community as Evident in the First Epistle of John.* Missoula, MT: Scholars Press.

Boismard, M. E. (1949). 'La connaissance de Dieu dans l'Alliance Nouvelle d'après la première épître de S. Jean'. *Revue Biblique* 56:365–91.

(1972). 'The First Epistle of John and the Writings of Qumran' in *John and Qumran*, Edited by J. H. Charlesworth; London: Geoffrey Chapman, 156–65.

Bolt, P. G. (1998). 'Life, Death and the Afterlife in the Greco-Roman World' in *Life in the Face of Death: The Resurrection Message of the New Testament.* Edited by R. N. Longenecker; Grand Rapids, MI: Eerdmans, 51–79.

Bray, G. L. (2000). *James, 1–2 Peter, 1–3 John, Jude.* Downers Grove, IL: InterVarsity Press.

Brooke, A. E. (1912). *A Critical and Exegetical Commentary on the Johannine Epistles.* Edinburgh: T. & T. Clark.

Brown, R. E. (1966). 'The Qumran Scrolls and the Johannine Gospel and Epistles' in *New Testament Essays.* Edited by R. E. Brown; London: Geoffrey Chapman, 102–31.

(1970). *The Gospel according to John: Introduction, Translation and Notes, Volume 2.* Garden City, NY: Doubleday.

(1982). *The Epistles of John: Translated with Introduction, Notes, and Commentary.* Garden City, NY: Doubleday.

Brown, T. G. (2003). *Spirit in the Writings of John: Johannine Pneumatology in Social-scientific Perspective.* London: T. & T. Clark International.

Bruce, F. F. (1979). *The Epistles of John.* 2nd edition. Grand Rapids, MI: Eerdmans.

(1982). *1 & 2 Thessalonians.* Waco, TX: Word.

Büchsel, F. (1933). *Die Johannesbriefe.* Leipzig: Deuchert.

Bultmann, R. (1973). *The Johannine Epistles: A Commentary on the Johannine Epistles.* Philadelphia, PA: Fortress Press.

Burdick, D. W. (1985). *The Letters of John the Apostle.* Chicago, IL: Moody.

Burge, G. M. (1996). *The Letters of John.* Grand Rapids, MI: Zondervan.

Callahan, A. D. (2005). *A Love Supreme: A History of Johannine Tradition.* Minneapolis, MN: Fortress Press.

Callow, J. C. (1999). 'Where Does 1 John 1 End?' in *Discourse Analysis and the New Testament: Approaches and Results.* Edited by S. E. Porter and J. T. Reed; vol.CLXX; Sheffield: Sheffield Academic Press, 392–406.

Campbell, C. R. (2007). *Verbal Aspect, the Indicative Mood, and Narrative: Soundings in the Greek of the New Testament.* New York, NY: Peter Lang.

(2008a). *Verbal Aspect and Non-Indicative Verbs: Further Soundings in the Greek of the New Testament.* New York, NY: Peter Lang.

(2008b). *Basics of Verbal Aspect in Biblical Greek.* Grand Rapids, MI: Zondervan.

Carson, D. A. (1987). 'The Purpose of the Fourth Gospel: John 20:31 Reconsidered'. *Journal of Biblical Literature* 106:639–51.

(1988). 'John and the Johannine Epistles' in *It is Written: Scripture citing Scripture.* Edited by D. A. Carson and H. G. M. Williamson; Cambridge: Cambridge University Press, 245–64.

(1991). *The Gospel According to John.* Grand Rapids, MI: Eerdmans.

(1994). 'The Three Witnesses and the Eschatology of 1 John' in *To Tell the Mystery: Essays on New Testament Eschatology in Honor of Robert H. Gundry.* Edited by T. E. Schmidt and M. Silva; vol. C; Sheffield: JSOT Press, 216–32.

(2004). '"You Have No Need That Anyone Should Teach You" (1 John 2:27): An Old Testament Allusion That Determines the Interpretation' in *The New Testament in Its First Century Setting: Essays on Context and Background in Honour of B. W. Winter on His 65th Birthday.* Edited by P. J. Williams, A. D. Clarke, P. M. Head and D. Instone-Brewer; Grand Rapids, MI: Eerdmans, 269–80.

(2005). 'Syntactical and Text-Critical Observations on John 20:30–31: One More Round on the Purpose of the Fourth Gospel'. *Journal of Biblical Literature* 124:693–714.

(2007). '1–3 John' in *Commentary on the New Testament Use of the Old Testament.* Edited by G. K. Beale and D. A. Carson; Grand Rapids, MI: Baker, 1063–7.

Cassem, N. H. (1972). 'A Grammatical and Contextual Inventory of the use of κόσμος in the Johannine Corpus with Some Implications for a Johannine Cosmic Theology'. *New Testament Studies* 19:81–91.

Childs, B. S. (1984). *The New Testament as Canon: An Introduction.* London: SCM Press.

Clark, D. J. (2006). 'Vocatives in the Epistles'. *The Bible Translator* 57:32–44.

Clines, D. J. A. (1993). 'Possibilities and Priorities of Biblical Interpretation in an International Perspective'. *Biblical Interpertation* 1:67–87.

Coetzee, J. C. (1979). 'The Holy Spirit in 1 John'. *Neotestamentica* 13:43–67.

Collins, R. F. (2002). *1 & 2 Timothy and Titus: a Commentary.* Louisville, KY: Westminster John Knox Press.

Culpepper, R. A. (1985). *1 John, 2 John, 3 John.* Atlanta, GA: John Knox Press.

(2001). 'Anti-Judaism in the Fourth Gospel as a Theological Problem for Christian Interpreters' in *Anti-Judaism and the Fourth Gospel.* Edited by R. Bieringer, D. Pollefeyt and F. Vandecasteele-Vanneuville; Assen: Royal Van Gorcum, 68–91.

Culy, M. M. (2004). *1, 2, 3 John: A Handbook on the Greek Text.* Waco, TX: Baylor University Press.

Curtis, E. M. (1992). 'The First Person Plural in 1 John 2:18–27'. *Evangelical Journal* 10:27–36.

Davids, P. H. (1982). *The Epistle of James: A Commentary on the Greek Text.* Exeter: Paternoster.

de Boer, M. C. (1988). 'Jesus the Baptizer: 1 John 5:5–8 and the Gospel of John'. *Journal of Biblical Literature* 107:87–106.

(1991). 'The Death of Jesus Christ and his Coming in the Flesh'. *Novum Testamentum* 33:326–46.

(2001). 'The Depiction of "the Jews" in John's Gospel: Matters of Behaviour and Identity' in *Anti-Judaism and the Fourth Gospel.* Edited by R. Bieringer, D. Pollefeyt and F. Vandecasteele-Vanneuville; Assen: Royal Van Gorcum, 260–80.

de Boor, W. (1982). *Die Briefe des Johannes.* 4th edition. Wuppertal: R. Brockhaus.

de Jonge, H. J. (2001). 'The "Jews" in the Gospel of John' in *Anti-Judaism and the Fourth Gospel*. Edited by R. Bieringer, D. Pollefeyt and F. Vandecasteele-Vanneuville; Assen: Royal Van Gorcum, 239–59.

de la Potterie, I. (1971). 'Anointing of the Christian by Faith' in *The Christian Lives by the Spirit*. Edited by I. de la Potterie and S. Lyonnet; New York, NY: Alba House, 79–143.

Deines, R. (2001). 'The Pharisees Between "Judaisms" and "Common Judaism"' in *Justification and Variegated Nomism: Volume 1, The Complexities of Second Temple Judaism*. Edited by D. A. Carson, P. T. O'Brien and M. A. Seifrid; vol. I; Tubingen: Mohr Siebeck, 443–504.

Derickson, G. W. (1993). 'What is the Message of 1 John?'. *Bibliotheca Sacra* 150:89–105.

Dodd, C. H. (1946). *The Johannine Epistles*. London: Hodder and Stoughton.

Dryden, J. d. W. (1999). 'The Sense of σπέρμα in 1 John 3:9 in Light of Lexical Evidence'. *Filologia Neotestamentaria* 11:85–100.

du Preez, J. (1975). '"Sperma autou" in 1 John 3:9'. *Neotestamentica* 9: 105–10.

du Rand, J. A. (1979). 'A Discourse Analysis of 1 John'. *Neotestamentica* 13:1–42.

(1994). *Johannine Perspectives*. Johannesburg: Orion.

du Toit, B. A. (1979). 'The Role and Meaning of Statements of "Certainty" in the Structural Composition of 1 John'. *Neotestamentica* 13:84–99.

Dumbrell, W. J. (1991). 'The Spirit in John's Gospel' in *Spirit of the Living God – Part 1*. Edited by B. G. Webb; vol. v; Homebush West, NSW: Lancer, 77–94.

Dunn, J. D. G. (1980). *Christology in the Making: A New Testament Inquiry into the Origins of the Doctrine of the Incarnation*. Philadelphia, PA: Westminster.

(1988). *Romans 9–16*. Dallas, TX: Word.

(1991). *The Parting of the Ways: Between Judaism and Christianity and Their Significance For the Character of Christianity*. London: SCM.

(1992). *Jews and Christians: The Parting of the Ways AD 70 to 135*. Tubingen: Mohr Siebeck.

(2001). 'The Embarrassment of History: Reflections on the Problem of "Anti-Judaism" in the Fourth Gospel' in *Anti-Judaism and the Fourth Gospel*. Edited by R. Bieringer, D. Pollefeyt and F. Vandecasteele-Vanneuville; Assen: Royal Van Gorcum, 47–67.

Eagleton, T. (1983). *Literary Theory: An Introduction*. Minneapolis, MN: University of Minnesota.

Edwards, R. B. (1996). *The Johannine Epistles*. Sheffield: Sheffield Academic Press.

Ehrman, B. D. (1988). '1 John 4:3 and the Orthodox Corruption of Scripture'. *Zeitschrift fur die neutesamentliche Wissenschaft* 79:221–43.

Ellingworth, P. (1993). *The Epistle to the Hebrews: A Commentary on the Greek Text*. Grand Rapids, MI: Eerdmans.

Ellis, E. E. (1978). *Prophecy and Hermeneutic in Early Christianity: New Testament Essays*. Tübingen: Mohr.

Evans, C. A. (1982). 'On the Quotation Formulas in the Fourth Gospel'. *Biblische Zeitschrift* 26:79–83.

(1987). 'Obduracy and the Lord's Servant: Some Observations on the Use of the Old Testament in the Fourth Gospel' in *Early Jewish and Christian Exegesis: Studies in Memory of William Hugh Brownlee*. Edited by C. A. Evans and W. F. Stinespring; vol. x; Atlanta, GA: Scholars Press, 221–36.

(2001). 'Polemics or Anti-Semitism? The New Testament and First-Century Judaism'. *Mishkan* 34:80–94.

Evans, R. J. (1997). *In Defence of History*. London: Granta Books.

Fee, G. D. (1987). *The First Epistle to the Corinthians*. Grand Rapids, MI: Eerdmans.

(1992). 'On the Text and Meaning of John 20:30–31' in *The Four Gospels 1992: Festschrift Frans Neirynck*. Edited by F. V. Segbroeck, C. M. Tuckett, G. V. Belle and J. Verheyden; vol. III; Leuven: Leuven University Press, 2193–205.

Fish, S. (1981). 'Why No One's Afraid of Wolfgang Iser'. *Diacritics* 11.1:2–13.

Francis, F. O. (1970). 'The Form and Function of the Opening and Closing Paragraphs of James and 1 John'. *Zeitschrift für die neutesamentliche Wissenschaft* 6:110–26.

Freyne, S. (2002). 'Christological Debates among Johannine Christians' in *The Many Voices of the Bible, Concilium 2002/1*. Edited by S. Freyne and E. van Wolde; London: SCM, 59–67.

Gaugler, E. (1964). *Die Johannesbriefe*. Zurich: EVZ-Verlag.

Goetchius, E. V. N. (1976). 'Towards a Descriptive Analysis of EINAI as a Linking Verb in New Testament Greek'. *Journal of Biblical Literature* 95:147–9.

Gore, C. (1920). *The Epistles of St John*. London: J. Murray.

Goulder, M. (1999). 'A Poor Man's Christology'. *New Testament Studies* 45:332–48.

Grayston, K. (1981). 'The Meaning of *Parakletos*'. *Journal for the Study of the New Testament* 13:67–82.

(1984). *The Johannine Epistles*. Grand Rapids, MI: Eerdmans.

Griffith, T. (1998). 'A Non-Polemic Reading of 1 John'. *Tyndale Bulletin* 49:253–76.

(2002). *Keep Yourselves from Idols: A New Look at 1 John*. Journal of the Study of the New Testament Supplement Series 233; London: Sheffield Academic Press.

Grundmann, W., Hesse, F., de Jonge, M. and van der Woude, A. S. (1974). 'χρίω, χριστός, ἀντίχριστος, χρῖσμα, χριστιανός' in *Theological Dictionary of the New Testament*. Edited by G. Kittel and G. Friedrich; vol. ix; Grand Rapids, MI: Eerdmans, 493–580.

Haas, C., Jonge, M. d. and Swellengrebel, J. L. (1972). *A Translator's Handbook on the Letters of John*. London: United Bible Society.

Harris, M. J. (1983). *Raised Immortal: Resurrection and Immortality in the New Testament*. London: Marshall Morgan and Scott.

Hartog, P. A. (2005). 'The Opponents of Polycarp, *Philippians*, and 1 John' in *Trajectories through the New Testament and the Apostolic Fathers*. Edited by A. Gregory and C. M. Tuckett; Oxford: Oxford University Press, 375–91.

Haupt, E. (1879). *The First Epistle of St. John: A Contribution to Biblical Theology*. Edinburgh: T. & T. Clark.

Hays, R. B. (1989). *Echoes of Scripture in the Letters of Paul*. New Haven, CT: Yale University Press.

Heckel, T. K. (2004). 'Die Historisierung der johanneischen Theologie im Ersten Johannesbrief'. *New Testament Studies* 50:425–43.

Hengel, M. (1989). *The Johannine Question*. London: SCM Press.

(1991). *The Pre-Christian Paul*. London: SCM.

Hiebert, D. E. (1991). *The Epistles of John: An Expositional Commentary*. Greenville, SC: Bob Jones University Press.

Hill, D. (1981). *The Gospel of Matthew*. Grand Rapids, MI: Eerdmans.

Hills, J. V. (1989). '"Little children, keep yourselves from idols": 1 John 5:21 Reconsidered'. *Catholic Biblical Quarterly* 51:285–310.

Hoffman, T. A. (1978). '1 John and the Qumran Scrolls'. *Biblical Theology Bulletin* 8:117–25.

Houlden, J. L. (1973). *A Commentary on The Johannine Epistles*. London: Adam and Charles Black.

Hultgren, A. J. (1976). 'Paul's Pre-Christian Persecutions of the Church: Their Purpose, Locale and Nature'. *Journal of Biblical Literature* 95:97–111.

Iser, W. (1972). 'The Reading Process: A Phenomenological Approach'. *New Literary History* 3:279–99.

(2000). *The Range of Interpretation*. New York: Columbia University Press.

Jenks, G. C. (1991). *The Origins and Early Development of the Antichrist Myth*. 59; Berlin: Walter de Gruyter.

Jensen, M. (2008). 'Being "Sons (Children) of God" in 1 John' in *Donald Robinson: Selected Works – Appreciation*. Edited by P. G. Bolt and M. D. Thompson; vol. III; Camperdown: Australian Church Record, 197–203.

(2009). '"You Have Overcome the Evil One": Victory over Evil in 1 John' in *Christ's Victory Over Evil: Biblical Theology and Pastoral Ministry*. Edited by P. G. Bolt; Nottingham: Apollos, 104–22.

(2012). 'The Structure and Argument of 1 John'. *Journal for the Study of the New Testament* (in press).

Jensen, P. D. and Payne, T. (1995). *The Blueprint: Christian Doctrine*. Sydney: St. Matthias Press.

Johnson, L. T. (1989). 'The New Testament's Anti-Jewish Slander and the Conventions of Ancient Polemic'. *Journal of Biblical Literature* 108:419–41.

Johnson, T. F. (1993). *1, 2, and 3 John*. Peabody, MA: Hendrickson.

Jones, P. R. (2009). *1, 2 & 3 John*. Macon, GA: Smyth & Helwys.

Jossa, G. (2006). *Jews or Christians? The Followers of Jesus in Search of their Own Identity*. Wissenschaftliche Untersuchungen zum Neuen Testament 202; Tubingen: Mohr Siebeck.

Judge, E. A. (1994). 'Judaism and the Rise of Christianity: A Roman Perspective'. *Tyndale Bulletin* 45:355–68.

Kauder, E. (1986). 'ἀντίχριστος' in *The New International Dictionary of New Testament Theology*. Edited by C. Brown; vol. I; Carlisle: Paternoster Press, 124–6.

Kennedy, H. A. A. (1916). 'The Covenant-conception in the First Epistle of John'. *Expository Times* 28:23–6.

Kim, D. (2004). *An Exegesis of Apostasy Embedded in John's Narratives of Peter and Judas against the Synoptic Parallels*. Lewiston, NY: Mellen.

Kinlaw, P. E. (2005). *The Christ is Jesus: Metamorphosis, Possession, and Johannine Christology*. Atlanta, GA: Society of Biblical Literature.

Klappert, B. (2001). 'The Coming Son of Man Became Flesh: High Christology and Anti-Judaism in the Gospel of John' in *Anti-Judaism and the Fourth Gospel*. Edited by R. Bieringer, D. Pollefeyt and F. Vandecasteele-Vanneuville; Assen: Royal Van Gorcum, 159–86.

Klauck, H. J. (1988). 'Internal Opponents: the Treatment of the Secessionists in the First Epistle of John' in *Truth and its Victims*. Edited by W. Beuken, S. Freyne and A. Weiler; vol. Concilium CC; Edinburgh: T. & T. Clark, 55–65.

  (1990). 'Zur rhetorischen Analyse der Johannesbriefe'. *Zeitschrift fur die neutesamentliche Wissenschaft* 81:204–24.

  (1991). *Der erste Johannesbrief*. Zurich: Benziger.

Knox, D. B. (2000). 'The Five Comings of Jesus' in *D. Broughton Knox: Selected Works. Volume 1: The Doctrine of God*. Edited by T. Payne; vol. I; Kingsford, NSW: Matthias Media, 213–27.

Kotzé, P. P. A. (1979). 'The Meaning of 1 John 3.9 with Reference to 1 John 1.8 and 10'. *Neotestamentica* 13:66–83.

Kramer, W. (1966). *Christ, Lord, Son of God*. London: SCM.

Kruse, C. (2003). 'Sin and Perfectionism in 1 John'. *Australian Biblical Review* 51:60–70.

Kruse, C. G. (2000). *The Letters of John*. Grand Rapids, MI: Eerdmans.

Lampe, G. W. H. (1973). '"Grievous Wolves" (Acts 20:29)' in *Christ and Spirit in the New Testament: Studies in Honour of Charles Francis Digby Moule*. Edited by B. Lindars and S. S. Smalley; Cambridge: Cambridge University Press, 253–68.

Larsen, I. (1990a). 'The Phrase ἐν τούτῳ in 1 John'. *Notes on Translation* 4:27–34.

  (1990b). 'Jesus Came through Water and Blood'. *Notes on Translation* 4:35–8.

  (1991). 'Boundary Features'. *Notes on Translation* 5:48–54.

Law, R. (1979). *The Tests of Life: A Study of the First Epistle of St. John*. 3rd edition. Grand Rapids, MI: Baker.

Lazure, N. (1969). 'La convoitise de la chair en 1 Jean, II,16'. *Revue Biblique* 76:161–205.

Legrasse, S. (1995). 'Paul's Pre-Christian Career According to Acts' in *The Book of Acts in its First Century Setting: Palestinian Setting*. Edited by R. J. Bauckham; vol. IV; Grand Rapids, MI: Eerdmans, 365–90.

Lentricchia, F. (1980). *After the New Criticism*. Chicago, IL: University of Chicago Press.

Lieu, J. M. (1981). '"Authority to Become Children of God". A Study of 1 John'. *Novum Testamentum* 23:210–28.

  (1991). *The Theology of the Johannine Epistles*. Cambridge: Cambridge University Press.

  (1993). 'What was from the Beginning: Scripture and Tradition in the Johannine Epistles'. *New Testament Studies* 39:458–77.

  (2008a). *I, II & III John: A Commentary*. Louisville, KY: Westminster John Knox Press.

  (2008b). 'Us or You? Persuasion and Identity in 1 John'. *Journal of Biblical Literature* 127:805–19.

Loader, W. (1992). *The Johannine Epistles*. London: Epworth Press.

Longacre, R. E. (1992). 'Toward an Exegesis of 1 John Based on the Discourse Analysis of the Greek Text' in *Linguistics and New Testament Interpretation*. Edited by D. A. Black, K. Barnwell and S. Levinsohn; Nashville, TN: Broadman, 271–86.

Louw, J. P. (1975). 'Verbal Aspect in the First Letter of John'. *Neotestamentica* 9:98–104.

Luna, R. F. (2004). *Structure littéraire et argumentation de la première épître johannique*. PhD Thesis: Université de Montréal, Montréal.

MacLeod, D. J. (2002). 'Christology in Six Lines: An Exposition of 1 Timothy 3:16'. *Bibliotheca Sacra* 159:334–48.

Malatesta, E. (1973). *The Epistles of St. John: Greek Text and English Translation Schematically Arranged*. Rome: Gregorian University.

(1978). *Interiority and Covenant: A Study of einai en and menein en in the First Letter of Saint John*. Analecta Biblica 69; Rome: Biblical Institute Press.

Marshall, I. H. (1978). *The Epistles of St John*. Grand Rapids, MI: Eerdmans.

(1980). *The Acts of the Apostles: An Introduction and Commentary*. Leicester: Inter-Varsity Press.

(2003). 'Review of *Keep Yourselves from Idols: A New look at 1 John*'. *Evangel* 21:93–4.

McGaughy, L. C. (1972). *Toward a Descriptive Analysis of EINAI as a Linking Verb in New Testament Greek*. Society of Biblical Literature Dissertation Series 6; Missoula, MT: Society of Biblical Literature for the Linguistics Seminar.

Metzger, B. M. (1994). *A Textual Commentary on the Greek New Testament: A Companion Volume to the United Bible Societies' Greek New Testament (Fourth Revised Edition)*. 2nd edition. Stuttgart: United Bible Societies.

Michaels, J. R. (1989). *John*. Peabody, MA: Hendrickson Publishers.

(2002). 'By Water and Blood: Sin and Purification in John and First John' in *Dimensions of Baptism: Biblical and Theological Studies*. Edited by S. E. Porter and A. R. Cross; Journal of the Study of the New Testament Supplement Series 234; London: Sheffield Academic Press, 149–62.

Minear, P. S. (1970). 'The Idea of Incarnation in First John'. *Interpretation* 24:291–302.

Moloney, F. J. (1998). *The Gospel of John*. Collegeville, MN: Liturgical Press.

Morgen, M. (2004). 'La Mort Expiatoire de Jesus d'Apres 1 Jean' in *The Catholica Epistles and the Tradition*. Edited by J. Schlosser; Leuven: Leuven University Press, 485–501.

(2005a). *Les épîtres de Jean*. Paris: Cerf.

(2005b). 'Le Prologue de la Première Épître de Jean sa Structure et sa Visée'. *Revue des Sciences Religieuses* 79/1:55–75.

Morris, L. (1965). *The Apostolic Preaching of the Cross*. 3rd edition. Grand Rapids, MI: Eerdmans.

Motyer, S. (1997). *Your Father the Devil?: A New Approach to John and the Jews*. Carlisle: Paternoster.

Mounce, W. D. (2000). *Pastoral Epistles*. Nashville, TN: Thomas Nelson.

Neufeld, D. (1994). *Reconceiving Texts as Speech Acts: An Analysis of 1 John*. Biblical Interpretation 7; Leiden: E. J. Brill.

Noack, B. (1959–1960). 'On I John II. 12–14'. *New Testament Studies* 6:236–41.

O'Neill, J. C. (1966). *The Puzzle of 1 John: A New Examination of Origins.* London: SPCK.

Olsson, B. (1999). 'First John: Discourse Analyses and Intepretations' in *Discourse Analysis and Other Topics in Biblical Greek.* Edited by S. E. Porter and D. A. Carson; Journal of the Study of the New Testament Supplement Series 113; Sheffield: Sheffield Academic Press, 107–16.

Ott, W. (1990). 'Marking the Sections in 1 John'. *Notes on Translation* 4:44–50.

Painter, J. (1975). *John: Witness and Theologian.* London: SPCK.

   (1986). 'The 'Opponents' in 1 John'. *New Testament Studies* 32:48–71.

   (2002). *1, 2, and 3 John.* Collegeville, MN: Liturgical Press.

Palmer, E. F. (1982). *1, 2, 3 John, Revelation.* Waco, TX: Word Books.

Peerbolte, L. J. L. (1996). *The Antecedents of Antichrist: A Traditio-Historical Study of the Earliest Christian Views on Eschatological Opponents.* Supplements to the Journal for the Study of Judaism 49; Leiden: E. J. Brill.

Perkins, P. (1979). *The Johannine Epistles.* Dublin: Veritas.

   (2005). 'Gnostic Revelation and Johannine Sectarianism: Reading 1 John from the Perspective of Nag Hammadi' in *Theology and Christology in the Fourth Gospel.* Edited by G. V. Belle, J. G. V. D. Watt and P. Maritz; Leuven: Leuven University Press, 245–76.

Persson, A. (1990). 'Some Exegetical Problems in 1 John'. *Notes on Translation* 4:18–26.

Pervis, J. D. (1986). 'The Samaritans and Judaism' in *Early Judaism and Its Modern Interpreters.* Edited by R. A. Kraft and G. W. E. Nickelsburg; Atlanta, GA: Scholars Press, 81–98.

Peterson, D. G. (2009). *The Acts of the Apostles.* Grand Rapids, MI: Eerdmans.

Piper, O. A. (1947). '1 John and the Didache of the Primitive Church'. *Journal of Biblical Literature* 66:437–51.

Plummer, A. (1911). *The Epistles of St. John.* Cambridge: Cambridge University Press.

Porter, S. E. (1994). *Idioms of the Greek New Testament.* 2nd edition. Sheffield: JSOT Press.

Porton, G. G. (1992). 'Sadducees' in *The Anchor Bible Dictionary.* Edited by D. N. Freedman; vol. v; New York, NY: Doubleday, 892–5.

Reicke, B. (1984). 'Judaeo-Christianity and the Jewish Establishment, A.D. 33–66' in *Jesus and the Politics of his Day.* Edited by E. Bammel and C. F. D. Moule; London: SCM, 145–52.

Rensberger, D. K. (1997). *1 John, 2 John, 3 John.* Nashville, TN: Abingdon Press.

   (2001). *The Epistles of John.* Louisville, KY: Westminster John Knox Press.

Richter, G. (1977). 'Blut und Wasser aus der durchbohrten Seite Jesu (Joh 19, 34b)' in *Studien zum Johannesevangelium.* Edited by J. Hainz; Regensburg: Pustet, 120–42.

Robinson, J. A. T. (1962). 'The Destination and Purpose of the Johannine Epistles' in *Twelve New Testament Studies.* Edited by J. A. T. Robinson; London: SCM, 126–38.

   (1976). *Redating the New Testament.* London: SCM.

Rogers, E. (1984). 'Vocatives and Boundaries'. *Selected Technical Articles related to Translation* 11:24–9.

Ross, A. (1954). *The Epistles of James and John.* Grand Rapids, MI: Eerdmans.

Salier, W. H. (1997). 'What's in a World? Κόσμος in the Prologue of John's Gospel'. *Reformed Theological Review* 56.3:105–17.

Schenke, L. (1997). 'The Johannine Schism and the Twelve' in *Critical Readings of John 6*. Edited by R. A. Culpepper; Leiden: Brill, 205–19.

Schmid, H. (2002). *Gegner im 1. Johannesbrief? Zu Konstruktion und Selbstreferenz im johanneischen Sinnsystem*. Beitrage zur Wissenschaft vom Alten Neuen Testament 159; Stuttgart: Kohlhammer.

(2004a). 'How to Read the First Epistle of John Non-Polemically'. *Biblica* 85.1:24–41.

(2004b). 'Tradition als Strategie: Zur Pragmatik des Traditionsargument im 1. Johannesbrief' in *The Catholica Epistles and the Tradition*. Edited by J. Schlosser; Leuven: Leuven University Press, 503–17.

Schnackenburg, R. (1982). *The Gospel according to St. John, Volume 3*. London: Burns & Oates.

(1992). *The Johannine Epistles: A Commentary*. New York, NY: Crossroad.

Schneider, J. (1964). 'ἔρχομαι, ἔλευσις, ἀπ-, δι-, εἰς-, ἐξ-, ἐπ-, παρ-, παρεισ-, περι-, προσ-, συνέρχομαι' in *Theological Dictionary of the New Testament*. Edited by G. Kittel; vol. II; Grand Rapids, MI: Eerdmans, 666–84.

Scholtissek, K. (2004). 'Die relecture des Johannesevangeliums im ersten Johannesbrief'. *Bibel und Kirche* 3:152–6.

Schurer, E., Vermes, G., Millar, F. and Goodman, M. (1986). *The History of the Jewish People in the Age of Jesus Christ (175 B.C.-A.D. 135)*, 2nd edition; Edinburgh: T. & T. Clark.

Schweizer, E. (1966). 'Zum religionsgeschichtlichen Hintergrund der "Sendungsformel" Gal 4 4f. Rm 8 3f. John 3 16f. 1 John 4 9'. *Zeitschrift fur die neutesamentliche Wissenschaft* 57:199–210.

Seifrid, M. A. (1992). *Justification by Faith: The Origin and Development of a Central Pauline Theme*. Leiden: Brill.

Sherman, G. E. and Tuggy, J. C. (1994). *A Semantic and Structural Analysis of the Johannine Epistles*. Dallas, TX: SIL.

Silva, M. (1995). 'Review of José Fernando Toribio Cuadradro <<El viniente>> Estudio exegetico y teologico del verbo ἔρχεσθαι en la literatura joanica'. *Novum Testamentum* 37.3:303–5.

Sloyan, G. S. (1995). *Walking in the Truth: Perseverers and Deserters: the First, Second, and Third Letters of John*. Valley Forge, PA: Trinity Press International.

Smalley, S. S. (1980). 'What about 1 John?' in *Papers on Paul and Other New Testament Authors*. Edited by E. A. Livingstone; Journal for the Study of the Old Testament Supplement Series 3; Sheffield: JSOT Press, 337–43.

(1984). *1, 2, 3 John*. Dallas: Word Books.

(2007). *1, 2, 3 John*, 2nd edition; Nashville, TN: Thomas Nelson.

Stott, J. R. W. (1988). *The Letters of John: An Introduction and Commentary*, 2nd edition; Grand Rapids, MI: Eerdmans.

Strecker, G. (1988). 'Der Antichrist: Zum religionsgeschichtlichen Hintergrund von 1 Joh 2,18.22; 4,3 und 2 Joh 7' in *Text and Testimony: Essays on New Testament and Apocryphal Literature in Honour of A. J. J. Klijn*. Edited by T. Baarda; Kampen: J. H. Kok, 247–54.

(1996). *The Johannine Letters: A Commentary on 1, 2, and 3 John*. Minneapolis, MN: Fortress Press.

Streett, D. R. (2011). *They Went Out from Us: The Identity of the Opponents in First John.* Beihefte zur Zeitschrift für die neutestamentliche Wissenschaft 117; Berlin: De Gruyter.

Tan, R. K. J. (2002). 'Should We Pray for Straying Brethren? John's Confidence in 1 John 5:16–17'. *Journal of the Evangelical Theological Society* 45:599–609.

Thatcher, T. (1994). 'A New Look at Asides in the Fourth Gospel'. *Bibliotheca Sacra* 151:428–39.

Thomas, J. C. (1998). 'The Literary Structure of 1 John'. *Novum Testamentum* 40:369–81.

——— (2003). *The Pentecostal Commentary on 1 John, 2 John, 3 John.* Sheffield: Sheffield Academic Press.

Thompson, M. M. (1992). *1–3 John.* Leicester: InterVarsity Press.

Thyen, H. (1988). 'Johannesbriefe' in *Theologische Realenzyklopadie.* Edited by G. Muller; vol. XVII; Berlin: W. de Gruyter, 186–200.

Tollefson, K. D. (1999). 'Certainty within the Fellowship: Dialectic Discourse in 1 John'. *Biblical Theology Bulletin* 29:79–89.

Toribio Cuadrado, J. F. (1993). *'El viniente': estudio exegâetico y teolâogico del verbo erchesthai en la literatura joânica.* Spain: Monografâicas de la Revista 'Mayâeutica'.

Towner, P. H. (2006). *The Letters to Timothy and Titus.* Grand Rapids, MI: Eerdmans.

Trebilco, P. (2004). *The Early Christians in Ephesus from Paul to Ignatius.* Tübingen: Mohr Siebeck.

Uebele, W. (2001). *'Viele Verfèuhrer sind in die Welt ausgegangen': die Gegner in den Briefen des Ignatius von Antiochien und in den Johannesbriefen.* Stuttgart: Kohlhammer.

Vermes, G. (1997). *The Complete Dead Sea Scrolls in English.* New York, NY: Allen Lane/Penguin Press.

von Wahlde, U. C. (1990). *The Johannine Commandments: 1 John and the Struggle for the Johannine Tradition.* New York, NY: Paulist Press.

——— (2001). '"You Are of Your Father the Devil" in its Context: Sterotyped Apocalyptic Polemic in John 8:38–47' in *Anti-Judaism and the Fourth Gospel.* Edited by R. Bieringer, D. Pollefeyt and F. Vandecasteele-Vanneuville; Assen: Royal Van Gorcum, 418–44.

——— (2002). 'The Stereotyped Structure and the Puzzling Pronouns of 1 John 2:28–3:10'. *Catholic Biblical Quarterly* 64:319–38.

Vouga, F. (1988). 'The Johannine School: A Gnostic Tradition in Primitive Christianity?' *Biblica* 69:371–85.

——— (1990). *Die Johannesbriefe.* Tubingen: Mohr Siebeck.

Wallace, D. B. (1985). 'The Semantics and Exegetical Significance of the Object-Complement Construction in the New Testament'. *Grace Theological Journal* 6:91–112.

——— (1996). *Greek Grammar Beyond the Basics: An Exegetical Syntax of the New Testament.* Grand Rapids, MI: Eerdmans.

Watson, D. F. (1989). '1 John 2:12–14 as Distributio, Conduplicatio, and Expolitio: A Rhetorical Understanding'. *Journal for the Study of the New Testament* 35:97–110.

——— (1997). 'Antichrist' in *Dictionary of the Later New Testament and its Developments.* Edited by R. P. Martin and P. H. Davids; Leicester: InterVarsity Press, 50–3.

(2003). '"Keep Yourselves from Idols" A Socio-Rhetorical Analysis of the *Exordium* and *Peroratio* of 1 John' in *Fabrics of Discourse: Essays in Honor of Vernon K. Robbins*. Edited by D. B. Gowler, L. G. Bloomquist and D. F. Watson; Harrisburg, PA: Trinity Press International, 281–302.

Watson, W. G. E. (1995). *Classical Hebrew Poetry: A Guide to its Techniques*. 2nd edition. Journal for the Study of the Old Testament Supplement Series 26; Sheffield: Sheffield Academic Press.

Weeks, N. (1976). 'Admonition and Error in Hebrews'. *Westminster Theological Journal* 39:72–80.

Weir, J. E. (1975). 'The Identity of the Logos in the First Epistle of John'. *The Expository Times* 86:118–19.

Weiss, K. (1967). 'Orthodoxie und Heterodoxie im I. Johannesbriefe'. *Zeitschrift fur die neutesamentliche Wissenschaft* 58:247–55.

(1973). 'Die 'Gnosis' im Hintergrund und im Spiegel der Johannesbriefe' in *Gnosis und Neues Testament*. Edited by K. W. Tröger; Gütersloh: Gütersloher Verlagshaus Mohn.

Wengst, K. (1976). *Haresie und Orthodoxie im Spiegel des ersten Johannesbriefes*. Gütersloh: Gütersloher Verlagshaus Gerd Mohn.

(1988). 'Probleme der Johannesbriefe'. *Aufstieg und Niedergang der Römischen Welt* 25.5:3753–72.

Wenham, G. J. (1987). *Genesis 1–15*. Waco, TX: Word Books.

Westcott, B. F. (1966). *The Epistles of St John: The Greek Text with Notes*. Appleford Abingdou, Berkshire: Marcham Manor Press.

Williams, M. A. (1996). *Rethinking 'Gnosticism': An Argument for Dismantling a Dubious Category*. Princeton, NJ: Princeton University Press.

Windisch, H. (1930). *Die katholischen Briefe*. 2nd edition. Tubingen: J. C. B. Mohr.

Witetschek, S. (2004). 'Pappkameraden? Die Auseinandersetzung mit den "Gegnern" im 1. Johannesbrief und die Darstellung des Judas im Johannesevangelium' in *The Catholic Epistles and the Tradition*. Edited by J. Schlosser; Leuven: Lueven University Press, 519–30.

Witherington, B. (1989). 'The Waters of Birth: John 3:5 and 1 John 5:6–8'. *New Testament Studies* 35:155–60.

(2006). *Letters and Homilies for Hellenized Christians*. Downers Grove, IL: IVP Academic.

Womack, M. M. (1998). *1, 2 & 3 John*. Joplin, MO: College Press.

Wright, N. T. (2003). *The Resurrection of the Son of God*. London: SPCK.

Wu, D. (1998). *An Analysis of the Structure of 1 John Using Discourse Analysis*. PhD Thesis: Southern Baptist Theological Seminary, Louisville, Kentucky.

Wurm, A. (1903). *Die Irrlehrer im ersten Johannesbrief*. Freiburg: Herder.

Yarbrough, R. W. (2008). *1–3 John*. Grand Rapids, MI: Baker Academic.

Yarid, J. R. (2003). 'Reflections of the Upper Room Discourse in 1 John'. *Biblicotheca Sacra* 169:65–76.

Young, R. A. (1994). *Intermediate New Testament Greek: A Linguistic and Exegetical Approach*. Nashville, TN: Broadman and Holman.

INDEX OF SUBJECTS

INDEX OF MODERN AUTHORS

INDEX OF ANCIENT SOURCES

Other Sources